Physical Education for Elementary School Teachers: Foundations of a Physical Literacy Journey

Authors

Doug Gleddie, PhD, University of Alberta
Clive Hickson, PhD, University of Alberta
Brent Bradford, PhD, Concordia University of Edmonton

Chapter Collaborators

Shannon Kell, PhD, Mount Royal University (Chapters 1 & 2)
Joanna Sheppard, PhD, Fraser Valley University (Chapter 3)
Hayley Morrison, MA, University of Alberta (Chapter 7)
Lauren Sulz, PhD, University of Alberta (Chapter 8)
Steve Berg, PhD, University of British Columbia – Okanagan (Chapter 8)
Ashleigh Evaniew, MEd, Edmonton Public School Board (Chapter 10)

Ripon Publishing 2018
A Division of Ripon Consulting Ltd.
Copyright Protected

ISBN 978-1-988921-00-6

Ripon Publishing 2018
ISBN 978-1-988921-00-6

[Library of Congress Info]
ISBN 978-1-988921-00-6
Copyright 2018 by Ripon Publishing a Division of Ripon Consulting Ltd.
Acquisitions Editor: Dr. G. J. Fishburne; Developmental Editor: Dr. G. J. Fishburne
Copyeditor: Dr. G. J. Fishburne
Cover Design: Shelley Smith, Graphic Designer
Book Layout: Shelley Smith, Graphic Designer
Printed by Capital Colour, Edmonton, Alberta, Canada T6E 5K1

Ripon Publishing
riponpublishing@gmail.com

Dedication

From all of us: We would like to dedicate this book to our students - the pre-service teachers who we are privileged to teach with and learn from. You are the future of the profession we hold most dear and it is our fondest hope that this book aids you on your own journey of becoming a teacher of physical education.

Doug: To Andrea, one of the best teachers of physical education that I know (even though you really, really like math...). To Isaiah and Megan, who put up with being test students, continuous teaching examples and my incessant physed t-shirt wearing. To my students: past, present and future - may we always continue to move and learn together!

Clive: Jill, as always, your constant support provides me with encouragement and confidence. Selena and Tim, you keep me grounded in what is important in education and provide me with wonderful teaching anecdotes to share with students.

Brent: To my family - Ashleigh, Kane, and Brooke. Thank you for your support throughout this writing process. Specifically, to Ashleigh - thank you for sharing your knowledge in the area of physical education teaching. To future teachers - may you recognize the importance of role modeling - it will prove to be an effective teaching tool.

Acknowledgements

The opportunity to write this book would likely have never materialized without the influence and support of Dr. Graham Fishburne. Graham has been a leader in the field of physical education throughout his most distinguished career. Over the years, the authorship team members of Doug, Clive, and Brent have worked closely with Graham in a variety of capacities. He has been a mentor, colleague and friend to each of us. Without doubt, Graham has had a most profound influence on our professional lives. His original book, Developmentally Appropriate Physical Education for Children and Youth, was both the foundation and inspiration for this text. Graham's thoughts and opinions always prompt ideas and consideration. We are indebted to his willingness to share his knowledge and advice.

We would also like to acknowledge the contributions of our collaborating authors:

Stephen Berg   Hayley Morrison
Ashleigh Evaniew   Joanna Sheppard
Shannon Kell   Lauren Sulz

These accomplished professionals enthusiastically shared their knowledge, experience and expertise with the readers of this text (and us!). Their willingness to collaborate, revise and write together makes the book so much stronger and benefits the physical education profession.

Both the authors and Ripon Publishing would like to thank the following people and agencies for providing permission to use their photographs, graphics, and other materials and content in this textbook.

A 'big' thank you to the children, parents, and teachers who generously gave their time to create many of the photographs in this textbook. Thank you to:

Souha Athmani, Francesco Cimino, Gavin Cimino, Kirby Fletcher, Andrea Gleddie, Isaiah Gleddie, Megan Gleddie, Nickolas Hall, Carson Haywood-Farmer, Lori-Lei Mecredi, Adrien Rootsaert, Dean Rootsaert, Heather Rootsaert, Jessica Rootsaert, and Melissa Valerio.

Thank you is also extended to Dr. Dean Kriellaars, University of Manitoba, and to Dr. Lee Schaefer, McGill Univesity, for their contributions, and providing permission to use their ideas and research findings in this textbook.

Finally, there are many agencies and organizations, local, national, and international, who support and advocate quality education and learning experiences for all people. Many of these organizations and agencies are cited and referenced in this book. However, the following are identified and thanked for sharing and allowing specific material and content to appear in this textbook. They are:

- Alberta Education
- Alberta Assessment Consortium
- Canadian Sport for Life and Sport for Life Society
- PHE Canada
- The Pan-Canadian Joint Consortium for School Health (JCSH)
- The United Nations Educational, Scientific and Cultural Organization (UNESCO) Quality Physical Education Policy Project (2014)
- World Health Organization

Author Biographies

Douglas Gleddie, PhD, is an Associate Professor in the Faculty of Education at the University of Alberta. He teaches physical education curriculum and pedagogy to undergraduate and graduate students. Doug researches narratives of physical education, school sport, physical literacy, meaningful physical education, and teacher education. Most importantly, he is a husband to Andrea, a father to Isaiah and Megan, a mediocre hockey player, and a decent mountain biker.

Clive Hickson, PhD, is a Professor and Associate Dean in the Faculty of Education at the University of Alberta, where he teaches physical education curriculum courses. With a keen interest in physical and health education programming in Canadian schools, Clive's research has focused on the effective teaching in physical education, physical education programming, mentorship, and the impact of school leadership on K-12 health and physical education programming. Clive enjoys participating in outdoor activities with his wife, Jill, and watching his children, Selena and Tim, in their sporting endeavours.

Brent Bradford, PhD, is an Assistant Professor in the Faculty of Education at Concordia University of Edmonton. He teaches physical education curriculum and pedagogy, health and wellness, and physical activity undergraduate courses. Brent's research interests include effective teaching, daily physical activity, symbolism of teacher clothing and teacher education. Brent enjoys hockey, swimming, cycling, and exploring beautiful western Canada during family drives with his wife Ashleigh and children Kane and Brooke.

Chapters 1 & 2: Shannon Kell, PhD, is an Assistant Professor in the Department of Health and Physical Education at Mount Royal University. She teaches a number of physical literacy courses, outdoor leadership, and an elementary physical education curriculum and pedagogy course in the Department of Education. Shannon researches the experiences of teacher candidates, post-secondary student mental health, and the benefits of spending time alone outdoors to recharge. She spends her free time with her two young children, Thomas and Janay, young husband, Jason, and dog, Mojo; together they all enjoy grass stains, searching for bugs, and long walks through the off-leash park.

Chapter 3: Joanna Sheppard, PhD, is an Associate Professor in the Department of Kinesiology and Physical Education at the University of the Fraser Valley (UFV) in Chilliwack, B.C. Her research focuses on physical and health education, life skills, curriculum development, and teaching games for understanding. Joanna's passion lies in the collaborative efforts of best practices with local, national, and international teaching colleagues. Working side by side within the elementary and secondary school system, Joanna strives at making strong pedagogical connections that meet the physical literacy needs of all our students.

Chapter 7: Hayley Morrison, MA, is an instructor, Graduate Student and PhD Candidate in the Faculty of Education at the University of Alberta. She teaches physical education curriculum and pedagogy to undergraduate students. Hayley's research is focused on inclusive physical education and professional development for teachers. She has a passion for dance and loves spending her time outside camping and playing baseball, volleyball, and soccer.

Chapter 8: Lauren Sulz, PhD, is an Assistant Professor in the Faculty of Education at the University of Alberta. She teaches physical education and health education curriculum and pedagogy to undergraduate and graduate students. Lauren's research focuses on enhancing the physical activity and health behaviours of children and youth through changes to school curricula, school policy, and school environments. She enjoys being active with her partner Jason, daughter Nora, and son Fletcher.

Chapter 8: Stephen Berg, PhD, is an Assistant Professor in the Faculty of Education at the University of British Columbia - Okanagan. He teaches physical and health education curriculum and pedagogy and researches children's physical activity, play, and well-being. He is married to Shelley, "dad" to Ashley, Brooke, and Scott, an avid skier, runner, and dancer in the Canadian School of Ballet's the Nutcracker.

Chapter 10: Ashleigh Evaniew, MEd, is an elementary school teacher with the Edmonton Public School Board, and has spent the majority of her teaching years specializing in physical education and early childhood education. Ashleigh has also taught classes at both the University of Alberta and Concordia University of Edmonton. Her research interests have included whole child development, cooperative learning, cross-curricular connections, and student wellness. Ashleigh's husband Brent, and children Kane and Brooke, proudly cheer her on during running races, soccer matches, and CrossFit training.

Disclaimer: Safety and Teaching Progressions, and Approved Resources

Safety and Teaching Progressions

All the activities contained in this textbook have been identified as developmentally appropriate for children and youth, providing recognized teaching progressions are followed, and recognized safety procedures adhered to and employed. Before using any of the ideas or teaching any of the activities identified in this textbook, the reader must be familiar with and cognizant of both recognized safety considerations and developmentally appropriate teaching progressions, and must follow these safety considerations and teaching progressions when teaching any of the activities identified in this textbook. All people who engage in any of the activities contained in this textbook do so completely at their own risk. Anyone who engages in any of the activities contained or suggested in this textbook will take full responsibility for any and all effects as a result of engaging in these activities. No blame, fault, or liability whatsoever of any kind can be made against the authors of this publication or the publishing company.

Using Approved Resources

The activities, ideas, and suggestions, together with the resources identified to support the teaching of elementary school physical education, have been created, identified, and selected to offer developmentally appropriate learning opportunities for children and youth in the area of physical education. However, the various Provincial and Territorial education departments, together with School Boards and different education districts, often publish their own lists of 'approved' physical education teaching resources for their jurisdiction. Hence, it is the personal responsibility of the individual using any of the ideas, activities and cited resources in this textbook to check to ensure the materials, plans, ideas, Internet websites, books, videos, and lesson plan ideas and topics covered in this textbook meet with the approval of the jurisdiction where they are to be used.

Table of Contents

Chapter 1
Why Physical Education?

Introduction: Do We Need Physical Education?

Our mission or challenge is to do all we can to enable ALL to make progress on their individual physical literacy journey.
Margaret Whitehead, 2013

*Our role as physical educators is to engage students with what we do in the **now**, however, we must also ensure that what we do is enduring and is more than just fun or agreeable. "...upon them devolves the responsibility for instituting the conditions for the kind of present experience which has a favourable effect upon the future."*
Dewey, 1938, p. 50

The question of whether or not we need physical education (or art, or music) is answered quite clearly when school authorities have tight budgets. The answer is most often a resounding "NO!" as these 'extra' courses are neglected, under-budgeted or outright cut. However, the question itself is valid. Do we really NEED physical education? Can we just add recess, or daily physical activity, or more sports? Why is it so important that children be physically educated? Our hope is that, by the end of this chapter, you will:

- Realize the benefits and impact of quality physical education
- Understand that physical education 'fits' naturally into a holistic, student-centered view of education
- Understand the concept of 'values' as applied to physical education
- Be introduced to the concept of physical literacy

The Benefit and Value of Physical Education

The following is a brief, but important overview of the benefits of quality physical education.

Health:
- Female students receiving a QDPE (Quality Daily Physical Education) program are more likely to report being more active and healthier twenty years later than female students who received a minimal physical education program (Shephard & Trudeau, 2010)
- Increased physical education instructional time is related to reduced obesity rates in grade 5 students (Cawley, Friswold & Meyerhoefer, 2013)
- Students who take more physical education in high school were more physically active after high school (Mears, 2005)

Academic Progress and Learning:

- Grades and standardized test scores for students enrolled in physical education, despite having almost an hour less of 'core academic instruction', were similar to those of students who did not have physical education but instead had more core academic instruction. (Coe, Pivarnik, Womack, Reeves & Malina, 2006)
- Students in grades 2-6 who received an additional hour of physical education per day had better scores in French, English, science and mathematics than their peers who participated in one period of physical education per day (Shephard, 1996)
- Adding time for physical education does not impact academic achievement negatively (Sallis et al., 1999; Trudeau & Shephard, 2008)
- Girls who had physical education for 70 or more minutes per week attained significantly higher reading and mathematics scores than did girls with 35 or fewer minutes per week (Carlson et al., 2008)

Mental Health:

- The Canadian Mental Health Association describes mental health as: *striking a balance in all aspects of your life: social, physical, spiritual, economic and mental.* Physical education is therefore part of a complete and holistic education.
- Physical activity can reduce depression (Mutrie, 2000; Dunn et al., 2001)
- Physical activity decreases anxiety levels, and improves behaviour and self-worth (Parfitt et al., 2009)

Motor Learning:

- Students motor skills improved with increased physical education and physical activity time (Ericsson, 2008)
- Students who did NOT have daily physical education were more likely to have motor deficits (Ericsson & Karlsson, 2014)

Social and Emotional Learning:

- Physical activity is associated with a stronger self-image, quality of life, and quality of peer and family relationships for children and youth (Iannotti et al., 2009)
- Adolescents who are more active have a stronger sense of self-efficacy (Valois et al., 2008)
- Physical activity has the potential to enhance mood and improve self-esteem and self-perception (Fox et al., & 2000)

Joy of Human Movement:

- Students who pursue a goal of physical literacy have, "...a love of being active, born out of the pleasure and satisfaction individuals experience in participation." (Almond & Whitehead, 2012, p. 69)

- "When movement is joyful and meaningful, it may even inspire us to do things that were never thought possible." (Kretchmar, 2008, p. 162)
- In order to access psychological benefits of physical activity, it needs to be enjoyed! (Wankel, 1993)

Despite a plethora of reasons why physical education should be an integral part of schooling, the facts continue to be ignored by many people in decision-making positions. This discrepancy has led to some very strong statements being made by researchers in the field. In an article entitled, 'Why We Should Not Cut P.E.', Trost and van der Mars (2010) came to the following three conclusions:

1. Policymakers must stop trying to justify cuts to physical education on the grounds that such cuts will strengthen school achievement or, ultimately, the economy.
2. Policymakers, school administrators, and teachers should stop arguing over whether physical education is essential.
3. School administrators must aggressively make room for physical education (p. 64).

It is important to note, these conclusions were arrived at after only reviewing the impact of more or less physical education on academic performance within the context of the United States, under the 'No Child Left Behind' policy. If all the results were considered from studies that have consistently shown the positive and lasting benefits of physical education in a person's life, then there is ***absolutely no reason to reduce or remove physical education.***

What do we know about the impact of physical education?

The United Nations Educational, Scientific and Cultural Organization (UNESCO), as part of its *Quality Physical Education Policy Project* (2014), developed a series of info-graphics illustrating the impact and benefits of quality physical education. These graphics provide an excellent overview of why we need quality physical education.

This first graphic from UNESCO (see Figure 1.1) provides a broad introduction to the way that quality physical education connects to quality education and society at large. First, it provides a connection to the concept of lifelong or lifecourse physical activity. Second, the graphic demonstrates how physical education supports the development of citizenship, a common goal of education. Third, there is an acknowledgement of the confidence competence loop and its connection to academic success. Finally, physical education is a learning gateway that allows students to acquire the knowledge and skills to solve 21st century problems.

A key element of a quality physical education program is inclusivity. Figure 1.2 illustrates how an inclusive class celebrates diversity and teaching for all (Chapter 7). Through this student-focused, strength-based approach, physical education can challenge common assumptions about mobility and participation. From gender to culture, socio-economic status to ableism – physical education can be a positive environment for understanding, appreciation and change.

QUALITY PHYSICAL EDUCATION CONTRIBUTES TO 21ST CENTURY EDUCATION

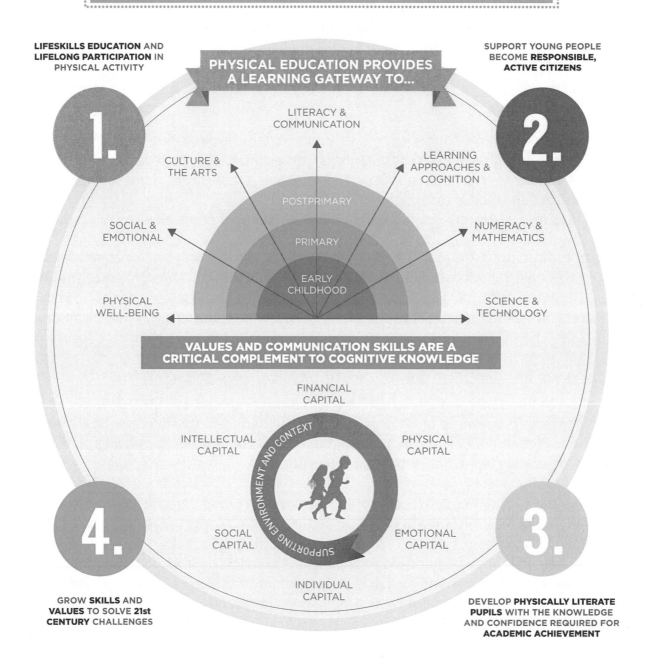

Figure 1.1 Quality Physical Education Contributes to 21st Century Learning

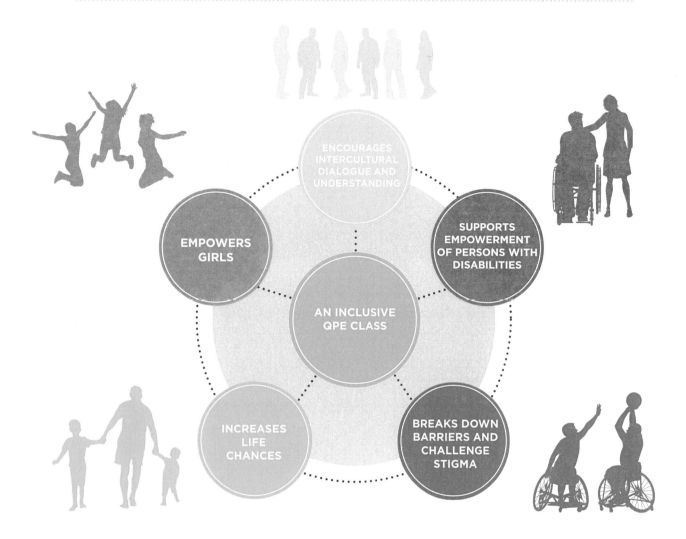

Figure 1.2 Quality Physical Education Drives Inclusion

Across Canada, on average, Provinces spend over 40% of their budget on health. Or actually, sickness! Very little funding goes to prevention or 'upstream' initiatives. Figures 1.3 and 1.4 demonstrate the impact that investing in lifelong physical activity, rooted in quality physical education, can have on a wide range of socio-economic measures. From unhealthy habits like smoking, to lifelong earning potential, to health costs, to active children – physical education makes a difference!

On a world-wide scale, NOT investing in quality physical education hurts society. The statistics and evidence presented above attest to the benefit and importance of physical education. We know that physical activity improves quality of life. Given all this evidence, it should be an easy decision to value physical education in today's society. Unfortunately this is not the case.

THE BENEFITS OF INVESTING

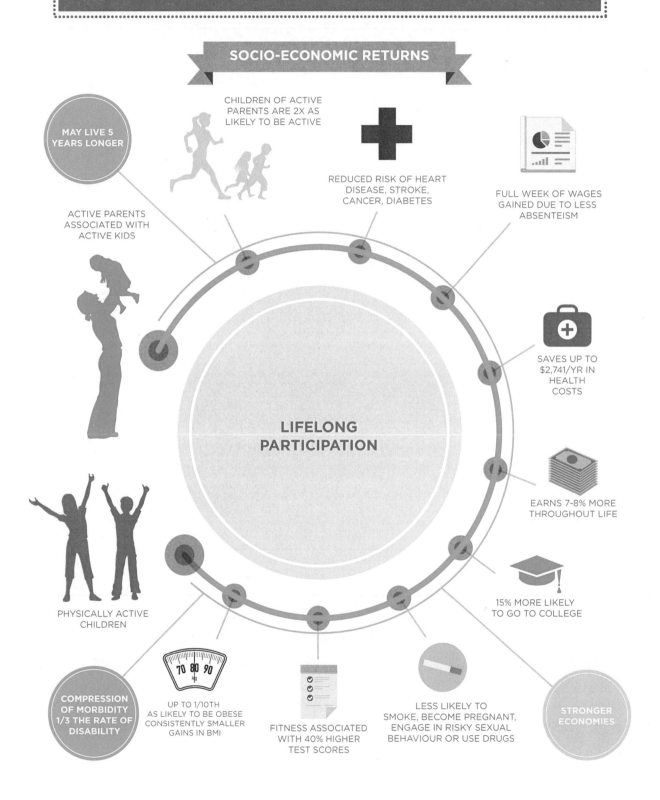

SOCIO-ECONOMIC RETURNS

MAY LIVE 5 YEARS LONGER

CHILDREN OF ACTIVE PARENTS ARE 2X AS LIKELY TO BE ACTIVE

REDUCED RISK OF HEART DISEASE, STROKE, CANCER, DIABETES

FULL WEEK OF WAGES GAINED DUE TO LESS ABSENTEISM

ACTIVE PARENTS ASSOCIATED WITH ACTIVE KIDS

SAVES UP TO $2,741/YR IN HEALTH COSTS

LIFELONG PARTICIPATION

EARNS 7-8% MORE THROUGHOUT LIFE

PHYSICALLY ACTIVE CHILDREN

15% MORE LIKELY TO GO TO COLLEGE

COMPRESSION OF MORBIDITY 1/3 THE RATE OF DISABILITY

UP TO 1/10TH AS LIKELY TO BE OBESE CONSISTENTLY SMALLER GAINS IN BMI

FITNESS ASSOCIATED WITH 40% HIGHER TEST SCORES

LESS LIKELY TO SMOKE, BECOME PREGNANT, ENGAGE IN RISKY SEXUAL BEHAVIOUR OR USE DRUGS

STRONGER ECONOMIES

Figure 1.3 The Benefits of Investing

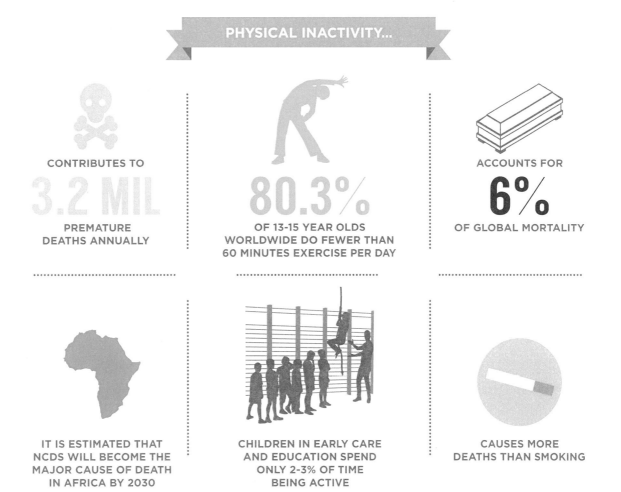

PHYSICAL INACTIVITY...

CONTRIBUTES TO
3.2 MIL
PREMATURE
DEATHS ANNUALLY

80.3%
OF 13-15 YEAR OLDS
WORLDWIDE DO FEWER THAN
60 MINUTES EXERCISE PER DAY

ACCOUNTS FOR
6%
OF GLOBAL MORTALITY

IT IS ESTIMATED THAT
NCDS WILL BECOME THE
MAJOR CAUSE OF DEATH
IN AFRICA BY 2030

CHILDREN IN EARLY CARE
AND EDUCATION SPEND
ONLY 2-3% OF TIME
BEING ACTIVE

CAUSES MORE
DEATHS THAN SMOKING

Figure 1.4 The Cost of Not Investing

Figure 1.5 clearly illustrates that regardless of the convincing arguments presented in the previous 4 figures, full implementation of quality daily physical education, taught by trained professionals, is far from ideal. This leads to the question: 'why do our current practices and behaviours not align with what we know is important?' When will we use what we know to change what we do? To help answer these questions we need to consider what is 'valued' in society.

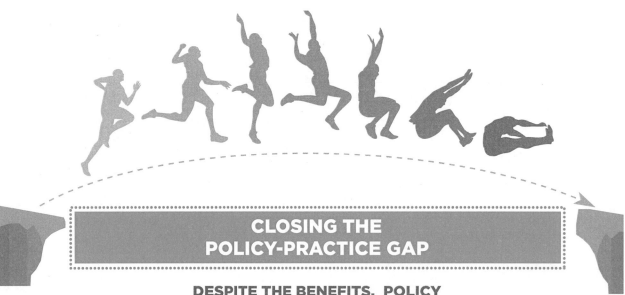

CLOSING THE POLICY-PRACTICE GAP

DESPITE THE BENEFITS, POLICY IS NOT BEING TRANSLATED INTO PRACTICE...

97% OF COUNTRIES GLOBALLY DECLARED PHYSICAL EDUCATION COMPULSORY

BUT..

ONLY
79%
OF COUNTRIES HAVE PRESCRIBED CURRICULA

IN
54%
OF COUNTRIES PHYSICAL EDUCATION HAS A PERCEIVED LOWER STATUS THAN OTHER SUBJECTS

ONLY
71%
OF COUNTRIES ADHERE TO IMPLEMENTATION REGULATIONS AND DELIVERY

ONLY
53%
OF PRIMARY SCHOOLS HAVE SUITABLY TRAINED PHYSICAL EDUCATION TEACHERS

Figure 1.5 Closing the Policy-Practice Gap

What Do You Value?

Values

Have you ever taken a moment to think about what you believe to be important? Chances are, these beliefs are the core of your own values. The Oxford Canadian Dictionary (1998) defines values as:

Principles or standards of behaviour; one's judgement of what is important in life.

Therefore, if you believe that family and friends are important, then you value relationships. If you perceive personal wellness to be important, then you value feeling good and being active. As will be discussed in Chapter 2, beliefs can also be based on your prior experiences. Beliefs help make up your personal values.

Educational Values

Just as individuals have values, educational systems also ascribe to certain values. These can be represented in a variety of ways at different levels.

Government: Each Provincial Ministry of Education establishes statements that broadly outline what they value. For example, the mission statement from Alberta Education communicates the values of inclusivity, student engagement, citizenship and entrepreneurship. Similarly, the statement from Ontario Ministry of Education identifies citizenship as well as including student success and productivity.

The ministry ensures that inclusive learning opportunities enable students to reach success as engaged thinkers and ethical citizens with an entrepreneurial spirit. Alberta Education, 2015	*Learners in the education system will develop the knowledge, skills and characteristics that will lead them to become personally successful, economically productive and actively engaged citizens.* Ontario Ministry of Education, 2015

Curriculum: In addition, Ministries of Education identify and specify certain values, which are directly or indirectly reflected in subject area curricular documents. These values are portrayed in documents such as Alberta Education's Program of Studies' under the heading *aim* and through broad 'goal statements' for the various subject areas. Table 1.1 summarizes the aims of the elementary education programs of study for physical education for a number of Canadian Provinces (Kilborn, Lorusso & Francis, 2015). (Note: some Provinces combine the subject areas of health and physical education.) A common value seen among these Aim statements is the desire for students to lead active, healthy lifestyles – lifestyles that last long after students complete their formal education from kindergarten through to grade 12.

Table 1.1 Curricular Aims	
Province	**Aim**
British Columbia & Yukon Territory	To empower students to develop a personalized understanding of what healthy living means to them as individuals and members of society in the 21st century.
Alberta (adopted by NWT)	To enable individuals to develop the knowledge, skills and attitudes necessary to lead an active, healthy lifestyle.
Saskatchewan	To support students in becoming physically educated individuals who have the understandings and skills to engage in movement activity, and the confidence and disposition to live a healthy, active lifestyle.
Manitoba (adopted by Nunavut)	To provide students with planned and balanced programming to develop the knowledge, skills and attitudes for physically active and healthy lifestyles.
Ontario	Based on the vision that the knowledge and skills acquired in the program will benefit students throughout their lives and help them to thrive in an ever-changing world by enabling them to acquire physical and health literacy and to develop the comprehension, capacity and commitment needed to lead healthy, active lives and to promote healthy, active living.
Quebec	To help students gain a sense of self-responsibility for their fitness and health by allowing them to develop a repertoire of movement skills, a repertoire of cognitive strategies, a knowledge base in the subject, behaviours consistent with safety and ethical rules, the critical sense they need to manage their health wisely, and positive attitudes in their relationships with others when participating in physical activities.
New Brunswick	To attain healthy levels of physical activity and fitness for all students; to encourage the acquisition of motor skills; to develop knowledge and attitudes supportive of continuing active living habits throughout life; and to develop specific objectives designed to meet the physical growth and developmental needs of all children and youth.
Nova Scotia	Active, healthy living is shaped by the vision of learners experiencing purposeful physical activity and developing knowledge of, skills for, and attitudes towards the health benefits of a physically active lifestyle.
Newfoundland & Labrador	Physical education fosters personal and community wellness by empowering students to attain healthy, lifelong attitudes and behaviours through physical activity as part of the total educational experience.
Prince Edward Island	To provide opportunities for students to develop knowledge, skills, and positive attitudes toward active living. The curriculum will support students in acquiring the understandings and skills to engage in movement activity and to develop a solid foundation for a balanced lifestyle.

At the teacher level, curricular documents usually contain another form of more specific values labeled as student outcomes, objectives, or competencies, which serve to indicate what we, as a society, represented by the Ministry of Education, believe to be important (value) for students to learn and demonstrate. Chapter 4 addresses student learning outcomes and curriculum in greater detail.

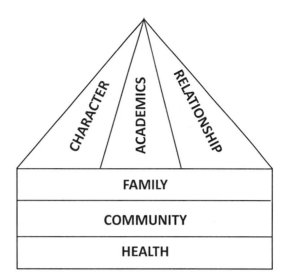

BATTLE RIVER SCHOOL DIVISION PYRAMID OF SUCCESS

Figure 1.6 BRSD Pyramid of Success

School Authorities: In addition, individual school authorities (e.g., boards, districts, etc.) within a Province have a specific philosophy or have identified certain larger goals that they prioritize and advertise as values. One such district, Battle River in Alberta, has expressed their common values through the "pyramid of success" shown in Figure 1.6 (Gleddie, 2012, p. 36).

Schools: Further, each school likely prides itself on certain educational values that it aims to achieve. Most often, these are reflected in a school's creation of culture and can often be found in its mission and vision statements.

Teachers: As a pre-service teacher, it is important to take some time to reflect on your own personal values as they relate to education, teaching and, especially, physical education.

- What is important to you?
- What do you believe students should know and be able to do before they graduate?
- What do you imagine a school to be like, perhaps one you may teach at?
- What do you value in your own teaching space (classroom, gymnasium, field, playground)?

Values and Physical Education

When it comes to the role of physical education in schools, it becomes clear that this subject is not valued as high as others such as literacy and numeracy (Trost & van der Mars, 2010). However, we have clear evidence (UNESCO, and all the evidence presented at the beginning of this chapter) of the benefits of physical education, and the critical and unique contribution it makes to education in the 21st century. So where is the problem? Why does this disconnect persist despite all the evidence?

As can be seen in the example above, the issue here is one of values. The parents and trustees value top scores in math and language arts. They do not value physical education at the same level, therefore decisions are made that negatively impact quality implementation of this curriculum subject area. As educators who believe (value) the importance of physical education and the fundamental need to truly teach the whole child, we have a moral obligation to advocate for the inherent value of movement and physical education and its quality implementation and inclusion in the school curricula. Consider this quote by Scott Kretchmar (1990):

> ...the sort of zeal we need in our profession is the kind that is grounded in values that are "larger" than any of us and that are selected on the basis of reason and evidence, not just personal opinion. Values that are not mere inventions, that cannot be dismissed simply as individual preferences cause us to pay attention and give allegiance to them— these kinds of values provoke us to persevere, take a stand, celebrate and, if necessary, suffer. (p. 97)

Perhaps part of the reason physical education is not valued is that we have not portrayed it as 'value-able'. Every time we trivialize physical education with concepts such as '*busy, happy, good*' (Placek, 1983); 'as long as they have fun' (O'Reilly, Tompkins & Gallant, 2001) and; 'it's just gym' (Robinson & Gleddie, 2011), we reduce the perceived value. Kretchmar's 'larger than any of us' values can be found in the UNESCO illustrations and include whole child education, physical and mental health, societal benefits and the joy of movement. These are the values we need to focus on and lift up! One of the ways to do this is through a concept called **physical literacy**.

Physical Literacy

An Introduction to Physical Literacy

The philosophy and concept of physical literacy has gained a lot of momentum in education, sport, recreation and the home – and for good reason! Margaret Whitehead (2013), a leading philosopher behind the concept, offers this definition:

> Physical literacy can be described as the motivation, confidence, physical competence, knowledge and understanding to value and take responsibility for engagement in physical activities for life.

The Elements of Physical Literacy

The definition of physical literacy includes four essential and interconnected elements whose relative importance may change throughout life.

 Motivation and confidence (Affective)

Motivation and confidence refers to an individual's enthusiasm for, enjoyment of, and self-assurance in adopting physical activity as an integral part of life.

 Physical competence (Physical)

Physical competence refers to an individual's ability to develop movement skills and patterns, and the capacity to experience a variety of movement intensities and durations. Enhanced physical competence enables an individual to participate in a wide range of physical activities and settings.

 Knowledge and understanding (Cognitive)

Knowledge and understanding includes the ability to identify and express the essential qualities that influence movement, understand the health benefits of an active lifestyle, and appreciate appropriate safety features associated with physical activity in a variety of settings and physical environments.

 Engagement in physical activities for life (Behavioural)

Engagement in physical activities for life refers to an individual taking personal responsibility for physical literacy by freely choosing to be active on a regular basis. This involves prioritizing and sustaining involvement in a range of meaningful and personally challenging activities, as an integral part of one's lifestyle.

Core Principles

Five core principles underlie the definition in this Statement.

Physical literacy:

- is an inclusive concept accessible to all
- represents a unique journey for each individual
- can be cultivated and enjoyed through a range of experiences in different environments and contexts
- needs to be valued and nurtured throughout life
- contributes to the development of the whole person.

Authors of this Statement

Canada's Physical Literacy Consensus Statement is the result of a collaborative process among ParticipACTION, Sport for Life Society, the Healthy Active Living and Obesity Research Group at the Children's Hospital of Eastern Ontario Research Institute, Physical and Health Education Canada, Canadian Parks and Recreation Association, and the Ontario Society of Physical Activity Promoters in Public Health. Representatives from the International Physical Literacy Association also contributed in an advisory capacity.

 This consensus process was made possible, in part, by the RBC Learn to Play Project, with funding from RBC and the Public Health Agency of Canada.

Figure 1.7 The Elements of Physical Literacy

A number of stakeholders in Canada, including representatives from education, sport, and recreation, have created a Canadian consensus statement for physical literacy based on the above definition (Canadian Sport for Life, 2015, p.2). See Figure 1.7.

Although we will take a deeper look at physical literacy in Chapter 3, let's examine why the concept resonates so clearly with educators. Corlett and Mandigo (2013) described how physical literacy, as a skill based competency, is similar to other educational skills and competencies that we value. They framed their illustration as an exercise in which 4 fictional teachers (language arts, mathematics, music and physical education) were asked to ensure that all grade 6 students in the school become literate in each teacher's specific subject area. Their article is summarized in table 1.2.

Table 1.2 Skill-Based Literacies				
Subject	**Language Arts (Literacy)**	**Mathematics (Numeracy)**	**Music (Music Literacy)**	**Physical Education (Physical Literacy)**
Building Blocks	"A,B,C's"	"1,2,3's"	"Do, Re, Mi's" check on this from music	Body, space, effort, relationships
Combinations	Sentences/paragraphs	Fractions, equations	Scales	Sequences
Abstractions	Stories, poems, essays	Problem solving, algorithms	Scores	Complex games, gymnastic routines
Life Application Examples	Read a novel for leisure Canadian Charter of Rights and Freedom	Program a computer game Pythagorean theorem	Perform in a band with friends. Beethoven's Symphony #9	Dance at a wedding. Cirque de Soliel

It becomes immediately apparent that each of these four subject areas follow a similar progression and seek to prepare students for a successful healthy life and good citizenship. Corlett and Mandigo conclude with this statement:

> *For now, we can at least be content that there is a literacy parallelism in the world of embodied life that links it to language, mathematics, and music and the work by PHE Canada on physical literacy through an education lens (www.phecanada.ca/ programs/ physical-literacy) has helped physical educators speak a language that is consistent with educators across various subject areas.* (p. 24)

The concept and application of physical literacy, as implemented in physical education, is consistent with the language and structure of education and therefore offers a means of connectivity and cohesion with all educators.

Conclusion

Throughout this chapter we have discussed the benefits of physical education and the importance of placing value on physical education as a curriculum subject area. However, and just as important, we need to be concerned that physical education continues to be undervalued in 'education' and society, even when compelling evidence is presented to show that our children, youth and general population need to be physically literate; they need to have positive physical education experiences. As you continue to engage in this text, take time to regularly pause and reflect on your beliefs which are influenced by your values and experiences. How can you be a positive advocate for quality physical education?

Checking for Understanding

I Can...

- State three different benefits of quality physical education in three separate categories (e.g., health, academics, etc.).
- Explain HOW physical education 'fits' into a holistic view of education.
- Share the value of physical education with a colleague.
- Explain how the concept of physical literacy is important for educators.

Chapter 2
Physical Education and You

Introduction: Why does your past matter?

The only source of knowledge is experience.
Albert Einstein

Life can only be understood backwards; but it must be lived forwards.
Soren Kierkegaard

Our past, which we can also label as our experience, has an incredible impact on both our present and future. For those who are considering entering the teaching profession, past experiences as students, with teachers and with education in general have power to define who we are now and who we will become. In fact, our very identities are linked with both our experiences and the places where our stories arise (Silko, 1996).

As an example, consider the following short excerpt from the article, *Remembering instructors: Play, pain and pedagogy.*

So, my major beef with the so-called physical education that I received as a kid is that it robbed me of the joy of physical activity for many years. It did nothing whatever to establish habits of balance in life between the cerebral and the physical. It did not promote habits of physical and mental health that can be derived from participation in physical play. Instead, the focus seemed to be on achieving excellence in a competitive setting. It destroyed my physical confidence. (Strean, 2009, p. 217)

Clearly, we can see this individual's past physical education experience had an impact (negative) long after leaving school. As teachers, we are shaped by our past but not controlled by it. It is possible to examine our experiences, analyze them and, regardless of whether they were positive or negative, learn from them (Gleddie & Schaefer, 2014). Therefore, the objective of this chapter is to help you:

- Comprehend the importance of experience,
- Explore personal experiences of physical education,
- Recognize how these experiences can impact our teaching and understanding of physical education – now and for the future,
- Understand that your students will each have their varied experiences of physical education and movement,
- Begin to develop a personal teaching philosophy of physical education.

Past Experiences with Physical Education

John Dewey and Experience

John Dewey was a philosopher, psychologist, social activist, and educator who argued that we must recognize and understand the connection between education and personal experience. His seminal work emphasized that learning is a social process; students can flourish when allowed to experiment and interact with their environment. In his influential book, Experience and Education (1938), he demonstrated that education and experience are not necessarily directly related because some experiences are not educative: "The trouble is not the absence of experiences, but their defective and wrong character – wrong and defective from the standpoint of connection with further experience" (p. 27). Dewey characterizes these "wrong and defective" experiences as mis-educative. Consider the quote below.

> *Experience and education cannot be directly equated to each other. For some experiences are mis-educative. Any experience is mis-educative that has the effect of arresting or distorting the growth of further experience.* (p. 25)

When we consider the earlier quote by Strean (2009) from *Play, Pain and Pedagogy*, it is clear the individual had a mis-educative experience in physical education. What we experience in our daily lives has an impact not only on the present, but also the future. Dewey went on to state that experience has two basic elements. First, there comes the immediate element of whether an experience is agreeable or disagreeable. The second element emerges when we consider the influence of the current experience on later experiences. Clearly, our job as physical educators is to engage students with what we do in the ***now***, however, we must also ensure that what we do is enduring and is more than just fun or agreeable. "… upon them devolves the responsibility for instituting the conditions for the kind of present experience which has a favourable effect upon the future." (Dewey, 1938, p. 50)

Mis-Education?

Think back to a few significant experiences in your life. Would you categorize any as mis-educative? Why? What were the specific aspects that turned you away from future similar experiences? Discuss these aspects with your colleagues/peers.

A large part of what we do in education is to create experiences for students. It is very important that we consider Dewey's views as we design and implement our lessons within a physical education program.

Hence, the central problem of an education based on experience is to select the kind of present experiences that live fruitfully and creatively in subsequent experiences.

Dewey, 1938, p. 27-28

Questions to consider:
  • Will my lesson/activity engage the student now?
  • Will my lesson/activity encourage and support future experiences?

Experiences also play a role in helping define and shape the things we believe are important – these tend to be the very things we believe our own students should find valuable.

Narrative, Experience and You

One of the ways we commonly share our experiences with each other is through stories or narratives. Writing and sharing narratives about your (mis)educative experiences in school, and physical education in particular, can be an effective way to examine our values and where they came from. Studying our narratives not only shapes what we currently believe but also how we might move forward into the future as a teacher of physical education.

The concept of story or narrative as a basis for research and learning in physical education, although still relatively new, has begun to gain momentum. An emerging number of researchers and authors have started to unravel the narratives of others by investigating the personal experiences of children and youth and the manner that these experiences have impacted their choices and decisions in adulthood (Armour & Jones, 1998; Garrett, 2006; O'Sullivan, 2006; Sparkes, 2002; Wrench & Garrett, 2012). Using a variety of methodologies and techniques, these authors are helping to show that the body is a "site" for lived experience; experiences that manifest themselves in pre-service teachers' construction of personal pedagogy (McMahon & Penney, 2013).

Autobiographical narrative inquiry is a specific methodology that involves studying experience through stories (Clandinin & Connelly, 2000). Gleddie and Schaefer (2014) engaged in a study of their own educative experiences of movement and physical education. Their process included writing and inquiring into stories of experiences from childhood, early days as elementary students, and physical education teaching. As narrative inquirers, they were able to shift their gaze from (inward) personal feelings, hopes and dispositions, to (outward) existential social conditions, to an examination of temporality, backwards and forwards (past, present and future) and, finally, to a consideration of place, "which attends to the specific concrete physical and topological boundaries of inquiry landscapes" (Clandinin & Connelly, 2000, p. 51).

Many educators and researchers have found that these methodologies offer insight into how experiences shape our identities, our practices and our beliefs as students, teachers and teacher educators. As well, they recognize the importance of understanding stories about physical education experiences that differed from theirs. This realization has resulted in a reconsideration of some of their pedagogical strategies. In the following text box, consider this portion of a story fragment from their article.

> **Longjohns**
>
> *"Doug, you forgot your gym clothes! Come over here!" I sheepishly slunk over to the centre of the basement and was ready to explain my situation when suddenly I was swept off my feet, lifted high into the air and pinned against the ceiling. "Why do you not have your gym clothes?!?" Three quick, relevant facts. Number one, there was no way I was explaining myself in front of the whole class. Number two, I could barely keep myself from peeing my pants, much less actually talk. Number three, I stutter badly when forced to respond verbally under pressure. Therefore, I said nothing except for a few stuttered grunts. After a little more uplifted condemnation for not being changed, I was forced to sit out for the rest of the class. Although I kept a brave face for my friends, ("That was so cool how he lifted me up so high"), inside I was embarrassed, frustrated, mad and ultimately – helpless.* (Gleddie & Schaefer, 2014, p. 9-10)

Obviously, this experience had a deep and lasting impact on the author, but it does not end with the telling of the story. Gleddie and Schaefer go on to analyze their stories using what is called the 'three-dimensional space.'

> *Narrative inquiry…begins with a pragmatic ontology that treats lived experience as both the beginning and ending points of inquiry. Various social and cultural influences may come into play during the inquiry… In a narrative inquiry, these social and cultural influences are not treated only as the occasions for critical exposure. They are treated as resources to be used in pursuit of always tentative and partial ameliorations of experience.*
>
> Clandinin & Rosiek, 2007, p. 55

Clandinin and Connelly's notion of narrative inquiry can be used to better understand your learning process as a pre-service teacher. Together, we can come to a better understanding of how autobiographical narrative inquiry not only provides opportunities to reflect on how past experiences shape pedagogy, but how a rich and reflective autobiographical inquiry process reveals possibilities to see the complexity, continuity, and interaction (Dewey, 1938) of your own experiences. If we can see how complex our own "stories to live by" (Clandinin, 1985; Schaefer & Clandinin, 2012 are, we can recognize, in a transactional way, how complex others' stories are as well. This phenomenon offers opportunities to "see otherwise" (Greene, 1995) and initiates possibilities for *world travelling* (Lugones, 1997).

Let us take a closer look at the process of autobiographical narrative inquiry, starting with a fragment from Shannon's 2012 story.

The Rink

I loved the rink. It was a place filled with familiar smells of musty, sweaty gear and greasy hamburgers from the canteen. I loved that it was always a bit chilly. My favourite rinks were the ones with the electric heaters hanging over the bleachers; the dry, warm radiation on my bare arms in the middle of winter was soothing. My dad and I would walk around the lobby looking at the same framed pictures of former hockey players to kill time, get a drink, and go to the bathroom. One day we were hanging around loitering and a lady approached us who I recognized as one of the parents but didn't know her name. She said to my dad as though I wasn't standing right there, attached to my dad's hip, "Oh, is this your little boy?" as she smiled. I slid behind my dad's leg a bit to hide from her, suddenly very conscious of my short haircut. I remember being embarrassed for my dad having to explain. "No, this is my daughter, Shannon," he said very matter-of-fact. And then for some reason I felt a wash of embarrassment come over me. I looked down at my feet because there was nowhere else to look. "Hi," I muttered to my shoes in a whisper. I could feel tears welling in my eyes but wasn't sure why. I quietly apologized to my dad as we walked away and he patted my head. "Don't listen to her. Maybe she just saw how good you were at hockey last week". My dad always knew what to say, even if he didn't say much. But as we hung around the rink for the rest of the practice and walked to the car afterward, I remember being very confused. (Remembered experience(s), story written September 2, 2012)

Thinking about this remembered experience using the narrative inquiry three-dimensional space (Clandinin & Connelly, 2000), Shannon looks back and recalls having a very uncomfortable realization and perhaps a moment when she began to try to socially shape her stories to live by, into acceptable frames. Outwardly, she remembers feeling that she didn't want her parents to be embarrassed of her. Looking backward and inward, she said she was also embarrassed for the lady, and now wonders about the assumptions the lady had made about her gender. Using Hay and Macdonald's (2010) notion of ability, Shannon wonders if she had demonstrated, while playing hockey, traits that had been associated with boys rather than girls, underlining a dominant discourse in society that boys have more ability in sports than girls. Shifting temporally to the present, Shannon thinks about her teaching experiences on the physical education landscape and sees how physical education can be a magnifying class for insecurities; too fat, too thin, uncoordinated, underdeveloped skill, etc. The experience of being mistaken for a boy has shaped how she, as an educator, responds to individuals who do not fit the dominant narratives of physical education.

To go back to the 'Longjohns' story, Gleddie and Schaefer (2014) come to several conclusions in their analysis. Temporally, this was a one time 'bad' or mis-educative experience with physical education. They postulate that perhaps other, educative experiences in a way 'inoculated' Doug and therefore he has been able to move past this one mis-educative experience to go on to a career in 'physical education' based on what he loves best. From the dimension of 'place,' physical education and the activity spaces were a place of enjoyment and safety for Doug, therefore, the 'Longjohns' story was disconnected from his normal feelings about those places. Finally, socially, what stood out was a lack of trust between Doug and his teacher. Looking forward, Doug currently strives as an educator to create trust with students and devotes a lot of time to that task (p. 9).

Autobiographical Inquiry Activity

The purpose of this activity is to allow you an opportunity to reflect on how you have become a teacher. Specifically, reflect on how you have come to conceptualize physical education and physical activity. You are all pre-service teachers because of past experiences you have had and these experiences are important to both your personal and professional identity. Our biases, values, and beliefs shape how we see the curriculum, how we treat colleagues, how we view ourselves as physical education teachers, and how we view the subject area. Therefore, it is important to inquire into where and how these important aspects of your identity have been shaped.

Part 1: Personal Reflection / Discussion
Take some time to think about your past experiences of physical education, sport and/or physical activity. What comes to mind right away? What kind of thoughts and memories emerge? These memories take place anywhere, at any time. They should not only be experiences with school.

Join with a small group and discuss your experiences. Similarities? Differences? Common themes or threads? As you engage in the discussion, consider which memories you may choose to expand upon as story fragments.

Part 2: Story Fragments
Write 1-2 short stories around particular memories you reflected on and discussed. Write the experience as if it is a narrative. Make it first person (use of 'me' and 'I'), detailed and focused on the actual event / memory. It should be engaging, and include enough information to allow the reader to catch a glimpse of the experience.

Part 3: Inquiry
In this section of the assignment, you have the opportunity to inquire into the narratives that you wrote. Think about why they are important to you. How have they shaped your path to education? How have they shaped your beliefs and values around PE? How will these stories play out in your own PE class? What are the resonances between the stories, the threads that hold them together?

(Adapted from Dr. Lee Schaefer's assignment, McGill University)

Through an acknowledgment of experience and by using narrative inquiry examples, we can understand how our past influences not only our present, but also our future. These stories, analyses and realizations help us to understand who we are and what we bring to our roles as teachers of physical education. In the next section, we will examine how these experiences also play a role in the development of a teaching philosophy for physical education.

Developing a Teaching Philosophy for Physical Education

Why a Teaching Philosophy?

Developing a teaching philosophy is a very important, if not the most important, aspect to becoming a teacher and continuing your career as an educator. Teaching is an expression of who you are; it is important that you first know yourself before you teach others (Beatty, Leigh, & Dean, 2009). Your philosophy will guide you through important and/or challenging decisions and will help you identify successes. From daily decisions about what you will teach and engage in for particular lessons, to more long-term decisions about how you imagine students learning in your classroom/gymnasium throughout the year. These decisions are all directly related to your teaching philosophy.

Although your teaching philosophy is always changing and evolving as you continue to experience unique people, contexts and content, you must recognize that you already have a philosophy about teaching. Learning to teach is an ongoing journey that began long before you entered post-secondary education. It has been estimated that pre-service teachers have already spent approximately 13,000 hours observing teachers by the time they enter teacher education (Britzman, 2003). To have a sense of what you believe in allows you to work toward meaningful goals both for you and the students and colleagues whom you work alongside. By developing your teaching philosophy, you will be able to navigate the complex world of teaching in a much more rewarding way. One way to think about your teaching philosophy is in relation to your identity.

What is Identity?

Your teaching philosophy is directly related to who you are or, in other words, your identity. As examined earlier, we can use a narrative approach to think about identity. Our experiences highlight the multiplicity of our lives and speak to the interrelationship between a person's personal practical knowledge and the landscapes on which they live and work. Identity can be thought of in terms of our "stories to live by" (Clandinin, 1985; Schaefer & Clandinin, 2012); we often speak about our experiences through stories and we are able to see how our stories have been shaped over time, in various places, and in different relationships. Our stories to live by have not been developed in isolation; our identities involve many complex personal and contextual factors, as you saw earlier in the autobiographical inquiry activity.

Richie and Wilson (2000) explained further that our identity is never determined by a single person, place or thing. We are often faced with multiple, often conflicting discourses and where these discourses intersect can be sites of examination. When we find ourselves in spaces of tension, where discourses collide or intersect, we may be called upon to critically reflect. These spaces of tension can be focal points for examination. Often schools are spaces of tension where we find ourselves questioning our identities; where our personal and professional selves come together. Beauchamp and Thomas (2009) stated that a sense of agency and empowerment can come from realizing one's identity.

Your Choice

As a teacher of physical education, you have a very important opportunity; you will be able to create an environment where all students will want to participate and will be able to enjoy

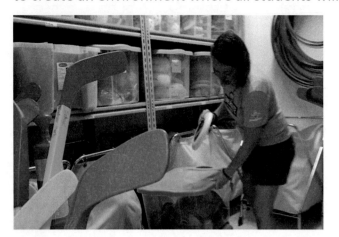

educative and enduring experiences. By building relationships and getting to know students individually, you may find your own educational philosophy shifting as you are influenced by students.

Physical Education Philosophy

Although you may not have considered yourself a physical education teacher prior to entering your teacher education program, it is important to reflect on what you believe about physical education and why you believe what you do. As mentioned earlier in the chapter, your beliefs about teaching physical education have been formed by:

- Your past experiences (and reflection)
- Your beliefs about education
- The curriculum (educational system)
- Your values
- Your identity

Your Experiences and Your Teaching

If you have mis-educative experiences in school, you are more likely to avoid similar uncomfortable situations as a teacher. For example, if you did not enjoy physical education while growing up, then you probably already perceive physical education as a challenging and undesirable subject to teach. However, you have a choice to change this perception and create a positive physical education experience for students in your class; you have the ability to use your experience to help construct educative and enduring experiences (Dewey, 1938). As well, just because you may have thoroughly enjoyed your physical education experiences growing up, we must remain cognizant that not everyone enjoyed a similar experience. For example, you may have participated in a variety of sport-specific activities and thrived during competition set up by your teacher(s) in class.

Both professionally and personally, it is a worthwhile exercise to consider your previous experiences (either educative or mis-educative) and examine how your identity and your teaching philosophy are shaped by these stories.

Developing a Physical Education Teaching Philosophy

As an elementary school teacher, you are responsible for teaching physical education. You have the ability to shape and influence your students' perceptions about physical activity, movement, their bodies, their health, and so many other important lifelong dispositions. You must be an advocate for physical education; this begins with shaping your own philosophy about physical education.

Although early in your career you may feel that creating a teaching philosophy is superficial because you do not know enough, this is not true. You have many experiences that create valuable knowledge within you; these experiences can help you create an authentic philosophy. In a recent study of teacher candidates over the course of their teacher education programs, first year students admitted they could not see a reason for making a teaching philosophy statement. That same group by their fourth year – after s chool and life experiences – agreed that they believed they owned their evolving philosophy and were beginning to make connections between their philosophy and teaching (Nickel, 2013).

The process of drafting a physical education teaching philosophy is just as important as the actual content or end product. Working through your philosophy increases your self-awareness as an educator and person (Beatty, Leigh, & Dean, 2009). It helps you clarify your values by reflecting on your experiences and beliefs.

Framing Your Philosophy

You may be wondering where to begin and feel overwhelmed by the idea of putting pen to paper. Remember that, even by starting, you are more likely to return to your philosophy statement to revise it than if you never began in the first place. One suggested method to begin a philosophy statement is to follow three steps: reflect, connect, and craft (Beatty, Leigh, & Dean, 2009).

1. **Reflect:** Ask yourself what a great day of teaching looks, sounds and feels like? Visualize this ideal day using all of your senses. Now consider the opposite experience; what might a challenging day look, sound and feel like? Be sure to jot everything down even if you may not use it later.
2. **Connect:** Group your ideas into themes or patterns. For example, if you notice that many of your positive visualization descriptions involve students working collaboratively and experiencing their surroundings without your intervention as a teacher, you may want to create a philosophy theme of 'collaboration' or 'experiential learning.'
3. **Craft:** Write a thesis statement or summary statement to begin your paragraph. Then start to add the themes or patterns you have identified in step 2. This paragraph can be your core framework from which you will add and remove ideas.

Another suggested method to begin a statement is to refer to a well-known document such as a provincial curriculum guide (Kell, 2015). You can begin your philosophy statement with your own beliefs about physical education and move into specific terminology that your school / Province uses. In order to keep the philosophy statement about your values and not the document, be sure to always revisit how your beliefs connect to the Provincial values. The following text box identifies a simple framework for outlining your ideas and beginning your physical education teaching philosophy using this method.

PE Philosophy Statement Activity

The purpose of this assignment is to engage in the process of writing a PE philosophy statement through reflection and continual reassessment. Developing a professional philosophy statement is ongoing; our experiences, backgrounds, contexts, and interactions help shape our identity. Although your 'PE Philosophy Statement' is specific to your current context, you are asked to reflect on your beliefs, values, and principles that you believe are most important personally and professionally when teaching. You will record a pre-course statement, revise it throughout the semester, and look back on it at the end of the course to develop a product you will share.

Part 1: Pre-Course Statement Draft
Record your statement
a. Print a hard copy
b. Bring to class each week

Part 2: Ongoing Reflection and Reassessment
Re-visit your statement after each class meeting
a. Make changes on the hard copy in coloured ink
b. Take a photograph of the 'new document' each week with changes
Consider: What did you learn or experience this week that has shifted...
        ...your philosophy about teaching?
        ...what you believe about how students learn?
        ...how you connect with students?

Part 3: Sharing
Re-write your statement in a polished form (typed or hand-written)
        a. Take a photograph (large enough to read)
Collect all photographs, capturing changes over time
        b. Create an electronic document (collage, time line, visual, etc.)
Share your PE Philosophy Statement with peers or online in your portfolio

Here is an example of a pre-service teacher's philosophy statement (Shared by Brittney Glinsbockel, Mount Royal University, 2014) based on the above process:

Sample of PE Philosophy Statement Activity

Created: September 23rd
The physical experience
- Inclusive – students with a variety of physical & emotional needs
- Accommodating – appropriate assessment for each group of students taught
- Engaging – students should feel same and supported in P.E class

Learning to maintain a healthy lifestyle
- Active for life – activity should be incorporated, not separated
- Character building – teamwork, responsibility, trust, cooperation, determination

Students should learn about their bodies for understanding what physical activity means

Revised: October 7th
The physical experience
- Inclusive – students with a variety of physical & emotional needs
- Accommodating – appropriate assessment for each group of students taught

- Engaging – students should feel same and supported in P.E class
- Student choice
- Body awareness & development – understanding the complexities of body movement and developing competence and confidence in a variety of skills

Learning to maintain a healthy lifestyle
- Active for life – activity should be incorporated, not separated
- Character building – teamwork, responsibility, trust, cooperation, determination

Students should learn about their bodies for understanding what physical activity means.

Educators should be sensitive to student development and preference, not single students out and put them on the spot. This might hinder them having a positive experience in the gym.
Revised: Weekly for semester (additional drafts not shown)

Final Revision: December 2nd
Students engaging in physical experiences will demonstrate a variety of physical and emotional needs. I believe it to be the educator's responsibility to recognize these needs and accommodate accordingly. Here it is important to consider means for inclusive practice and what that might mean in a physical education (P.E.) setting. For example, accounting for diversity might look like providing appropriate equipment and space for students and designing tasks tailored to their needs. I believe this to be important in any educational setting where students should feel equally supported and remember that educators should be sensitive to student development and preference; no singling students out and putting them on the spot. This might hinder them having a positive experience in the gym.

I believe it is significantly important for students to learn about what it means to maintain a healthy lifestyle and becoming active for life; meaning activity should be incorporated, not separated. Assisting students in building the foundation for living a healthy lifestyle will lay in their understanding of the ways physical activity engages the whole person physically, emotionally, cognitively, and socially. Young people will be empowered by learning about body awareness and development, and understanding the complexities of body movement to develop competence and confidence in a variety of skills. Students should learn about their bodies simply to understand what physical activity means for them.

Not only will a positive physical education experience encourage students in becoming active for life, but gain skills in communication, cooperation, teamwork, determination, and build character along the way. Students will take ownership of their learning in P.E. by participating in self-assessments and student choice activities. I value a teaching environment where students are the stewards for their own learning, but are guided by an educator who oversees safety and encourages success. Safety and classroom management are essential to providing a structured and secure physical education environment. Educators and students will collaborate about what safety standards in P.E. should look like before entering the gym and maintain consistency in these criteria throughout the year. Some key concerns to address might be fair play, appropriate clothing, control signals, and respecting yourself, others, and the environment.

A teaching philosophy is by no means a static document. Following are the physical education teaching philosophy statements from Doug and Shannon with over 35 years of experience between them. These philosophies have been revisited and revised multiple times over many years of teaching; life and school experiences are appropriate to refer to when you draft and finalize your own teaching philosophy.

Doug: Over the length of my career, I have developed a fundamental belief in the absolute, critical, elemental, life-changing and life-giving need for human movement. For me, there are two critical elements that form the core of my teaching philosophy for physical education.

1. Movement for the sake of movement. Movement can stand on its own – it has inherent worth and efficacy all by its lonesome. Thelen (1995) stated, "People perceive in order to move and move in order to perceive. What, then, is movement but a form of perception, a way of knowing the world as well as acting on it?" Movement is essential to who we are as human beings and is absolutely critical to growth and development across the lifespan. The health and academic benefits are a great bonus, but are really just an extension of how movement is part of our human identity and helps us negotiate the treacherous terrain of life. Therefore, education should not be considered "whole-child" unless it includes education of the physical. Physical literacy is a concept that has gained momentum recently in Canada and globally. The definition is based on the United Nations renewed literacy definition, "Literacy is crucial to the acquisition, by every child, youth and adult, of essential life skills that enable them to address the challenges they can face in life..." (UN, 2002).

2. The intrinsic JOY of movement. As Kretchmar (2008) writes, "When movement is experienced as joy, it adorns our lives, makes our days go better, and gives us something to look forward to. When movement is joyful and meaningful, it may even inspire us to do things we never thought possible" (p. 162). The fact is, kids (and adults!) are motivated by joy and will work / play extremely hard to find it. As a bonus, they'll also get all the health and academic benefits. If you want to see an example of this ethic in action, go visit a skate park. There you'll see people finding joy in learning – intrinsic motivation at its best and not a trophy or rubric in sight.

Quite often, students will approach me and express their apprehension about taking a class on PE pedagogy. Their fears may be grounded in a negative experience, a misguided perception or a stereotype – it really doesn't matter. My teaching philosophy allows me to meet them where they are, provide joyful movement experiences, and help them establish an identity as a teacher of PE.

Shannon: I believe that a foundation to quality teaching is building relationships. This can include, but is not limited to, learning about each student in class; their name, their experiences, their background, their challenges, their successes. Effective and meaningful teaching begins with knowing who your students are and what their expectations are for the teacher and the course. At the outset, for example, expectations should be negotiated and communicated clearly. Communication requires open dialogue and begins to build trust within the professional relationship.

I also believe that students should own their learning. In other words, learning that occurs in a course should be student-centered, relevant, and challenging. For this to occur, a course must be organized in a way that allows students to ask deep questions about the content and/or context, explore the content/ context, and assess their learning alongside the teacher. The teacher, ideally, becomes a facilitator for and supporter of each student.

Finally, I believe that teaching should involve collaboration with the larger community. Students need to be engaged with community members beyond the course and their peers for deeper learning to occur. As a result, students may find networking opportunities, places for volunteerism, spaces of enjoyment and fulfillment, and/or real-life learning experiences.

Depending on the nature of where you will be sharing your philosophy statement, you may choose to include more or less personal content. As well, there is no set standard for tone and content. However, do not hesitate to include your values and beliefs. Your philosophy statement should be authentic and true to who you are as a person and a professional.

Importance of Reflecting and Intentional Professional Development

Creating and revising a teaching philosophy offers the opportunity for both reflection and professional development. Through the process you may realize that you feel strongly about specific aspects of physical education. On the other hand, you may identify areas that you would like to know more about. As a teacher, it is your obligation to commit to lifelong learning, especially since this is what we ask of our students.

You have the ability to shape your professional development. Nickel (2013) agreed with Beauchamp and Thomas (2009) who emphasized teacher candidates, who are aware of their strengths and the unique contributions they can make to the profession, are better able to target their own professional growth to those priorities they value. Although your teaching philosophy may initially be aligned closely to the discourse of your teacher education program, it will progressively develop to align with your own aspirations and evolving identity as a teacher.

Sharing your Teaching Philosophy with Others

Once you have created a draft of your physical education teaching philosophy, it is important to share it with others. Sharing helps ground your thinking by employing peers and colleagues as sounding boards; your ideas will become more refined as you are asked questions about your values and beliefs. In addition, your teaching philosophy may help generate ideas for others' developing philosophies and vice versa. It is also important to share your philosophy with parents and students. This will help them understand your process and rationale within physical education.

Conclusion

As you have learned, your past is part of both your present, and your future. Although you can't change what happened to you in the past, you can ensure that the result now and in the future will be positive. This is especially important if you have had a poor experience with physical education in the past. Reflecting on those experiences can help you to become a better teacher – over your whole career!

Checking for Understanding

I Can…
- Make positive educational choices based on how my past experiences shape and impact my teaching of physical education.
- Understand that each of my own students will have varied experiences of physical education and make teaching decisions based on that knowledge.
- Share two key elements of my physical education teaching philosophy with a colleague.

Chapter 3
Foundations of a Quality Physical Education Program

Just as youngsters learn to read, to compute, to analyze in classrooms over their school years, effective physical education teachers provide a wealth of lasting experiences in gyms and on fields that lead youngsters to enjoyably participate in physical activity for a lifetime.

George Graham, blog post, 2015

Introduction

A house is only as good as its foundation. Although there are different types of building materials used in foundations, the goal is the same: to provide a stable and strong platform upon which to build something that is functional, appealing and will last for a long, long time. Building a quality physical education program is really not that much different. Without the proper elements united in a solid foundation, how can we ever expect to build a program that has efficacy, strength and longevity? Foundations are critical.

This chapter is designed to take you on a tour of some of the crucial elements that underlie quality physical education programs. Therefore, the objectives of this chapter are to:

- Understand that the foundation of quality physical education rests on the intrinsic joy of human movement

- Gain an understanding and appreciation of physical literacy and why the concept belongs in education

- Explore the relationship between physical activity, physical education, and physical literacy

- Understand curricular outcomes in physical education and how they relate to program aims

- Develop an understanding of the principles and concepts of motor learning and how they apply to elementary school physical education

- Understand the importance of developmental appropriateness and how it impacts planning and teaching decisions

- Appreciate the key role that physical and emotional safety play in a quality physical education program and understand how to create a supportive culture

The JOY of Physical Education!

When movement is experienced as joy, it adorns our lives, makes our days go better, and gives us something to look forward to. When movement is joyful and meaningful, it may even inspire us to do things we never thought possible.

Kretchmar, 2008, p. 162

Currently, the two most common arguments put forth when advocating for quality programs of physical education, and more physical education for children and youth, include benefits to health and improved academic performance. For example:

- **Health Benefits:**
  - 6 Dimensions of Wellness (Fishburne, 2005; Hales & Lauzon, 2015)
  - Leadership opportunities (Lieberman, Arndt, & Daggett, 2007; Martinek & Schilling, 2003)
- **Academic Benefits:**
  - Higher levels of self-efficacy, greater academic performance, less disruptive behaviour, less anxiety (Medina, 2008)

Great! The more benefits associated with physical education that can be identified (refer back to Chapter 1 for a more comprehensive list of benefits), the stronger the rationale when advocating for quality programs of physical education. There is a wealth of valid evidence available to show the many benefits of physical education. Such evidence should not be ignored (although sadly, it often is).

The kind or type of evidence often put forth to justify the benefits of physical education also causes a problem - A BIG PROBLEM. The identifiable benefits are often 'extrinsic' or 'functional' in nature – improved academic achievement score, improved fitness score, etc. When all the focus is on extrinsic or functional rationale, two very important aspects of movement itself are missed.

#1: Movement for the sake of Movement!

Movement can stand on its own – it has inherent worth and efficacy. Therefore, physical

education as a subject area also has value all by itself – not just because it helps 'students do better in school' or 'be healthy.' We NEED physical education just like we need mathematics, science and all the other curriculum subjects (including art and music!). Consider this quote:

People perceive in order to move and move in order to perceive. What, then, is movement but a form of perception, a way of knowing the world as well as acting on it?
Thelen, 1995, p. 89

So, in physical education, we teach students how to not only know their bodies and their environments, but also how to act on this knowledge. In other words, movement is essential to who we are as human beings; it is absolutely critical to growth and development across the lifespan (Haywood & Getchell, 2014). For example: infants who averaged 41 days of creeping (movement) experience were more likely to avoid a "visual cliff" (plexi-glass covered drop-off) than infants with 11 days of similar movement experience (Witherington, et al., 2005). At the other end of the spectrum, women over 80 years of age who participated in a targeted exercise program (e.g., strength and balance) had significantly less falls than the 80 year-old women who did not (Campbell, et al., 1999). The health and academic benefits of physical education is very important, but such benefits can be considered merely a 'bonus' as they are truly just an extension of how movement is part of our human identity that helps us negotiate the diverse terrain of life. Therefore, education should not be considered "whole-child" unless it includes education of the physical.

If educators want to create an education environment that directly opposes how the human brain works most effectively, a design that resembles a school classroom would be the most effective choice.

Medina, 2008

#2: The Intrinsic Joy of Movement!

"…physical education is important because movement is joyful, pleasurable, provides intrinsic satisfaction, and can be personally meaningful and central to the human experience" (Blankenship & Ayers, 2010, p. 171). A joy-based approach to physical education speaks to the natural motivation found in satisfying movement activities and focuses on developing students who become lifelong, joy-seeking movers (Blankenship & Ayers, 2010; Kretchmar, 2008).

Imagine two Grade 3 children having the following conversation:

"So, I was thinking of increasing my cardiovascular fitness by running around and tagging people."

"Great! I'll join you, and afterwards, we can work on our core strength and dynamic balance as we swing on the swings"

"Right – I am looking to reduce my co-morbidity and manage my ADHD!"

"You got that right – I don't want to get diabetes. And, this running around really helps me focus on science after lunch!"

It even sounds funny to say it out loud, but this is sometimes how movement and physical education are treated. The fact is, students are motivated by joy and will work/play extremely hard to find it. As a bonus, they'll also get all the health and academic benefits. Think of those times in your life where you experienced joy through physical activity. Didn't you want more (Chapter 2)? Take some time to go and watch young children engaged in free play. Observe the joy in movement and the educative nature and motivation that exists. Learn from it!

Want to advocate for physical education? Want healthier children and a less sedentary society? Want your students to love physical education and to be lifetime movers? Become an advocate and role model for the inherent worth of movement itself. Be a joy-facilitator and find ways to allow others to also discover their own joy through movement.

Physical Literacy

Where did Physical Literacy come from?

Literacy is crucial to the acquisition, by every child, youth and adult, of essential life skills that enable them to address the challenges they can face in life, and represents an essential step in basic education, which is an indispensable means for effective participation in the societies and economies of the 21st century.
United Nations, 2002

The United Nations 2002 declaration has opened the door to new interpretations of what it means for students in our schools to be "literate." There is a growing recognition that literacy no longer refers to reading and writing alone. Literacy is being able to read and respond to the world we live in. We have become very familiar with terms such as media literacy and computer literacy as our society changes. In Canada, our children are also facing the following challenges:

- 14% of children aged 5-11 do not meet the recommended guidelines of 60 minutes of Moderate to Vigorous Physical Activity (MVPA) per day
- Only 24% of children aged 5-17 walk or wheel to school
- Children aged 5-11 spend 7.6 hours per day being sedentary
- Only 24% of children aged 5-11 meet the recommended guidelines of 2 hours or less of screen time per day (ParticipACTION, 2015)

> Take a closer look at the bolded words in the United Nations quote above. Why might these phrases be important for elementary school physical education?

Clearly, it is time to recognize and act upon a long-neglected form of literacy – physical literacy. Margaret Whitehead is a physical education philosopher from the United Kingdom who has been working on the term and its ramifications for the past 25 years. In her words,

...as appropriate to each individual's endowment, physical literacy can be described as a disposition in which individuals have: the motivation, confidence, physical competence, knowledge and understanding to value and take responsibility for maintaining purposeful physical pursuits/activities throughout the lifecourse. (2010)

Whitehead's definition aligns perfectly with the United Nations literacy definition. We need students to embark on a physical literacy journey. This lifelong journey will prepare them to meet the challenges of inactivity, poor health, and sedentary lifestyles. Students who are engaged in physical literacy will be able to effectively participate in society as we move further into the 21st century.

What is Physical Literacy?

Chapter 1 provided both the Canadian consensus statement on Physical Literacy as well as a glimpse of how physical literacy "fits" in education.

"A B C's, 1 2 3's, Do Re Mi's,
Run Jump Throw!"

Let us take a closer look at the concept itself and highlight some important pieces for educators. In partnership with Physical and Health Education (PHE) Canada, several researchers wrote a key position paper entitled, ***Physical Literacy for Educators.*** They proposed the following definition for Canadian physical educators:

Individuals who are physically literate move with competence in a wide variety of physical activities that benefit the development of the whole person.

Physically literate individuals consistently develop the motivation and ability to understand, communicate, apply, and analyze different forms of movement. They are able to demonstrate a variety of movements confidently, competently, creatively and strategically across a wide range of health-related physical activities. These skills enable individuals to make healthy, active choices throughout their life span that are both beneficial to and respectful of themselves, others, and their environment.

Mandigo, Francis, Lodewyk & Lopez, 2009, p. 6-7

The position paper goes on to describe why these specific characteristics are so critical to a journey of physical literacy.

1. **Motivation:** belongs to the affective domain and ensures participation and commitment to improvement. Teachers will focus on cultivating intrinsic motivation and the desire for lifelong physical activity.

2. **Understanding, communicating, applying and analyzing:** these terms refer to the cognitive domain and also speak across disciplines to the broad nature of education. Teachers will use similar terms, vocabulary or core competencies across curricula (e.g., ***problem solving)*** to reinforce common learning strategies and goals.

3. **Diversity of movement:** psychomotor skills need to be developed across the spectrum of activities. Dance, games, fitness, gymnastics, individual activities, outdoor pursuits – all provide unique aspects and the whole is greater than the sum of the parts. Teachers will ensure a breadth of movement opportunities and provide rich and diverse learning environments.

4. **Confidence and competence:** perhaps the most critical relationship of the definition – these two terms are inextricably linked. Self-esteem plays a critical role in skill development, however, there is an equal reciprocal relationship. Teachers will help students to build self-esteem and fundamental/complex motor skills – together, these can be applied in authentic movement contexts.

5. **Creativity:** another cross-curricular competency that can be further developed in physical education. Teachers will encourage creativity through the inclusion of aesthetic, expressive movement (e.g., dance), but also through creative skill application in games or cooperative activities.

6. **Strategically:** this cognitive element can certainly apply to games (tactics, decision making), but can also be found in a variety of decision opportunities in individual activities, dance, and the outdoors. Teachers will ensure that students are able to think strategically in a variety of ways, most importantly, about how and when to apply their skills.

7. **Health-related, healthy active choices:** physical literacy is an important component of a healthy lifestyle and also fits within the goals of a healthy school community (see Chapter 8). Teachers will encourage the development of fitness goals and plans, home and community connections as well as healthy decision making.

8. **Lifespan:** for our students, physical literacy is important now and for the rest of their lives. Teachers will help students understand and apply the concept of a physical literacy journey that lasts a lifetime.

9. **Beneficial to and Respectful of themselves, others and their environment:** personal, social, and environmental responsibility are important educational and societal goals. Teachers will provide opportunities for reflection and pursuit of these goals through physical education.

(Adapted from: Mandigo, Francis, Lodewyk & Lopez, 2009, p. 7-8)

As well, the world of sport has also embraced physical literacy as a key component of the Long-Term Athlete (Participant) Development model (LTAD). See Figure 3.1. This alignment provides opportunities for discussion and consistency across applicable sectors like health, recreation, sport and education.

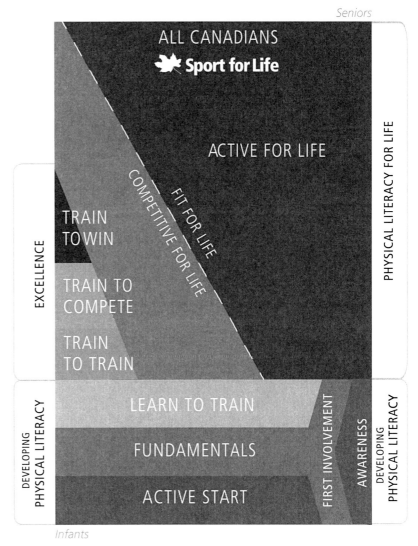

Figure 3.1 Long Term Athlete Development Model (canadiansportforlife.ca)

Dr. Dean Kriellaars(University of Manitoba) is one of the foremost advocates for physical literacy in Canada and around the globe. He has developed and shared some excellent models and research with a goal to further the physical literacy of Canadian children. After looking at the model in Figure 3.2, complete the task in the text box (*Examining the Model*).

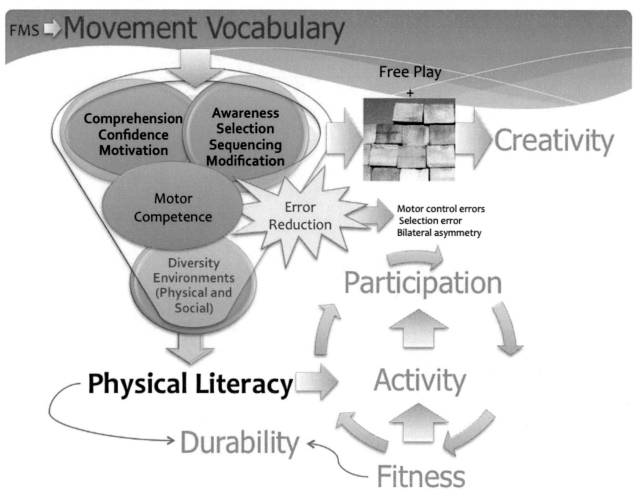

Figure 3.2 Physical Literacy (Kriellaars, 2014)

Why do we care about Physical Literacy?

First, as we saw in Chapter 1, there is an entire structure of values embedded into our schools and educational systems. One of the reasons that the concept of physical literacy has so much potential is the "fit" it has with educational structures, vocabulary, and, most importantly, values. Consider the following:

- **Whole child education?** Yes! You can't claim to teach the whole child without the development and care of their physical self. Besides, as Margaret Whitehead argues, physical literacy is a *monist* not a *dualist* approach. In other words, you can't separate the mind from the body. When we educate the whole person (physically and intellectually) we get much further than if we try and only focus on one aspect at the expense of another.
- **Core competencies?** Yes! In physical education we can effectively teach problem solving, creativity, decision making, and many other cross-curricular competencies we want to see in students. Elementary school teachers have a distinct advantage as they often see students across disciplines and are capable of making these connections and acting upon them.
- **Social-emotional learning?** Yes! As we saw in the position paper, *Physical Literacy for Educators*, self-esteem and care for self and others is a key aspect of physical literacy. As in the example above, elementary school teachers are uniquely situated and can teach social-emotional elements across subject areas.

Second, Dr. Dean Kriellaars has conducted a unique piece of research that also speaks to the value of physical literacy – from the children's perspective. He asked almost 7,000 students to rate the importance of three skill-based literacies in three contexts.

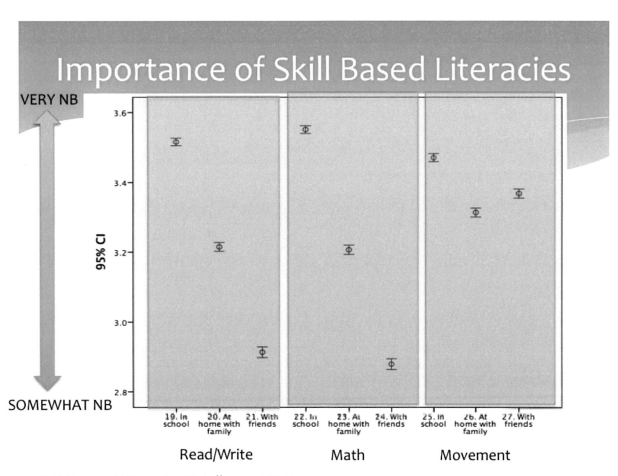

Figure 3.3 Skill Based Literacies (Kriellaars, 2014)

As can be seen in the graph, students perceive reading/writing and math as very important at school (Note: NB in the graph stands for importance). These areas are not seen as important at home and certainly not seen competencies that are needed with their friends. However, not only does movement score quite high at school (just below the other two!), but it is perceived as almost equally important at home and extremely critical with friends. What this indicates is that children themselves care very much about movement skills and find them extremely critical to the three most important parts of their lives: school, home, and friends.

Third, physical literacy as a lifecourse or lifelong approach is consistent with the aims or purposes of physical education curricula across the country. Table 1.1 in Chapter 1 highlights the consistency of the aims. "Active for life" is a common thread and a valuable goal that aligns extremely well with physical literacy.

Fourth, we care about physical literacy because as elementary school teachers, it is part of our job to educate the physical. When we add ***education*** we also add learning, potential for growth and value to the equation.

Physical Activity + Physical Education = An Enhanced Physical Literacy Journey

Finally, one of the key founding principles of public education is just that – access to education for all. Egerton Ryerson, one of the key advocates for public education in Canada, firmly believed that schooling should not be a class privilege and should be not only universal but free (Alberta Teachers' Association, 2015). As such, public education is the ONE PLACE where we should be able to guarantee that EVERY student is able to access support for their individual journeys of physical literacy. Although other sectors such as sport, recreation, and health also support the concept, school is the only mandated place where all children can develop physical literacy regardless of gender, race, or socio-economic status and it is best achieved by quality, daily physical education.

Domains in Physical Education

The United Nations has stated that students are multi-dimensional and have a right to full development of the "whole child" (UNESCO, 1978). First discussed by Heatherington (Noddings, 2005) in the early 20th century, the whole child philosophy is based on the premise that the interplay amongst the three domains of physical or moving, cognitive or thinking, and affective or feeling creates the "whole child" (Noddings, 2005; Rink 2010; Wall & Murray, 1994). See Table 3.1.

You may be thinking, of course this makes sense. Our students are not one-dimensional. But what this philosophy allows for in the physical education context, is the ability to refocus the inappropriate assumption that students are blank slates or the dualist notion that the mind and body function separately. Whole child education supports the understanding that children require learning environments that recognize the interplay between a child's physical, cognitive, and affective needs - a holistic approach to learning. (Manzo & Casale, 2000).

Therefore, it is equally important to discover and implement the most effective teaching practices to suit the individual needs of all learners and be reminded of the fact that within the physical education learning environment students may feel more at ease and/or tense and may display a different personality while in participation (Lu & De Lisio, 2009). Therefore, trying to enhance the physical education learning environment to one of positive movement experiences for all students is one way in

which the 'whole child' approach could be implemented (Lu & De Lisio, 2009).

The Physical Domain: The physical domain concentrates on the fundamental movements of the child. Also called the moving or psychomotor domain, it encourages the physical learning of locomotor skills such as running, jumping, and dodging, non-locomotor skills such as balancing and creating shapes with the body, and manipulative skills such as throwing, catching, and striking (Lloyd & Smith, 2013; Wall & Murray, 1994). An environment where teachers create learning experiences that scaffold upon previous learning, students will learn and adapt their movements to match their growth and development (Lloyd & Smith, 2013).

The Cognitive Domain: The cognitive domain concentrates on the knowledge, understanding, and thought processes of the child (Wall & Murray, 1994). Also named the thinking domain, this domain requires educators to constantly refine their own teaching strategies and ideas to enhance their students' movements and cognitive understandings (Espiritu, 1987). Students must feel safe in their learning environments in order to actively discover their own thought processes and apply new knowledge appropriately.

The Affective Domain: The affective domain concentrates on the emotional aspects of the child including moods, attitudes, self-concept, motivation, and social awareness (Holt & Hannon, 2006; Rink, 2010; Wall & Murray, 1994). Also called the feeling domain, this domain prompts teachers to focus on providing positive class environments that encourage learners to focus on their individual needs, as well as their social needs (Wall & Murray, 1994). While being involved in physical education class, students can develop sportspersonship, fair play, respect for others, self-control, and responsibility (Holt & Hannon, 2006). Even though they are hard to measure, it is essential to understand the rationale and motivation behind students' participation in physical education so that researchers and educators can discover how best to address the affective domain of every student.

Physical Literacy for Life

Physical and Health Education (PHE) Canada has created a model for physical education which stems from the understanding of the "whole child." More importantly, what specific areas of learning can be accomplished within each of these domains. We can use this information as an educational check-up to ensure not only that our breadth in physical education is being covered, but also that our students are understanding the connections to physical literacy.

Table 3.1 Domains in Physical Education		
Cognitive Domain **'THINKING'**	**Physical Domain** **'MOVING'**	**Affective Domain** **'FEELING'**
• Knowledge: what, how, when and why • Beliefs, Valu es and Morals: commitment, self confidence • Decision-Making: overcoming challenges • Self-Regulated and Aware: ongoing management • Healthy Living • Motivation: enjoyment, self-confidence	• Fundamental Movements • Movement Combinations • Cooperative Activities • Games • Dance • Educational Gymnastics • Alternative Environments • Individual Activities	• Social Well Being: empathy and cooperation with others • Emotional Well-being: self-control, resilience, managing stress • Spiritual Well-being: sense of purpose, personal accomplishment • Environmental Health: active transportation, connection to nature • Culturally Responsive

Learning to Move

Laban's Principles

Historically taught through dance, gymnastics and games, Laban's Movement concepts have changed the way we, as educators, approach physical education pedagogy. As the cornerstone of movement education (Wall & Murray, 1994), Laban's Movement concepts enable our students to look outside just the physical domain of learning, but also connect our bodies to the cognitive and affective domains needed to move. Through exploration of movement, students are able to develop and appreciate how they move their bodies, in space, weight, and relational to others by answering these questions "what, where, how, and with whom or what did you move?" For instance, when a student is asked "how did you use your body in physical education today, some may answer "well ...I ran around a lot" whereas students with an understanding of physical education vocabulary may answer "well...I curled my body into a tight shape when I rolled across the mat and I stretched a lot in my balances."

Body Awareness: The concept of body awareness teaches our students "what" the body can perform (Pangrazi & Gibbons, 2009) or more importantly what the body can do, while emphasizing locomotor, non-locomotor, and manipulative skills. Laban's movement framework organizes these movements into 6 themes or categories: body actions; body parts; activities of the body; body shapes; body symmetry and asymmetry; and continuity (Langton, 2007). See Table 3.2.

Table 3.2 Body Awareness	
Body Actions	• *Curl* • *Bend* • *Stretch* • *Twist* • *Swing*
Body Parts	• *Hand, foot, head, etc.* • *Support Body Weight* • *Lead Action* • *Apply and Receive Force of Weight* • *Flow-simultaneous/successive* • *Symmetry or Asymmetry*
Body Activities	***Locomotor*** • *Games: walk, run, jump, gallop, roll* • *Dance: walk, run, gallop, jump, leap, hop, skip, step* • *Gymnastics: jump, flight, rock, roll, slide, step, climb* ***Non-Locomotor*** • *Games: bend, stretch, twist, shift in weight, pivot, stop* • *Dance: gesture, curl, stretch, twist, spin, step & jump turns, rise, sink, open, close, stillness* • *Gymnastics:* ○ *balance/off balance, counterbalance, countertension, spin, jump, circle turns, hang, curl, step, twist* ***Manipulation*** • *Games: Throw, catch, strike, collect, carry, dribble, volley, kick*
Body Shapes	• *Straight, wide, round* • *Narrow, twisted* • *Symmetrical/Asymmetrical*
Symmetrical/ Asymmetrical	• *Locomotion/phrasing* • *Both sides/one side*
Continuity	• *Continuous/ non-continuous*

Body Awareness Activity (Example)
Jumping Beans (Grades K-3)

Equipment: A posted description of an activity for different kinds of beans, obstacle free area.

Instruction: Demonstrate bean shapes or body actions with students. The group will act out each bean shape as it is called out by the teacher.

Baked Beans: make body as small as possible
Jumping Beans: two-foot jump
Runner Beans: run on the spot
Chili Beans: shiver and shake
Jelly Beans: wobble and shake like jelly with a wide shape
French Beans: do the can-can with a partner
Lima Beans: with a partner, make a fat and narrow shape
Coffee Beans: be very energetic

Variation/Inclusion: Create movements for different kinds of bean (navy beans, kidney beans).

Space Awareness: The concept of space awareness teaches our students "where" the body is moving. Whether in areas, directions, levels, pathways, extensions, or planes, focusing on where we are moving, students will understand the intention of space within movement. See Table 3.3.

Table 3.3 Space Awareness	
Space Area	*General*
	Personal
Directions	*Forward*
	Backward
	Sideward
	Up
	Down
Levels	*High*
	Medium
	Low
Pathways	*Straight*
	Curved
	Zig, zag
	Twisted
Extensions	*Near*
	Far
Planes	*Sagittal (wheel)*
	Frontal (door)
	Horizontal (table)

Space Awareness Activity (Example)

Ship to Shore (Grades 2-5)

Equipment: Open space (a gymnasium or field)

Instructions:

- This game transforms your gymnasium into a pirate ship!
- Lines on the 4 sides of the basketball court become the bow, stern, port, and starboard side of the boat. When you make a call for one of these locations, have your students run and touch the wall that was called.
- You can add other actions for additional variety or have students invent their own.

Demonstrate the different ship commands or actions with students.

Captain's Coming: students stand at attention and salute the captains.

Swab the Deck: students drop to their hands and knees and pretend to scrub the floor.

Sailor Overboard: students find a partner, link arms, and pull each other back and forth.

Submarine: students lie on their stomachs with their hands pointed forward.

Crow's Nest: students move in space on their tiptoes while searching out to sea.

Effort Awareness: The concept of effort awareness teaches our students "how" the body is moving. Generally used incorrectly through physical education assessment, Laban's principal of effort focuses our students on how time, weight, space, and flow can affect the quality of their movements. See Table 3.4.

Table 3.4 Effort Awareness	
Time	Sudden/fast or with Acceleration
	Sustained/slow or with deceleration
Weight	Strong/Firm
	Light/Fine
Space	Straight/direct
	Flexible/indirect
Flow	Free/ongoing
	Bound/stoppable

Effort Awareness Activity (Example)
Pinwheel (Grades 3-4)

Equipment:

6 bowling pins

3 pylons per group

1 beanbag per student

Instructions:

- Divide students into small groups (e.g., 3-4).
- Students set up their area using bowling pins to create a circle approximately 1metre in diameter.
- Students place 3 pylons at various distances from the target to identify three lines that the participants will throw from
- Students take turns using an underhand throw to send a beanbag into the circle without knocking down any of the bowling pins.
- Students start at the closest distance and move farther away with each successful throw.
- Students keep track of how many attempts it takes them to get the bean bag into the target from each distance.
- Once a student has been successful at each line, the student starts at the beginning again and attempts to complete the game with fewer throws.

Relationship Awareness: The concept of Relationship awareness teaches our students "with whom" the body or "what" the body is relating to while moving. With objects, with others, with the rules, and with our own body parts, these relationships coincide with most movement our students are introduced to and developed through the elementary physical education classroom. See Table 3.5.

Table 3.5 Relationship Awareness	
Body Parts to Each Other	In front of/Alongside/Behind Far/Near Above/Below Meet/Part Over/Under
Individual or Groups	In front of/Alongside/Behind Far/Near Above/Below Meet/Part Lead/Follow Around/Between/Through Toward/Away Over/Under Match/Mirror/Copy/Contrast Unison/Cannon Simultaneous/Successive Supporting/Being supportive Offensive/Defensive Attack/Defend spaces Create space/Cover space Cooperation/Competition
Rules	Rules/Boundaries/Goals/Etiquette

Relationship Awareness Activity (Example)
Tail Chase (Grade 4-6)

Equipment:
1 tail/student (e.g., flag football belt with attached flags)

Instructions:
- Divide students into pairs.
- Give a "tail" to each participant and have them put it on.
- Remind students that no body contact is allowed and that they can only grab their partner's tail.
- At the signal, each student tries to grab the tail of their partner without having their own tail taken.
- When a student's tail is removed, it is returned and the participant puts their tail back, and the participants play again.
- Have students count how many times they can remove their partner's tail in the allotted time.

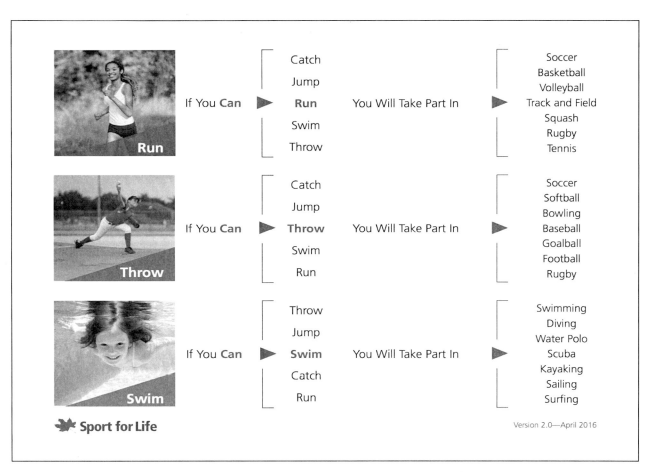

Figure 3.4 Fundamental Movement Skills (Canadian Sport for Life, 2016)

Fundamental Movement Skills

Fundamental movement skills (FMS) are described as an essential vehicle to all sport and physical activity. Take a moment to reflect on this statement as you peruse the Canadian Sport for Life graphic (Figure 3.4). What does this mean to you and how will this impact your planning and teaching? It looks simple enough, you teach your students how to run and they might be able to play a plethora of different sports. Or can they? When considering complex activities such as rugby, skating, or kayaking, many fundamental movements are at play and therefore must all be taught with progression in mind. With the physical literacy movement across Canada, fundamental movement skills have also been highlighted as a building block to further our students' development of physical skills as well as a precursor to our students' lifelong attitudes toward physical activity. Mastery of FMS can also be seen as an important motivation factor. For example, students will not want to play soccer if they cannot kick a ball. Further, if a child cannot run effectively, combining running with other fundamental movements such as dodging, will probably result in frustration even within a basic game of tag. It is this opportunity as educators to inspire our students with effective and progressive movement opportunities.

Viewed as the basic skills required for the foundation to complete and sequence more complex skills, fundamental movement skills enable our students in the early years (K-3) to move with confidence and competence if taught correctly and critically.

Fundamental movement skills have been broken down into three categories: locomotor, non-locomotor and manipulative. These skills can be described through action words, meaning our bodies are in motion or in motor control. These categories will be discussed in more detail and examples will be provided.

Locomotor Skills move the body from one place to another (e.g., Point A to B) or can project the body upward (Pangrazi & Gibbons, 2009). Walking, running, skipping, galloping, and jumping are all examples of skills to be taught at an early age.

FMS: Running

Move fast by using one's feet, with one foot off the ground at any given time

Characteristics of the Run	Cue Words for Students
Leg Action:	
Foot contact is with the heel, or as speed increases, with the ball of the foot under the body	Balls of feet
Swing knee is raised high	High knees
Support leg moves from slight bend to complete extension	
Arm Action:	
Elbow is bent at right angles (stay at this angle)and move in opposition to legs	Hands brush hips in backswing
Upper arm drives forward and back	Drive arms; elbows in

(PHE Canada, 2011)

FMS: Skipping

A rhythmical flow of the step-hop pattern, skipping combines two FMS, the step and the hop. This skip is the rhythmical flow of the step and hop on one foot, then step and hop of the other foot

Characteristics of the Skip	Cue Words for Students
A rhythmical repetition of the step-hop on alternate feet	Step-hop, step hop
Foot of non-support leg is carried near surface during hop	Keep back foot near the ground
Arms alternatively moving in opposition to legs	Arm/leg opposite
Toes and ball of foot are first landing	Land toes first

(PHE Canada, 2011)

Non-Locomotor Skills (sometimes referred to as balance and stability) are performed in place and with control (Pangrazi & Gibbons, 2009). Bending, stretching, pushing, pulling, balancing, curling and twisting are all examples of skills to be taught at the fundamental stage.

FMS: Log Roll	
A straight body rolling around a long axis	
Characteristics of the Log Roll	**Cue Words for Students**
Preparation:	
Lie on stomach with arms stretched overhead	Be as LONG as you can
Legs together and straight	
Palms facing floor	
Rolling Action:	
Roll to side, tummy, side, and then back	Stiff like a pencil
Keep body rigid	

(PHE Canada, 2011)

Manipulative Skills typically describe movements used within games and more specifically how one handles objects (Pangrazi & Gibbons, 2009). Throwing, catching, dribbling with your hands or feet, and striking are all examples of skills to be taught at the fundamental stage.

FMS: Overarm Throw	
Propelling the ball toward a given objective (object)?	
Characteristics of the Overarm Throw	**Cue Words for Students**
Preparation:	
Side facing	Side
Weight on the back foot	
Throwing arm circles downward and backward to make a W-shape with arms and body	Make a "W"
Eyes on the target	Look
Throwing Action:	
Foot opposite to throwing hand steps forward	
Hips rotate first, then the upper body	
Weight is transferred from the back foot to the front foot	Back to front
Release ball just in front of head	
Follow through:	
Point throwing hand to target	
Throwing hand drops down and points toward the opposite knee	Across body

(PHE Canada, 2011)

FMS: Sidearm Strike

Propelling an incoming object using the hand or an implement using a side arm action

Characteristics of the Overarm Throw	Cue Words for Students
Preparation:	
Stand facing the incoming object to be struck	Front face
Legs bent with hands out in front	Watch
Watch the object to be struck all the time	
Striking Action:	
Turn so that the shoulder opposite the striking hand is facing the object to be struck	
Take striking hand back and point to the incoming object with the non-striking hand to make a "W" shape with the arms and body	Back "W"
Contact the object in front of the foot, opposite the striking hand (foot closest to the incoming object)	Hitting zone
Transfer weight from back foot to front foot	Back to front
Strike through the object	
Striking hand follows through high to the opposite shoulder	Follow high
Return to front facing	

With the introduction and description of the FMS categories and a practical example by PHE Canada on how to break down each skill, we must turn our attention to the progressive phases of motor learning.

What is Motor Learning?

Motor learning is the dynamic process of development through the combination of physical and psychological factors that affects the ability of one to perform a task. This learning begins at birth as we explore with the help of those around us how to grasp, keep our head up, balance while sitting, creeping, crawling, and walking across the living room floor. As well, children develop and grow both cephalocaudally and proximodistally (Fishburne, 2005). The first term refers to the way we gain control of our head first, then the trunk and so on down the body. The second term refers to growth that occurs from the centre of the body outward. This development, while beginning with shakiness and uneasiness as our bodies learn a new task, becomes more fluid with time and practice and one day comes to be what we could call 'automatic'. The same can be said about our students and their development of fundamental movement skills. While your students explore these skills for the first time, observations will be similar. As explained by Temerzeglou (2014), these movements will seem jerky and uncoordinated; they will, however, become seamless and well executed with time and practice. Fitts and Posner (1967) in their seminal work, created the 3-part model in which most students will fall into with predictability and sequential stages. These three stages or phases are the cognitive, associative, and autonomous phases. This important research is the foundation for providing developmentally appropriate teaching and learning experiences in physical education.

Cognitive Phase of Motor Learning

Students share characteristics of learning such as:
- Questioning their personal performance
- Creating mental plans of how to complete the skill
- Experiencing uncoordinated and tentative attempts of the skill
- Using multiple attempts at completing the skill; not all successful; lacks consistency

---

To support this phase, teachers can provide simple, clear and consistent cues or teaching tips, accurate and developmentally appropriate demonstrations and, lots of personal practice opportunities.

Associative Phase of Motor Learning

Students share characteristics of learning such as:
- Being highly engaged in problem solving
- Being less dependent on the external cues
- Being better able to utilize internal cues; beginning to refine the skill
- Experiencing more successful and consistent practice attempts

---

By providing activities that exaggerate the skill being practiced, students begin to understand how the skill is used within game play. For example, having "ghost" or "mock" defenders introduced while working on the skill of dribbling with their feet will promote authentic learning experiences without overwhelming them with the rules of soccer.

Autonomous Phase of Motor Learning

Students share characteristics of learning such as:
- Performing skills somewhat effortlessly
- Experiencing automatic skill performance
- Requiring minimal conscious attention
- Making adjustments in the performance of the skill
- Be able to apply skills to many different settings

By challenging our students in game play, in the creation of sequences in gymnastics or dance, or in outdoor pursuits, students should be able to be viably able to move with poise, and economy as echoes the definition of physical literacy. Please keep in mind that the autonomous is not an 'end stage' per se; students should continue to develop, albeit more slowly.

Principles of Learning Movement Skills (x7)

How do we set up a positive learning environment for our students in physical education? One that promotes the learning and understanding of motor skills from a holistic approach? A number of principles have been identified that can assist in the preparation and planning of quality motor skills teaching:

- **Principle of Interest:** A student's interest toward learning a skill should indicate how much time is needed in teaching and practicing the skill. For instance, if you are starting to hear rumblings of "when are we going to play the game?" this can tell you that your students for the most part feel prepared to move on. Whereas, if frustration or behaviour issues seem to arise, the importance of taking more time to practice the skill may be needed. A great example is learning how to throw a flying disc. Gauging the practice of throwing for accuracy rather than throwing for distance can tell you how in tune your students are with the task at hand.

- **Principle of Practice:** Perfect practice makes perfect. This resonates especially when our students are trying out these skills for the first time. Positive and adjustment driven feedback will allow our students to move through the phases of motor learning more effectively. Positive feedback such as "Way to step with your opposite foot!" will highlight this to the student as well as motivate them to step successfully every time.

- **Principle of Distributed Practice:** Provide your students with short periods of concentrated practice rather than long sessions, which will keep your students focused with more learning. By stopping your students to ask them open-ended questions about what they were just working on, or by simply modifying the activity (see the REPS model in Chapter 4), can lead to practical understanding of the skill.

- **Principle of Skill Specificity:** One must remember that even if our students may be successful in one movement skill, this does not always mean the next movement skill you teach will be just as effective. Dribbling a basketball is much different than 'dribbling' a soccer ball. Make sure to allow your students time and space to develop the next skill, and provide effective progressions that make sense.

- **Principle of Whole-Part Learning:** As you prepare to teach your students a motor skill, how complex the skill is must be taken into consideration. For instance, should the skill be broken down into component parts, or can it be taught as one fluid movement.

- **Principle of Transfer:** The more identical two skills are, the greater possibility that positive transfer will occur. Taking the overhand throw, for example, with proper breakdown of this complex FMS can be transferred into striking an object.

- **Principle of Feedback:** Providing our students with external feedback as well as opportunity for peer feedback will allow them to feel the confidence to internally learn the skill taking place. Whether using self-talk or correction after every practice, students can effectively take accountable action on their own to be successful. Student ownership of tasks and skill development is the end goal!

Developmental Appropriateness

As stated by Fishburne (2005) and echoed in curriculum guidelines across Canada, physical education should take a developmental approach toward learning. Developmental appropriateness means the activities we choose for our students to participate in meet the learning needs for optimal student growth and development which could in turn lead to lifelong physical activity (Council of Physical Education for Children, 2000). More importantly, developmentally appropriate physical education integrates the concept of the whole child (physical, cognitive, affective domains), the phases of motor learning, as well as providing a safe learning environment for all students. See Table 3.6.

Belka's (1994) principles for developmental games highlight many areas we, as teachers, should embed within our elementary school physical education programs. These principles are as follows:

1. Provide for maximum participation, giving everyone many high quality opportunities.
2. Provide for safe play for everyone
3. Focus on skills and strategies considered to be "good to learn"
4. Meet the needs of participants with varying abilities
5. Support a developmental principle
6. Encourage efficient and effective movement
7. Build upon and use skills, concepts, and strategies to help participants become better game players
8. Enhance social and emotional status, including humane considerations of individuals and their differing abilities

Newell's Model of Constraints

While we build our developmentally appropriate physical education environments, we must also know and understand the different constraints we could be managing as we move from lesson to lesson. More importantly, it is critical to understand how Individual, Task, and Environmental constraints can affect successful participation within your classes. See Figure 3.5.

- **Individual constraints** refer to peoples unique mental and physical abilities that affect their movement towards physical education, and could be two-fold, structural and/or functional. **Structural constraints** is most effectively explained as the individual growth patterns and biological make up of our students. Whereas, **functional constraints** describe our students' behavioural make-up (e.g., attention span, anxiety towards an activity) (Haywood & Getchell, 2009).

- **Task constraints** can be described as the rules, goals, and equipment that are used within motor tasks (e.g., the basketball may be too large, the volleyball net may be too high, the music may be too fast)
- **Environmental constraints** can be the social and/or physical environments which could affect the performance of a motor task.

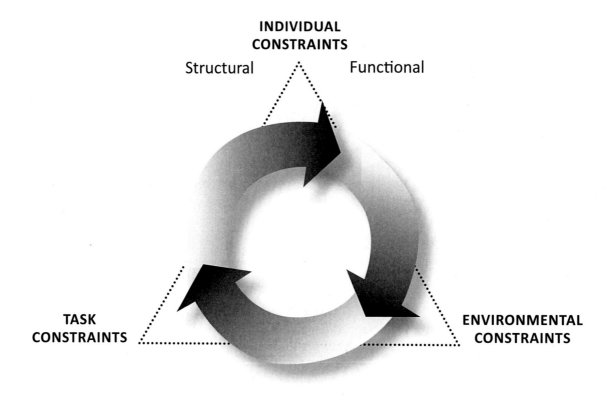

INDIVIDUAL
CONSTRAINTS

Structural   Functional

TASK
CONSTRAINTS

ENVIRONMENTAL
CONSTRAINTS

Figure 3.5 Newell's Model of Constraints (Haywood & Getchell, 2009, p. 6)

Constraints? What Constraints?

Using Newell's model, discuss the scenario below with your group. Come up with a positive and negative constraint in each of the four categories.

Jezzerha and Sam, Grade 2 students, are getting very frustrated trying to play basketball on the hoop installed in the gym. The high school students have left several size 7 basketballs out and the two grade 2's watched them shoot the balls into the hoops on the wall over and over. Jezzerha can hit the rim from time to time, Sam can't even come close!

- How could we change this situation to ensure that both Jezzerha and Sam's motor learning needs are being met?

- Can you make a change in each of the three constraints categories?
    - Individual: structural and functional
    - Task
    - Environment

Table 3.6 Characteristics of Developmental Levels - Approximation of Grade and Age

	Level 1: Grades K-2 5-7 Years of Age	Level 2: Grades 3-4 8-9 Years of Age	Level 3: Grades 5-6 10-12 Years of Age
Physical Growth and Development	• Height and weight gains are moderate and steady • Heart and breathing rate are high • Steady increase in strength and muscular endurance • Flexibility is high • Hand-eye coordination improves • Tires quickly, needs short breaks • Tends to have high centre of gravity	• Height and weight gains continue • Heart and lungs develop steadily • Slight decrease in flexibility can be noted • Muscle strength and endurance continues to increase • Early signs of poor posture • Some may be entering puberty • Centre of gravity lowers	• Rapid height and weight gains after puberty • Heart and lungs grow proportionate to size • Changes in strength and flexibility due to socialization, environment, etc. • Muscle strength and endurance still increasing • Able to sustain activity levels • Centre of gravity continues to lower
Motor Skill Development	Introduction to Fundamental Movement Skills: • Basic locomotor: walk, run, leap, jump, hop • Combined locomotor: skip, slide, stop, dodge • Basic non-locomotor: bend, stretch, twist, turn, push, swing • Basic manipulative (receptive, propulsive, retentive): catch, throw/strike, control	Refinement of Fundamental Movement Skills: • Combination and refinement of one or more fundamental movement skills (e.g. run and jump, catch and throw, dribble and kick, etc.)	Application of Fundamental Movement Skills and Specific Sport, Dance, or Specialized Skills • Advanced and refined versions of sports, dance, or other specialized skills (running long jump, football pass, hand spring) • Application of movement skills to multiple settings • Able to apply movement skills to new activity choices
Cognitive Development	• Gradual increase in attention span • Creative and curious • Enjoy rhythm and music • Desire to repeat activities they enjoy • Can follow simplistic instructions	• Attention span increases • Curious about own abilities • Able to handle more group activities • Interested in personal performance and achievement	• Marked increase in attention span • Increase in intellectual curiosity and a need to 'challenge' rationale • Genuine interest in learning about the body: health and performance
Affective Development	• Egocentric and curious • Need to explore without pressure and be praised • Requires short time frames for activity • Moving towards cooperative • Needs adult attention and approval • Sensitive to feelings and critique	• Group interests come more to the fore • Is aware of others • Able to focus over longer periods of time • Increased complexity of movement and strategy • Enjoys adult supervised activities • Need lots of opportunities to be successful	• Transition towards independence • Takes ownership of actions • Requires peer approval • Social acceptance is peer related rather than adult • Some differences begin to emerge: socialization and media influence

Adapted from Fishburne, 2005

Including All Learners

Although inclusion will be covered in more detail as part of Chapter 7, it is important to remember that one of the key foundational aspects of physical education is that IT IS FOR EVERYONE!

- Not 'just' for athletic children
- Not 'just' for those who can afford it
- Not 'just' for those students who are awkward or clumsy

Physical education is designed as part of public education so that all can move forward on their individual journeys of physical literacy.

One thing we do NOT do in physical education is leave people out. It would not go over well in mathematics to have students who solved problems the slowest be left out of the next round of questioning! We learn from making mistakes; students need to be included if we expect them to learn.

Consider the following game and how you might use it to teach your students (and yourself) the value of inclusion.

IT TAG for Inclusion

Purpose of the Activity:

- help students understand the relationship between cooperation and competition
- spatial awareness (movement through general space)
- introduction to strategy and tactics in game play
- understanding of how it might feel to be excluded or left out

Set up:

- you'll need an open, obstacle free space defined by lines or markings of some sort - that's it!

Phase #1: Individual

- Ask students to stand on the boundary lines so everyone is aware of the space.
- "This is it tag, everybody is it. Stay in bounds and don't get tagged. If you get tagged, or go out of bounds, you sit." - Any questions? 3,2,1 - go!
- What will happen is that some are tagged before they even know the game has started, others will last longer. Let it happen! Use the opportunity after the game to have a discussion about who had fun, how it feels to be out before you even have a chance to learn and play, etc.

Phase #2: Partners

- Ask students to stand on the boundary lines so everyone is aware of the space.
- Find a partner and hold hands (hands on shoulders, etc.) (you can have one group of 3 or the teacher can join in). "This is it tag, everybody is it. Stay in bounds and don't get tagged. If you get tagged, or go out of bounds, you sit. If your partner touches you on the shoulder, you are back up." Any questions? 3,2,1 - go!
- After one or two rounds, debrief again - How did this round go? Challenges? Opportunities? Did anyone feel left out? Why?

Phase #3: Quads

- Ask students to stand on the boundary lines so everyone is aware of the space.
- Take your pair, find another, and make a "quad" and hold hands (hands on shoulders, etc.) (you can have one larger or smaller group or the teacher can join in). "This is it tag, everybody is it. Stay in bounds and don't get tagged. If you get tagged, or go out of bounds, you sit. If your team-mate touches you on the shoulder, you are back up." Any questions? 3,2,1 - go!
- Continue the discussion started earlier about how things are much more fun if everyone is involved. As well, how can we learn if we are left out?

Using Newell's Model of Constraints

- Choose a game or activity you may have played as a student that was "exclusive" (sit out!)
- How can you modify the constraints so that all are included?

Safety First

Within the entire school environment, we, as elementary school teachers, must ensure that our students are safe, physically, socially, and emotionally. This element of safety becomes even more apparent within the physical education learning environment. Each province will have broad guidelines for safety. For example, the Safety Guidelines for Physical Activity in Alberta Schools' (2013) intent is two-fold:

1. To focus teacher attention on safe instructional practices in order to minimize inherent risk

2. To encourage school authorities to develop policies, and schools to develop plans and procedures, for the student safety and security

Although each school, jurisdiction and province will have unique and specific regulations and policies, Rink (2010) listed the 7 common safety issues created by teachers in physical education that should be avoided.

1. Students are trying to perform skills they are not yet capable of
2. Students are working too closely together with striking equipment (e.g., bats, racquets, sticks)
3. Activities that require students to move fast do not have enough room to slow down
4. Choosing activities that put students at risk (dodgeball)
5. Students have not been taught proper spatial awareness when moving around the gymnasium
6. Choosing equipment that is being used for a different purpose than intended
7. Leaving equipment out when not being used

Rink, 2010

Even though we can prepare and try to plan for every physical activity movement our students will attempt to make, a physical education class will always have a minimal amount of risk. Factors such as "cognitive ability and developmental maturity, skill level, previous experience of student and teacher, weather conditions, facilities and available equipment" could decrease or increase the level of risk our students may experience. Therefore, being proactive and preventative will not only create a safer environment for your students, but a more comfortable and enjoyable experience for all.

Physical Safety – Personal
Being proactive about our students' personal safety, more specifically, physical safety is one of the top priorities every physical education teacher should be prepared for. Whether a student has tripped and sprained an ankle, to presenting concussion symptoms, management for safety is essential. Universal precautions dealing with blood and bodily fluids should also be followed up with Provincial Guidelines.

Equipment and Space (Adapted from the Alberta/Ontario Safety Guidelines, 2013)

Pre-Check and Check it out: Before using any equipment with students, teachers should check it all. By creating a pre-activity check list of the equipment to be used that lesson, hazards, such as broken equipment, sharp edges, slippery surfaces, and/or missing of protective mats can be eliminated or isolated as a factor in the activity. This check could be either visual or recorded on a tracking form in order to make preparations or notes needed for ordering new equipment. Because the equipment is usually shared among many different groups (e.g., classes, sports teams, community groups), this is always a good check before use.

Protective Equipment: If the lesson you are considering has any need for protective equipment such as helmets (e.g., cycling, hockey,) teachers and supervisors are responsible to make sure this equipment is being properly worn by the students (e.g., properly fitting cycling helmets with chin straps done up).

Pump it up: All balls must be properly inflated. With seasonal changes and over usage, balls deflate quite frequently. This may cause injuries due to sharp edges, or incorrect skill movements due to adjusting for the equipment. Keeping an inexpensive ball pump handy and accessible is easy and efficient.

Home-made Equipment: Creativity and physical education do go hand-in-hand, but try to keep any student-made equipment at home. Examples such as bleach bottle scoops or homemade hockey sticks could cause harm due to what they were made out of. Therefore, if you would like to include making your own equipment for your lessons, which is a great idea, make sure to supervise this innovative idea and check school and district protocol as well as Provincial Guidelines.

Outside Equipment: Sometimes you may need a few more pieces of equipment for your plan. Make sure if you allow your students to bring their favourite racquet, stick, or in-line skates that parents/guardians have determined that the equipment is good to go; this means the equipment should be age suitable and in good working order.

An emphasis on a few safety issues that should be prepared for in advance when dealing with equipment needs were noted here, however, please see the provincial safety guidelines and school jurisdiction policies for a complete list.

Procedures and Policy

"At all times, teachers and instructors must comply with policies relating to the physical activities conducted as specified by the board/authority for which they are employed." (p. 11)

As the teacher, YOU are responsible to know what those policies are. These may include:
- Temperature/weather condition restrictions
- Field trip protocol
- Adult-to-student ratios
- Prohibited activities
- Record keeping, Etc.

Social Emotional Safety

As teachers of physical education, we are also responsible for creating and supporting a learning environment that is safe from a social-emotional standpoint as well as the physical. Our activity spaces should be bully-free, encourage appropriate risk-taking, provide positive feedback and, overall, be an environment where students believe they can be their best. Essentially, you are creating a culture of social-emotional safety in your class.
One model that can assist with the creation of such a culture is Teaching Personal and Social Responsibility through Physical Activity (TPSR, Hellison, 2011). This model focuses on teaching students five levels of responsibility, each with appropriate goals. See Table 3.7 and 3.8.

TPSR provides for one-on-one time with you, the teacher, to discuss a variety of aspects related to learning in physical education. As well, the model encourages the opportunity for students to reflect on their own learning, through discussion as well as game play with their peers. As such, the model becomes an effective way to solve class problems or other relationship breakdowns that may occur. For example, setting up a cooperative game environment focusing on working together could positively impact class dynamics. Alternatively, challenging your students to create their own game including rules and etiquette could highlight the practical importance of following classroom management. These are two ideas that you could try in your class.

Table 3.7 Five Levels of Responsibility

1. Respecting rights and feelings
    a. Self-control
    b. Respect for inclusivity
    c. Peaceful, democratic conflict resolution

2. Participation and effort
    a. Self-motivation
    b. Explore self-effort and try new things
    c. On-task persistence

3. Self-direction
    a. Independent work
    b. Goal setting progression
    c. Courage to resist negative peer pressure

4. Helping others / leadership
    a. Caring & compassion
    b. Sensitivity and responsiveness
    c. Inner strength

5. Outside the gym
    a. Trying ideas outside PE
    b. Role modeling

Implementation of the model includes key strategies and activities (Hellison, 2011) such as:

Table 3.8 Key Strategies and Activities of the TPSR model	

Relational (Counseling) Time	• 4 goals of encounters: to recognize…
	   i. strengths
	   ii. individuality
	   iii. voice
	   iv decision-making

Awareness Talks	• Discuss and explain 5 levels/goals • Don't overload – remind • Focus on what the goal is for THIS class
The Lesson	• How will you reach your goals?
Group Meetings	• Small and large (class) • Focus on goals and issues • Purpose can often be Levels 1 and 4 • Provides feedback to educator • Establish guidelines
Reflection time	• Self-evaluation; journal; thumbs up/down; checklists etc. • Connection to GO's and SO's
Counseling Time #2	• Same as #1 but an additional opportunity

Consider the following scenarios

A. A very awkward student who fails at most things...
B. The super-competitive student who mocks those below...
C. Laughter at a student whose pants tear during gymnastics...
D. A student hit in the head in a vigorous game of dodgeball...

Discuss with your group how you would:
- prevent the incident in the first place through the creation of a safe and caring PE culture
- deal with the incident appropriately to reinforce the culture you have built
- consult/apply provincial, district, and school guidelines, as appropriate

Conclusion

The key to building a quality physical education program, like a house, lies in the foundation. Once these critical elements are understood and put into place, you can be assured of a stable future! The joy of human movement, physical literacy, curriculum, motor learning, developmental appropriateness and safety all work together in a quality physical education program.

Checking for Understanding

I Can...
- Apply concepts of physical literacy and joy to my understanding of physical education
- Explain the differences and connections between physical activity, physical education and physical literacy
- Understand principles of motor learning for children
- Recognize the importance of developmentally appropriate physical education and share the benefits for students
- Understand and apply concepts of physical and social-emotional safety to create a culture of success

Chapter 4

Building Quality Physical Education Programming

Teachers who are enthusiastic towards the content being taught create more positive, welcoming learning environments.

Vidourek et al., 2011

Introduction

Teaching and learning must occur in quality physical education. Just like other subject areas such as Math, Science, Music, and Art, students require learning opportunities. In physical education, this learning must include the development of fundamental movement skills (PHE Canada, 2015). The focus of this chapter, therefore, is on the content of a quality Physical Education (PE) program. Our hope is that, by the end of this chapter, you will:

- Understand the rationale behind the quality physical education content
- Recognize the benefits of offering breath and variety in quality PE programming
- Understand the five dimensions of activity common across Canada
- Know a variety of activities within the five dimensions
- Develop an understanding of planning quality PE according to students' developmental levels

Physical Education across Canada

When looking at the aim and rationale within physical education curricular documents across Canada, it is clear that some commonalities exist. For example:

- The knowledge, skills, and attitudes developed in Kindergarten to Grade 12 physical education are necessary to lead active, healthy lifestyles (Alberta Learning, 2000)
- Physical education helps students develop an understanding of what is required for them to commit to "...healthy, active living and develop the capacity to live satisfying, productive lives." (Ontario Ministry of Education, 2010, p. 4)
- Physical and Health Education is "...to develop educated citizens who have the knowledge, skills, and understanding they need to be safe, active, and healthy citizens throughout their lives (British Columbia, 2016)

Additionally, general categories/outcomes exist in a variety of provincial curricula across Canada (see Table 4.1). In terms of these common general categories/outcomes, teachers must develop a deep understanding of their importance so that students are exposed to these curricular outcomes (Alberta Learning, 2000) which can be met through breadth and variety across the five dimensions of activities. It is important to recognize that Table 4.1 illustrates a common language that exists across a variety of provincial physical education curricula.

Table 4.1 Physical Education Curricula in Canada (General Categories)	
Alberta	• **Activity:** Acquire skills through a variety of developmentally appropriate movement activities; dance, games, types of gymnastics, individual activities, and activities in alternative environments • **Benefits Health:** Understand, experience and appreciate the health benefits that result from physical activity • **Cooperation:** Interact positively with others • **Do It Daily...For Life!:** Assume responsibility to lead an active life
Manitoba	• **Movement:** Demonstrate competency in selected movement skills, and knowledge of movement development and physical activities with respect to different types of learning experiences, environments, and cultures • **Fitness Management:** Demonstrate the ability to develop and follow a personal fitness plan for lifelong physical activity and well-being • **Safety:** Demonstrate safe and responsible behaviours to manage risks and prevent injuries in physical activity participation and for daily living • **Personal and Social Management:** Demonstrate the ability to develop self-understanding, to make health-enhancing decisions, to work cooperatively and fairly with others, and to build positive relationships with others • **Healthy Lifestyles Practices:** Demonstrate the ability to make informed decisions for healthy living related to personal health practices, active living, healthy nutritional practices, substance use and abuse, and human sexuality
Ontario	• **Active Living:** The skills and knowledge that will enable them to enjoy being active and healthy throughout their lives, through opportunities to participate regularly and safely in physical activity and to learn how to develop and improve their own personal fitness • **Movement Competence:** The movement competence needed to participate in a range of physical activities, through opportunities to develop movement skills and to apply movement concepts and strategies in games, sports, dance, and other physical activities • **Healthy Living:** An understanding of the factors that contribute to healthy development, a sense of personal responsibility for lifelong health, and an understanding of how living healthy, active lives is connected with the world around them and the health of others
Prince Edward Island	• **Active Living:** Enjoying and engaging in healthy levels of participation in movement activities to support lifelong active living in the context of self, family and community • **Skillful Movement:** Enhancing quality of movement by understanding, developing, and transferring movement concepts, skills, tactics, and strategies to a wide variety of movement activities • **Relationships:** Balancing self through safe and respectful personal, social, cultural, and environmental interactions in a wide variety of movement activities
Saskatchewan	• **Active Living:** Enjoy and engage in healthy levels of participation in movement activities to support lifelong active living in the context of self, family, and community • **Skillful Movement:** Enhance quality of movement by understanding, developing, and transferring movement concepts, skills, tactics, and strategies to a wide variety of movement activities • **Relationships:** Balance self through safe and respectful personal, social, cultural, and environmental interactions in a wide variety of movement activities

Reflection Corner…

Why do you think the general categories of student outcomes for these five Canadian provinces are so similar?

Physical education in elementary schools should be perceived by educational stakeholders (e.g., teachers, administrators, parents) as a subject that plays a primary role in child development. It is, therefore, of the utmost importance to provide students with both the breadth and variety of activities for development and to facilitate knowledge, skills, and attitudes required for lifelong physical activity.

The Importance of Breadth and Variety

Offering breadth and variety is integral to quality physical education programming (Fishburne, 2005). Table 4.2 offers a visual explanation of what breadth and variety can look like. For example, alternative environment-type activities and game-type activities are two of the possible dimensions that add to the breadth of physical education programming. Table 4.2 also identifies, within each dimension, a variety of activities that can be taught throughout the school year. Providing breadth and variety affords students a greater chance of obtaining high levels of confidence and competence across physical activities which can enhance their physical literacy journeys (Mandigo, 2010; Mandigo, Francis, Lodewyk, & Lopez, 2009; Whitehead, 2010). In support of this outcome, curricular documents across Canada clearly emphasize the importance of breadth and variety in physical education, such as:

- Students must have opportunities to learn "through a variety of physical activities" (Alberta Learning, 2000, p. 4)

- Students will develop the movement competence needed to participate in a range of physical activities, through opportunities to develop movement skills and to apply movement concepts and strategies in games, sports, dance, and other physical activities (Ontario Ministry of Education, 2010, p. 3-4).

- Students are expected to develop and apply a variety of fundamental movement skills in a variety of environments (British Columbia, 2016)

Unfortunately, based upon our experience, it is all too common to hear of a distinct lack of breadth and variety occurring in today's physical education programming. For example, some programs seem to follow a timetable based on extra-curricular sports: soccer in the fall, volleyball and basketball in the winter, track and field and slow-pitch in the spring. Additionally, it is still all too common to hear stories from pre-service teachers that include massive amounts of dodgeball, a lack of dance, the elimination of gymnastics, and a predominant 'throw out the ball' mentality. It is this lack of breadth and variety that hinders student development (Fishburne, 2005). Phillips and Silverman (2012) contended that our physical activity behaviour as adults (e.g., whether or not we decide to be physically active) are strongly influenced by our physical education experiences. Hence, students require opportunities to experience a wide range of physical activities in a positive learning environment. This range of physical activities should, in turn, help students enhance their fundamental movement skills, progress on their physical literacy journeys, discover new skills, and engage in new and innovative physical activities, games, dances, and sports. In support of this, British Columbia (2016) stated that daily engagement in a variety of physical activities influence physical literacy and personal health and fitness goals.

To place this issue in the broader context of education, imagine if all we did in English Language Arts (ELA) was read poetry. Of course, there is nothing wrong with poetry, however, ELA also should include breadth and variety such as works of fiction, non-fiction, etc. If we do not take the time to consider how to properly provide breadth and variety within physical education, students will not be exposed to learning environments that help them develop, refine, and master the wide range of skills required for their physical literacy journeys. According to Tompsett, Burkett, & McKean (2014), physical literacy educates students about "using their bodies in different contexts" (p. 56), which speaks clearly to the importance of breadth and variety in physical education. Environments such as swimming pools and outdoor areas add to the quality of physical education programming. For example, PHE Canada (2011) contended that being physically active in swimming pools and other water environments is not only advantageous when developing physical literacy, but can also save lives. Every student should learn to swim and, by extension, learn to move comfortably without fear in water environments. As Canadians, we spend a great deal of time in snowy, icy, and cold environments for months at a time. Therefore, activities such as snowshoeing, tobogganing, and skating at a young age can translate into confidence and competence on a snowboard, kicksled or icy sidewalk later in life (PHE Canada, 2011).

Describing Breadth and Variety. When describing the breadth in physical education programming, we use the word 'dimensions' to identify the broad categories of activities that should be taught in quality physical education programs. Despite slightly different wording and organization, essentially there are five common dimensions found in physical education curricula across Canada. These five dimensions, which are listed alphabetically as there is no hierarchical order, are identified across the second row in Table 4.2. Variety, on the other hand, refers to the array of possible activities that can be taught within each dimension.

Table 4.2 Breadth and Variety in Physical Education

	← *BREADTH* →				
	Alternative Environment Activities	**Dance Activities**	**Games Activities**	**Gymnastics Activities**	**Individual Activities**
↑ *VARIETY* ↓	• Cycling • Orienteering • Skating • Skiing • Swimming • Wall Climbing	• Aerobic • Creative • Cultural • Folk • Hip-Hop • Line	• Cooperative • Invasion • Net-Wall • Playground • Striking/Fielding • Target	• Acrobatic • Artistic • Educational • Rhythmic	• Fitness Circuits • Jogging • Track & Field • Yoga • Zumba
Consult your provincial curricular guide for additional information regarding breadth and variety.					

Considerations for Developmental Levels

As teachers develop quality physical education programming, which includes breadth and variety (see Table 4.2), it is imperative to constantly think about developmentally appropriate activities. Chapter 3 introduced you to the concept of addressing specific characteristics of developmentally appropriate levels. When teachers attend to delivering lessons that are developmentally appropriate, students become better equipped to achieve success. The following section describes specific information for each developmental level found in elementary schools (Fishburne, 2005) which applies across all five dimensions of activities. The five dimensions require variation such as equipment used, locations taught, levels of intensity required, and assessment procedures. Hence, attention toward developmentally appropriateness is critical when planning for quality physical education.

- **Developmental Level One (Kindergarten – Grade Two):** Regardless of the activity, teachers should ensure that the activities are simplistic in nature, require few rules, promote safety, allow for enjoyment and maximum participation, and support the development of basic fundamental movement skills.

- **Developmental Level Two (Grade Three – Four):** Regardless of the activity, teachers should ensure that the activities are simplistic in nature with more attention on the refinement of the basic fundamental movement skills developed in Developmental Level One, provide students with opportunities to test their limits in safe learning environments, require few rules, and allow for enjoyment and maximum participation. Within this developmental level, students should begin to engage in deliberate practice and be exposed to working in larger group settings than in Developmental Level One.

- **Developmental Level Three (Grade Five – Six):** Regardless of the activity, teachers should ensure that the activities help students apply skills to multiple situations, are challenging, provide students with opportunities to perfect their motor skills, require heightened levels of thinking skills, and allow for enjoyment and maximum participation. Within this developmental level, students should develop strategies individually, in partners, and in large groups.

Dimension: Alternative Environment Activities

Purpose: Active Healthy Kids Canada (2014) indicated that 95% of Canadian adults report local availability of parks and outdoor spaces. Outdoor areas provide students with numerous opportunities to be physically active. However, the Canadian Fitness and Lifestyle Research Institute (CFLRI) (2011) indicated that only 1/4 to 1/3 of the Canadian population actually report regular use of these spaces. This can be attributed to an array of factors such as safety concerns, lack of time (for both youth and parents to provide supervision), weather, and/or a preference for indoor screen-based activities (ParticipACTION, 2013). If students, therefore, are to realize the physical activity potential of these spaces, teachers of physical education must help them identify parks, recreational facilities, and other alternative learning environments as enjoyable and exciting places where they can engage in physical activities (e.g., swimming pools, skating arenas, sports facilities, trails).

Students have been found to take 35% more steps when physical education is held outdoors.

ParticipACTION, 2015

When students experience enjoyment and learning in a variety of alternative environment activities (e.g., orienteering, swimming, skiing), they will be more likely to engage in these activities in adulthood with families and friends (Hall, Bradford, & Hickson, 2015). According to Schaefer et al. (2014), Canadian children and youth aged 9-17 who play outside after school get 20 more minutes of heart-pumping activity per day, and are three times more likely to meet the Canadian Physical Activity Guidelines. Alternative environment activities enhance the breadth and variety in physical education programming, and serve several purposes, such as:

- Introducing students to alternative learning environments
- Fostering integration with other curricula (e.g., social studies, science)
- Supporting fundamental movement skill (FMS) development
- Enhancing levels of strength and endurance
- Applying FMS in activities that are held in different learning environments
- Encouraging decision making, leadership, communication, and teamwork skills

To increase children's safety, encourage more time outdoors, in nature. Natural play strengthens children's self-confidence and arouses their senses – their awareness of the world and all that moves in it, seen and unseen.

Louv, 2008

Teacher considerations for Alternative Environment Activities are shown in Table 4.3.

Table 4.3 Teacher Considerations For Alternative Environment Activities	
Communication	• Explain the activity to the school administrators (for school approval) • Consider the activity's cost • Choose to fundraise, collect money from each student • Ensure all funds are collected, if required • Complete all consent forms (including administrator's signature) • Contact the activity's organization (e.g., ski hill) to choose a date and time • Write/send home consent forms (to be signed by parents/guardians) • Collect the consent forms (signed hard copies) and attend to any that have not been returned/signed • Contact the transportation company to arrange rides to and from the activity, if required
Instruction	• Consider student knowledge and skill level • Obtain knowledge/experience of the activity site • Consult the "safety guidelines" document for safety considerations • Consider the student/teacher ratio (e.g., number of volunteers required) • Have a "What if" emergency plan • Plan accordingly to help students obtain the intended learning outcomes • Inform the students of the specific learning outcomes expected from participation • Ensure the students and off-site instructors know that the activity has a purpose rather than being organized play time • Consider, when possible, providing students with experiences participating in the activity at school prior to going off-site • Plan developmentally appropriate activities • Consider safety always (e.g., equipment, clothing, supervision, medications) • Ensure the facility provides proper equipment • Inform off-site instructors of student knowledge and skill level • Ensure the volunteers understand their roles and how to supervise
Differentiation	• Consider student medical concerns • Consider modifications for students with special needs • Provide off-site instructors with information about students with special needs • Attend to the variety of developmental levels of all students • Consider the variety of individual experience/skill levels of students (e.g., when at the skating rink, you could have a student who has figure skated for 6 years and a new-immigrant student who has never been on skates)

Activity Examples

The following section describes a variety of activities for the Alternative Environment dimension. The activities are divided into the three developmental levels present in elementary schools (Fishburne, 2005), and cover different types of environments (see Table 4.4).

Table 4.4 Activity Examples – Four Types of Environments	
LAND • Orienteering • Hiking • Cycling	**ICE/SNOW** • Cross-Country skiing • Tobogganing • Curling
WATER • Canoeing • Swimming • Spray parks	**AIR** (not as common for K-6 students) • Diving • Rope swings (swimming pools) • Climbing walls

To modify a type of activity, such as Orienteering across the three developmental levels, adjustments must be made to support the learning needs of the students in the different grade levels. Let's take a look at how Orienteering can be modified in this way:

Developmental Level One: Kindergarten – Grade Two

Orienteering: Introduce students to String Orienteering. This activity promotes the skills of discovering each Control Point, while ensuring the students follow the required pathway outlined by the string. String Orienteering is a perfect way for students to be introduced to mapping skills, and all the other benefits that stem from orienteering. Students can be encouraged to work individually or in partners.

Developmental Level Two: Grade Three – Four

Orienteering: After becoming comfortable with String Orienteering activities, students can participate in orienteering activities that do not require string. The Control Points can include problem-solving opportunities from other subject areas (e.g., Science) which can enhance the opportunities for cross-curricular connections. The Orienteering course could also promote enhanced levels of physical activity (e.g., push-ups at Control Point 1), and can incorporate strategic problem-solving in partners or small groups.

Developmental Level Three: Grade Five – Six

Orienteering: To improve students' fitness levels, more challenging and demanding courses can be developed, and more opportunities for cross-curricular connections can be promoted. For example, including Math Trails can put a more academic stamp on the orienteering experience while maintaining a high level of physical activity expectation.

Developmental Level One (Kindergarten – Grade Two)

String Orienteering (Land)

String orienteering is simply orienteering with the course route marked by a "string" that participants follow. Students can be provided string orienteering experiences outside the school walls. Although this activity requires some preliminary teacher preparation, students benefit greatly from working by themselves or in partners when searching for "control points" while following the string. While being provided with an easy-to-read map, students can follow the string and establish they have passed each control (e.g., collect a flag or some other object from each control). Additional strategies can include:

- adding physical tasks to do at control points (e.g., 10 jumping jacks)
- having students respond to directional questions at control points based on reading their map and/or observing their natural surroundings (e.g., did you go uphill or downhill since the last control point?)

Spelling Snowshoes (Snow)

In small groups, have students find a fresh patch of snow that has not been trampled upon yet. Each small group of students will be asked to spell out a variety of words using their snowshoes. The words could be from other subject areas, or could be ones they come up with. The activity can include criteria such as the group must spell out a total of five words in a certain time limit, or to spell out a variety of words with different numbers of letters (e.g., 2-letter word, 3-letter word, etc.). Additional challenges can include certain restrictions on the spelling activity such as working individually, adding more challenging words, etc.

Water Balance Relays (Water)

Each student will require a float. Have the students line up against one side of the pool about an arm's length apart from those beside them. After counting the students by two's (i.e., 1, 2, 1, 2...), have them travel to the other side of the pool balancing the float on different body parts (e.g., forehead, back of the hand and forearm). Challenge the students by asking if they can swim/walk to the other side of the pool without the float falling off! The student who covers the greatest distance (or quickest) can be recognized as the winner. Have the students explore different ways to balance the float while travelling from one side of the pool to the other, and try to include some partner balances.

Developmental Level Two (Grade Three – Four)

What Time Is It...Wet Whale? (Water)

In the swimming pool, have all students line up against one side of the pool (shallow end). Either you or a selected student, as Wet Whale, will stand on the opposite side of the pool facing away from the group of Fast Fish. The Fast Fish will all shout loudly together, "What Time Is It Wet Whale?" and Wet Whale must shout back the time. If Wet Whale shouts "5 o'clock!" all the Fast Fish must step, hop, or perform a swimming stroke 5 times towards Wet Whale. If Wet Whale shouts "11 o'clock!" the Fast Fish must move forward 11 steps, hops, or swim strokes, and so on. After the Fast Fish have asked Wet Whale what time it is 3-4 times, Wet Whale can shout "It is Feeding Time!" and try and catch some Fast Fish to feed on (by touching them on the shoulders)! When Wet Whale catches a Fast Fish (or more), they become Wet Whales, too. The activity continues until there are three Fast Fish remaining.

Frisbee Golf (Land)

Create a golf-like course around the playing field using boxes, sticks, etc. as "holes," and hand each student a Frisbee. Number the holes consecutively by attaching large-printed numbers on pylons. To eliminate standing for long periods of time, have the students, in groups of four, go to a specific hole "tee" (so all groups begin the activity at different holes). However, it is important for students to then move to the next 'higher numbered hole." After finishing Hole 18, groups will go onto Hole 1. In the groups of four, have the students take turns throwing their Frisbees at their specific hole. Ensure students understand their Frisbees must land in the hole (e.g., inside a box) or on it (e.g., pile of sticks). Have the students count and record the number of throw attempts it takes to get their Frisbee in the hole. After completing all the holes, have the students count up their number of individual attempts.

Milk Jug Curling (Ice/Snow)

The following is a game for 8 students in a 4 vs. 4 activity.

Preparation

- Fill up 8 four-litre plastic milk jugs with water and food colouring (i.e., 4 blue & 4 red)
- Where available and safe on the playing field, create curling sheets with a set of 3 food colouring rings indicated at each end of the sheet (as in regular curling), or use pylons, etc. to represent a target for students to slide the milk jugs toward

Activity Description

In teams of 4, students will take turns curling a milk jug (sliding it along the ice) towards the target, while striving to have their milk jugs stop closer to the target than those of the opposing team (i.e., red milk jugs vs. blue milk jugs).

To lead to greater accuracy when curling the milk jugs towards the target, a sock can be worn over the toes of the students' boots (better for sliding).

Developmental Level Three (Grade Five – Six)

Over/Under (Ice)

On an ice surface, this activity will require one regular-sized (water proof) ball, and each student will wear properly fitting skates and helmets. Two equal-numbered and heterogeneous teams (Team A [TA], Team B [TB]) will be selected by the teacher. TA will form a straight line (parallel to the playing space's center line) at one end of the ice surface. After the first in line (P1) throws the ball past the center line, P1 will then skate quickly around TA collecting one point each time "home plate" is passed (Note: home plate will be located at the beginning of Team A's line). P1 will continue running until the teacher calls out the word "Freeze" which will indicate that Team B has fulfilled its responsibilities. After P1 is asked to "Freeze," P1 will then skate to the end of Team A's line. Once P1 arrives at the end of the line, the next player in line (P2) will throw the ball and strive to collect points for TA by skating quickly! Every player on TA will have an opportunity to throw the ball and collect points.

At the opposite side of the ice surface, TB will spread out in the "outfield." Once the ball is thrown into the outfield, the ball will be retrieved by one player who will most likely be the closest player to the ball. The ball may be caught or picked up from the ice. Once the ball is retrieved by a player on TB, the rest of TB will form a straight line behind the player with the ball. The player with the ball will place it over his/her head in order to pass it backwards to the next player in the line. The ball will then travel to the end of the line following the sequence "Over the Head-Under the Legs-Over the Head-Under the Legs" and so on until it reaches the last player in the line. When the ball reaches the last player in line, the teacher will call out the word "Freeze" for both teams to hear.

When the word "Freeze" is called out, that will mark the exact time for TA's thrower-skater to "Freeze" and to add the earned points to the team's accumulated total! After each "thrower" on TA has had a turn to throw the ball, the two teams will switch sides/roles. Players from both teams will cross the center line by giving a high-five and a positive comment to an opposing player to promote good sportsmanship (cooperative learning)!

Water Pong (Water)

Each student will have a float (resembling a racquet). Have the students hit a ping pong ball back and forth together (partners/groups) as a warm-up. Instead of trying to bounce the ping pong balls off the water (as would be done on a ping pong table), the students will strive to keep the ball in the air while passing (striking) it to group members. As students become comfortable with passing to group members, challenge them to count how many times they can keep the ball in the air (for points). This activity can lead into a more structured game that could resemble a badminton-like activity. A team of 4-6 students could challenge another team with a few pool noodles acting as the net separating the two teams.

Lacrosse (Land)

Each student will have a lacrosse stick. In partners/small groups, have the students warm up by passing the lacrosse ball back and forth to each other, and ask them to move around while passing. Split the class into two teams, and ensure the two teams are aware of the game's boundaries on the playing field outlined by pylons. The students will play 7 against 7 with a goaltender. To score a goal, at team must make at least 3 passes after gaining possession, and shooting the ball into the opposing team's net (while staying outside the crease area).

Dimension: Dance Activities

Purpose: According to PHE Canada (2015), the most effective place to begin teaching dance activities is by looking at the dance-related learning outcomes that students should meet in quality physical education programming. The teaching of dance activities can include an  array of music (e.g., cultural), equipment, and stimuli. However, it is critical to ensure that consistent attention is given to listening and moving to the music. Students will discover a connection to their learning of dance skills when they relate to various pieces of music that interest them (according to developmental levels). According to Pavlovic, Popovic, and Zrnzevic (2015), traditional dances are significant in raising awareness of national affiliation, improve moral and aesthetic components of student personalities, improve students' musical capabilities including a sense of rhythm, melodic phrase, voice, musical hearing, sense of tempo and dynamics, musical memory, ability of active listening, and offer the opportunity to experience music.

Because the language of dance is embodied knowledge, it allows the students to express their knowledge about many subjects through their bodies. (Richard, 2013; p. 9)

As supported by Pavlovic et al. (2015) and other educational researchers (e.g., Fishburne, 2005; Hastie & Martin, 2006; Richard, 2013), when participating in dance activities, students problem-solve, develop a sense of time, rhythm, balance, and grace while listening to a variety of musical selections and moving through space simultaneously. Specifically, Barrett and Winters (2013) contended that "dance enables the body to guide students' thinking – opportunities that are often unique to physical education and arts education" (p. 17). Including dance activities in physical education programming enhances the breadth and variety, and serves numerous purposes, such as:

- Presenting ideas in kinesthetic form
- Relating dance movement and musical knowledge to other knowledge domains
- Supporting fundamental movement skill (FMS) development
- Enhancing student capabilities of responding to external stimuli
- Improving understanding of time and rhythm, and levels of coordination
- Enhancing strength, endurance, balance, and grace
- Supporting creativity, problem-solving, and higher level thinking skills
- Providing cross-curricular connections (e.g., language arts)
- Developing social skills
- Enhancing opportunities for lifelong physical activity

See Table 4.5 for more teaching considerations for Dance Activities.

Table 4.5 Teaching Considerations For Dance Activities	
Communication	• Explain the types of dance and musical selections that may be used (e.g., school newsletters, website) to parents, so they have all the information required • Explain to students the varying cultural music selections that will be used throughout the dance lessons (understanding of different cultural views) • Be aware of religious/cultural differences that may not allow for dance between sexes or not at all
Instruction	• Create a safe learning environment in which all students understand that the activities are intended to enhance an array of their skills (e.g., locomotor) • Select objectives from each of the 3 learning domains (i.e., psychomotor, cognitive, affective) which are all very closely integrated and contribute to the development of each other (PHE Canada, 2015) • Choose lyrics of popular music when the opportunity presents itself • Introduce students to traditional dances, primarily from their own nations, and sequently of other ones, which can be of great significance for improving intercultural education (Pavlovic et al., 2015) • Consider student knowledge and skill level • Plan accordingly to help students obtain the intended learning outcomes • Inform the students of the specific learning outcomes expected from participation • Plan developmentally appropriate activities • Consider safety always (e.g., space, music, groups) • Ensure that students have proper stimuli/equipment
Differentiation	• Consider modifications for students with special needs • Consider the cultural backgrounds of all students when selecting music • Remember to attend to the variety of developmental levels of all students • Ensure every student feels safe, comfortable, and willing to listen and move to the music

Activity Examples

The following section describes a variety of activities for the Dance dimension. The activities are divided into the three developmental levels present in elementary schools (Fishburne, 2005), and can include a variety of musical selections and movement criteria. Following is an example of how Dance activities can be taught across the three developmental levels (also see Table 4.5). Examples of types of dance activity and musical selection are shown in Tables 4.6 and 4.7 respectively.

Developmental Level One: Kindergarten – Grade Two

Clapping Games: Simple movement and clapping games and songs are an ideal way to introduce and practice important dance concepts such as beat and rhythm to young students. Choose songs with simple vocabulary and easy to follow actions. Classic dance-type learning activities include: Wheels on the Bus; Itsy, Bitsy, Spider; Head, Shoulders, Knees and Toes; and Patty Cakes.

Developmental Level Two: Grade Three – Four

Movement Cards: Have students create cards with words and/or pictures to match the four categories in Laban's Movement Analysis (Body Awareness, Spatial Awareness, Effort and Qualities, Relationships). For example, a card based on effort and qualities might read "rising". Shuffle, distribute, and have students create a movement sentence based on the chosen cards. Other ideas include cards based on animals (e.g., bear crawl, duck walk, etc.), athletics (e.g., soccer kick, ballet, etc.), common directions (e.g., up, down, sideways, etc.), etc.

Developmental Level Three: Grade Five – Six

Community Connections: Invite an Elder or a representative from a local cultural organization to share with your students the role of music and dance in their culture.

Poetry in Motion: Print out poems with notable 'movement' words. In groups, have the students create movements that match the mode/theme/idea of the poems.

Table 4.6 Types of Dance Activity Examples		
Developmental Level 1	**Developmental Level 2**	**Developmental Level 3**
Singing Games	Tapping Sticks to the Beat	Coming Around the Mountain (Square)
Clapping to the Beat	Skipping Games	Alley Cat (Folk)
Hopping to the Rhythm	Creative Movement	Flying Ace (Line)
Line Dances	Folk Dances	Square Dances
		Fishburne, 2005

Table 4.7 Musical Selection Examples		
Developmental Level 1	**Developmental Level 2**	**Developmental Level 3**
Baa, Baa, Black Sheep (Singing)	Skip to my Lou (Folk)	Coming Around the Mountain (Square)
Ring Around the Rosy (Singing)	Oh Susanna (Folk)	Alley Cat (Folk)
Macarena (Line)	Electric Slide (Line)	Flying Ace (Line)
		Fishburne, 2005

Developmental Level One (Kindergarten – Grade Two)

Clapping to the Beat

Have students sit cross-legged in a scattered formation on the floor.

1. Have students clap, individually, in the following ways (without music):
    a. Clap knees four times, repeating measure (1, 2, 3, 4; 1, 2, 3, 4; etc.)
    b. Clap hands four times, repeating measure (1, 2, 3, 4; 1, 2, 3, 4; etc.)
    c. Tap the floor four times, repeating measure (1, 2, 3, 4; 1, 2, 3, 4; etc.)
    d. Make up combinations of four claps on knees, then four taps on the floor, and four claps with the hands

2. Have students listen to "music" for the 4/4 meter (4 beats/measure) and the accent on the first beat
    a. Repeat 1a through 1d with music playing

Moving to the Beat (Standing & Shaking in One Spot)

From a standing position, have students shake different body parts to repeating measure (1, 2, 3, 4; 1, 2, 3, 4; etc.) with music. For example:

1. shake the right hand (1, 2, 3, 4)
2. add other body parts
3. shake the right hand/right leg

Moving to the Beat (Locomotion)

From a standing position, have students perform different locomotor movements to the rhythm of the music (e.g., run, jog, hop, slither) (see Chapter 1). Throughout this activity, students can be asked to imitate animals moving around (e.g., bear). Although students may imitate animals moving around, focus must remain on "moving to the music."

Baa, Baa, Black Sheep

Musical Accompaniment: Childhood Rhythms, Series 7, No. 701 (Folkcraft 1191)
Formation: Single circle, all facing center.
Skills: Stamp, bow and curtsy, turn, and walk.

Measures	Song	Action
1	Baa, baa, black sheep,	Stamp three times.
2	Have you any wool?	Shake fingers.
3	Yes sir, yes, sir,	Nod head twice.
4	Three bags full.	Hold three fingers up.
5	One for my master,	Turn right and bow or curtsy.
6	One for my dame,	Turn left and bow or curtsy.
7	And one for the little boy,	Turn around.
8	Who lives in the lane.	Face center and bow or curtsy.
9-12	Chorus	Join inside hands and take 16 steps counterclockwise.

Variations: All join hands and take 8 slides to the right, then 8 slides to the left. Raise hands and take 4 steps into the circle and 4 steps out. Repeat 4 in and 4 out. Drop hands and skip 16 steps counterclockwise.

Developmental Level Two (Grade Three – Four)

Let's Perform!

In partners, students sit cross-legged approximately 2 feet apart facing each other which will allow the partners to develop routines using the floor and the partner's stick for tapping. A few sample routines include:

1. Without Music (individuals):
   a. Tap sticks on the floor
   b. Tap both sticks together in front
   c. Tap sticks on floor (with both arms sideways)
2. Without Music (partners):
   a. Tap sticks on the floor
   b. Tap their own sticks together
   c. Exchange right sticks with partner
   d. Exchange left sticks with partner
3. With Music:
   a. Repeat 1 and 2
4. Without Music (partners):
   a. Partners will perform numerous calisthenic-like and other rhythmic routines while standing face-to-face, side-by-side, or back-to-back
5. With Music:
   a. Repeat 4
6. With Music (groups):
   a. After students have learned basic tapping skills and gained experience using hoops, balls, skipping ropes, etc. while moving to music, they can now develop creative rhythmic routines in groups … "Performances to Follow!"

Hoop Activity 1 (Individuals)

Have students place their hoops flat on the floor. Present challenges, such as the following, that involve applying locomotor skills and a change of direction

1. "Make up a jumping routine, moving in and out of your hoop." Later, add other challenges such as "in and out, around, and over." (Use even rhythm, 4/4 or 3/4 music.)
2. Use two or more hoops on the floor and repeat 1
3. Introduce ball bouncing with a hoop

Hoop Activity 2 (Partners)

In partners, twirling, throwing, catching, and stability and balance skills can be incorporated into an array of challenging matching, contrasting, and follow-the-leader routines.

1. Develop a series of challenges involving partners and music, using one or more hoops
2. Repeat the challenges involving partners and music, one or more hoops, while also incorporating different locomotor skills (e.g., run, hop, leap)
3. Repeat 1 or 2, adding a ball or other small equipment to the original challenge
4. Repeat 1 or 2, while changing the music from fast to slow, etc.
5. Repeat 1 or 2, while increasing the number of participants from partners to groups

Oh Susanna

Musical Accompaniment: Folkcraft 1186 – Lloyd Shaw E-14

Number the students 1s & 2s

Formation: Partners standing in a single circle facing center, with hands joined, the #1 on the 2's right side

Skills: Walk, slide, do-si-do, promenade

Measures	Call	Action
1-8	Slide to the left	All take 8 sliding steps and slide to the right & 8 sliding steps to the left
9-12	Forward and back.	All take 4 steps to the center and 4 steps back
13-16	1s forward and back	Release hands. 1s walk 4 steps toward the center of the circle & 4 steps back. 2s stand in place & clap hands
17-20	2s forward and back	2s go to center while 1s clap hands
21-24		Do-si-do with partners.
25-28		Do-si-do with corner 1s
29-32		Everyone promenades around the circle

Developmental Level Three (Grade Five – Six)

Electric Slide (Line Dance – Developmental Levels Two and Three)

Musical Accompaniment: "Get Ready for This" (U2 or Electric Boogie) – Marcia Griffiths (artists)

Formation: Lines facing front

Skills: Slide, clap, stomp, step

Measures	Action
	Slide to the left (3x), clap.
1	Slide to the right (3x), clap.
2	Step back with right foot, step back with left foot,
3	Step back with right foot, lean back and clap.
4	Lean forward, clap, lean backward, clap.
	Step 1/4 turn counterclockwise, scuff right foot forward.
	Repeat.

Variations: Substitute slides with full turns

Have the students try creative movements in groups of 4 – 6.

Alley Cat (Folk Dance)

Musical Accompaniment: ATCO 45-6226 (Columbia CL-2500)

Formation: Scattered with all facing the same direction

Skills: Touch step, turn, jump

Measures	Action
1	Slide right foot and touch toe to floor
2	Close right toe to left foot
3	Shift right foot to right and touch toe to floor
4	Close right foot to left and shift weight to right foot
5-8	Repeat 1 to 4 with left foot
9-12	Repeat 1 to 4 with right foot being extended back and returning to side of left foot
13-16	Repeat 1 to 4 with left foot extending back
17-18	Raise right knee up in front of left knee; repeat
19-20	Raise left knee up in front of right knee; repeat
21	Raise right arm in front of left knee
22	Raise left knee up in front of right knee
23-24	Clap hands and jump a 1/4 turn to the right
	Repeat dance, making a 1/4 turn toward the right during the last measure of each dance

"Day-O" (Creative Movement)

In groups of 6-8, have the groups listen to the musical selection "Day-O" (Raffi). After having a chance to listen to the music and discuss what types of movements can be expressed to "tell a story through their movements," have the groups develop a movement sequence together that creatively tells the story being sung in "Day-O." As a culminating activity, the groups can perform their "stories" to the class after they developed a beginning, middle, and end to the story. Within their stories, students can assume the identity of familiar stories (e.g., king and queen travelling to the castle, animals in the wild, circus events, etc.). Groups should include different levels, speeds, and qualities when "telling their stories" through their movement while also incorporating a variety of equipment.

Dimension: Games Activities

Purpose: Games provide students with opportunities to move with control, agility, speed, and balance in relation to a target, object, opponent, and/or space. With specific curricular outcomes, such as to "experience and develop ways to receive, retain and send an object, using a variety of body parts and implements and through a variety of activities" (Alberta Learning, 2000, p. 6), engaging in games can help students meet these learning outcomes. Additionally, students develop a deeper understanding of their body awareness, spatial awareness, relational awareness,

and quality of movement while cooperating with others, competing against others, and/or working individually. Including games in quality physical education programming enhances the breadth and variety, and serves several purposes, such as:
- Supporting fundamental movement skill (FMS) development
- Enhancing personal fitness and sport-specific skills
- Developing cooperative and competitive skills
- Being physically active in a multitude of game settings
- Enhancing creativity, problem-solving, and higher level thinking skills

When participating in games, students develop movement skills and the transferability of tactical solutions from one game to another.
PHE Canada, 2015

Table 4.8 identifies a number of important teaching considerations when teaching Games.

Table 4.8 Teaching Considerations For Games	
Communication	• Explain to the students about variety of games that will be taught (for an understanding of providing "variety") • Explain the difference between and benefits of, cooperative and competitive games • Help students develop skills and game sense vs. worrying about winning/losing
Instruction	• Consider student knowledge and skill level • Plan accordingly to help students obtain the intended learning outcomes • Inform the students of the specific learning outcomes expected from participation • Plan developmentally appropriate activities • Ensure that students have proper equipment • Consider safety always (e.g., space, equipment, teams) • Consider maximum practice opportunities and participation
Differentiation	• Consider modifications for students with special needs • Consider the cultural backgrounds of all students when planning various traditional/cultural games • Attend to the variety of developmental levels/experiences of all students • Create a safe learning environment for all students to understand that the learning environment is intended to enhance an array of their game skills (e.g., throwing a softball) (PHE Canada, 2015) • Ensure every student feels safe, comfortable, and willing to participate in the activities

Activity Examples

The following section describes a variety of activities for the Games dimension. The activities are divided into the three developmental levels present in elementary schools (Fishburne, 2005), and cover different types of fundamental movement skills. For each activity, a variety of possible modifications are shared using the REPS Model (Hickson & Saby, 2008).

To modify a type of activity, such as Volleyball (traditional game) across the three developmental levels, adjustments must be made to support the learning needs of students in the different grade levels. An example follows to show how Volleyball can be modified to achieve this:

Developmental Level One: Kindergarten – Grade Two

Volleyball: Introduce students to passing and receiving a developmentally appropriate ball (individually, partners). Provide students with opportunities to hit the ball against the wall (high) and either catch it or strike it again with two arms. Having maximal opportunities to "touch" the ball is essential for student learning in this developmental level.

Developmental Level Two: Grade Three – Four

Volleyball: After having a significant number of opportunities to pass and receive a ball, students should be comfortable enough to begin working in small teams engaged in modified volleyball-type games. Rules can include: the ball can bounce once prior to passing it to a teammate or moving it across the net; students can catch the ball then pass it; teams can have up to five passes prior to moving it to the other team.

Developmental Level Three: Grade Five – Six

Volleyball: Students can engage in volleyball games while developing strategies to earn points and to try to outplay the opposing team. Serves can be overhand or underhand, and positional play can be discussed in detail.

Developmental Level One (Kindergarten – Grade Two)

Alphabet/Number Soup

In small groups, students can be asked to create letters/words/numbers using only their bodies.

Possible Modifications based on the REPS Model:

R: Ask students to move at different levels (e.g., low) and/or use capital/lower case letters

E: Ask students to include/add different pieces of equipment

P: Allow more or less students

S: Ask students to ensure their letters/words/numbers take up a set space

  e.g., "As a group, create the largest/smallest letter B possible"

  e.g., "Your group's word must fit into the area marked by pylons"

Animal Introduction

In a circle formation, one student can be asked to say his/her name and to create an animal-like movement. The rest of the group is asked to repeat the name and the movement. Students will continue this process until each group member has had a turn.

Possible Modifications based on the REPS Model:

R: Ask students to restrict movements to specific levels, speed, body parts

E: Ask students to include/add different pieces of equipment

P: Allow more or less students

S: Ask students to perform in different spaces (e.g., small/large space, gymnasium, outdoors, classroom)

Cars on the Road

When the teacher says aloud "Go!" in the middle of a large circle of students, the students will then run around the circle, pretending to be "cars." A student (i.e., car) may move out to "pass" another, but the passing car must then move back into the circle. No student (i.e., cars) may reverse directions. As the teacher calls out "Stop," everyone must come to a full stop. A student (i.e., car) who fails to stop or who bumps into another "car" must run and give the teacher a high-five, then return to their place in the circle.

Possible Modifications based on the REPS Model:

R: Play the same game moving in a reverse direction

E: Substitute the calling out of "Go" and "Stop" with hand signals or flash cards

Developmental Level Two (Grade Three – Four)

Triangle Tag

Create groups of four (i.e., 3 students form a triangle holding hands and the 4th person is "it"). One student in the triangle is designated as the person to be caught. The "it" has to run around the triangle trying to tag the designated person on his/her back. "It" cannot reach across the triangle. The two other students act as "blockers" to try and save their group member from being tagged. Ask students to change roles frequently to give all participants a chance to experience each role.

Possible Modifications based on the REPS model:

E: "It" tries to tag with an implement; student being caught has a tail

S: Each group must stay within a set boundary

Hoop Circle

In small groups of 4–6, each group member will stand in a circle and hold hands. A hula hoop will be rested between two students' clasped hands. Without releasing hands, students will pass the hoop around the circle.

Possible Modifications based on the REPS model:

R: Change the hoop direction; perform the activity with closed eyes; stand on one foot

E: Use multiple hoops and/or different sized hoops

P: Allow more or less students

Instant Goal

In groups of three, students begin dribbling and passing the ball to each other. Suddenly, "Student A" moves away from the other two students and spreads his/her legs to make a goal. "Student B" and "Student C" then must dribble and pass the ball at least two times before one of them tries to kick the ball between "Student A's" legs (i.e., the goal). The game then continues, with "Student B" and "Student C" taking their individual turns at making a goal.

Possible Modifications based on the REPS model:

R: Instead of using feet to dribble, pass and shoot the ball, have students use their hands

E: Use different sized balls

P: Allow more students (e.g., four)

Developmental Level Three (Grade Five – Six)

Group Juggle

Divide students into small groups. Provide each group with an object that can be thrown. Each group member should stand in a circle facing each other. One group member will be asked to choose an object and to throw it to someone across the circle. The person receiving the object will then throw it to another group member until everyone has received and thrown the object once. The object cannot be thrown to a group member next to the thrower. The object should return back to the student who started. This throwing sequence must be remembered and followed in all future attempts.

Possible Modifications based on the REPS model:

  R: Throw with one hand; roll the ball; run around the circle after throwing; change direction

  E: Use a bean bag, larger/smaller objects; add objects

  P: Allow more or less students

  S: Every group member takes a step back or moves closer together

Shufflecurl

The rules are similar to shuffleboard, but the objective is to slide the disks as close to the center of the circle as possible. Students also try to knock the opponent's disks out of scoring position. When each student has slid four disks to the opposite circle, one "end" has been completed. Two "ends" make one round. A game may be five, ten, or more number of rounds. To score points, students are awarded one point for each disk which sits closer to the center of the circle than the closest disk of the opposing students.

Possible Modifications based on the REPS model:

  E: Use different disks (e.g., beanbags)

  S: Students take a step back or move closer to the circle

Group (Soccer) Keep Away

A group of four students try to keep the soccer ball away from partner defenders by passing, dribbling, dodging, stopping, and pivoting. As soon as one of the defensive partners touches the ball, the group of four is broken to switch roles (e.g., 2 of them become the partner defenders) and the activity is repeated.

Possible Modifications based on the REPS model:

  E: Use different sized balls

  P: Add more students to act as offensive and/or defensive players

  S: Make the playing space larger/smaller

Teaching Games for Understanding (TGfU)

An approach to teaching games in elementary school physical education can be through "teaching games for understanding" (TGfU). Bunker and Thorpe (1982) developed TGfU around the concept of teaching children games by playing games. Butler et al. (2008, as cited on OPHEA, 2014) identified six Basic TGfU Concepts:

1. Teach games through games
2. Break games into their simplest format – and then increase the complexity
3. Participants are intelligent performers in games
4. Every learner is important and is engaged
5. Participants need to know the content matter
6. Need to be developmentally appropriate (e.g., skill, challenge)

By creating an easy-to-understand illustration for teachers and students by outlining the similarities and linkages of strategy that can be transferred throughout the games in each category, TGfU is divided into four categories. When utilizing the TGfU approach, students are afforded a variety of opportunities to learn new aspects of sports (Pearson & Webb, 2008). Each category (see Table 4.9) includes games that involve similar goals, tactics, skills, rules, and concepts.

Table 4.9 TGfU – Four Categories & Activities			
Invasion/Territory	**Striking/Fielding**	**Target**	**Net/Wall**
• Floor hockey	• Baseball	• Curling	• Tennis
• Soccer	• Kickball	• Golf (Frisbee golf)	• Volleyball
• Handball	• Softball	• Bocce	• Badminton
• Basketball	• Cricket	• Bowling	• Racquetball

TGfU is a child-centred approach; the teacher acts as a facilitator and the students make their own adaptations in order to maximize the level of challenge and enjoyment. According to OPHEA (2014), the steps required for TGfU include:

- **Activity Appreciation:** trying out a version of the activity in a small-group
- **Tactical Awareness:** developing understanding of common elements of games and tactics needed for success
- **Decision-Making:** learning and practicing making decisions in action, in response to different situations
- **Application of Skills:** identifying and practicing the skills needed to improve play
- **Performance:** putting it all together, applying the skills, decision-making and tactics in game situations

The process is a cyclical one with students continuing to adapt and change as needed for the best playing experience (OPHEA, 2014).

Dimension: Gymnastic Activities

Purpose: Gymnastic activities provide students with opportunities to move with control, strength, and power. With specific curricular outcomes, such as bending, balancing, twisting, rolling, etc. (British Columbia, 2016), students will benefit from experiencing gymnastic activities. For example, students develop a deeper awareness of their body awareness, spatial awareness, relational awareness, and quality of movement. According to Lešnik, Glinšek, and Žvan (2015), mastery of gymnastic elements is a good base for developing different movement skills required in other physical activities, games, and sports. Including gymnastic activities in quality physical education programming enhances the breadth and variety, and serves several purposes, such as:

- Supporting fundamental movement skill (FMS) development
- Enhancing levels of strength, agility, balance, coordination, flexibility, endurance
- Supporting movement with grace and safety
- Incorporating movement that involves the whole body (upper, lower, left, right)
- Developing a deeper understanding of perseverance
- Improving fitness levels
- Enhancing creativity, problem-solving, and higher level thinking skills

Gymnastics is an excellent vehicle for the teaching of fundamental movement skills and promoting health-related fitness for elementary school students.
Coelho, 2010; Donham-Foutch, 2007

Educational vs. Traditional Gymnastics

Most schools today are deciding to not purchase large apparatus and equipment that can support gymnastics development (e.g., climbing ropes, climbers, box horses). Therefore, this section focuses on educational gymnastics using a variety of basic equipment such as mats, skipping ropes, and benches to support learning in this dimension.

A number of important teaching considerations for Gymnastic s Activities are identified in Table 4.10.

Table 4.10 Teaching Considerations for Gymnastic Activities	
Communication	• Explain to students about the variety of gymnastic activities that will be taught (for an understanding of providing "variety")

Instruction	• Consider student knowledge and skill level
	• Plan accordingly to help students obtain the intended learning outcomes
	• Inform students of the specific learning outcomes expected from participation
	• Plan developmentally appropriate activities
	• Ensure that students have proper equipment, apparatus, etc.
	• Consider safety always (e.g., space, equipment, teams)
	• Consider maximum practice opportunities and participation
	• Consider referring to "movement concepts" established by Rudolph Laban in 1974 as a classification system that allows for the identification and analysis of all movement (Fishburne, 2005; PHE Canada, 2011)
	  o Body Awareness (What can the body do?)
	    Shapes; Balance; Transfer of weight
	  o Space Awareness (Where does the body move?)
	    Personal/General; Direction/Pathways; Levels
	  o Qualities (How does the body move?)
	    Speed; Force; Bound and flow
	  o Relationships (To whom/what does the body relate?)
	    People; Objects

Differentiation	• Consider modifications for students with special needs • Consider the cultural backgrounds of all students when planning various activities • Attend to the variety of developmental levels of all students • Create a safe learning environment in which all students understand that the learning environment is intended to enhance an array of their gymnastic skills (e.g., rolls, balances) and to develop physical literacy (PHE Canada, 2015) • Ensure all students feel safe, comfortable, and willing to participate

Activity Examples

The following section describes a list of activities for the Gymnastics dimension. The activities are divided into the three developmental levels present in elementary schools (Fishburne, 2005) along with the six dominant movement patterns specific to gymnastics.

Dominant Movement Patterns (DMPs)

- **Landings:** body control on landing is an important skill because it enables students to control the movement of their body; landings are used in all jumping activities and in a range of games
- **Statics:** the "held" or "still" positions in gymnastics, and this should be the starting point for any gymnastics program
- **Swings:** play a central role in gymnastics as students develop spatial awareness, body tension, and grip strength
- **Rotations:** any turn or spin around an internal axis
- **Springs:** involve students projecting themselves into the air. It can involve springing from both legs, one leg or even from two hands and two feet. Landing techniques must also be proficient before students perform any springing activities
- **Locomotor Skills:** involve students travelling from one spot to another - Point A to Point B (e.g., running, sliding, galloping, crawling, hopping)

When considering developmental appropriateness for gymnastic-type activities, keep the DMPs in mind to ensure students are engaged in activities they are comfortable with, able to perform safely, and are able to meet success with some challenge. Examples of gymnastic activities follow for each of the three developmental levels.

Developmental Level One (Kindergarten – Grade Two)

Log Roll (Rotations)
The log roll is the simplest roll to perform. Individually, students will lie on their backs, with their arms extended over the head and the hands clasped together. The body will be kept in a straight line while rolling to the side (hips and shoulders should rotate at the same time) and then around to the starting position.

Inverted V (Statics)
Individually, while beginning in a squat position, with hands on the floor, students will lean forward, raise their hips, and look back through the legs. Holding this balance for 3 seconds, students can then be challenged to raise one leg, raise one arm, etc. Also, challenge students to balance:
- on one, two, three body parts

Have students practice different statics through problem-solving activities (e.g., on a bench, partners)

Animal Movements (Locomotions)
Have students spread out and stand individually. On the teacher's signal, students will begin to move using a variety of "animal-type" (and other living things) walks/jumps/movements. For example, the teacher can call out the following: bear; kangaroo; elephant; snake; etc., and observe the students moving in all directions and at various levels while demonstrating these animals' walking/jumping/movement styles.

Developmental Level Two (Grade Three – Four)

Fall and Land (Landings)

Students will begin on their knees with their bodies erect and arms at the sides. They will then fall forward and land on their hands, with a gradual bending of the arms to break the fall safely. As an extra challenge, students can perform 3 push-ups after they land safely.

Carousel (Swinging)

Partners will stand facing each other with their toes touching, arms extended and holding hands. On the teacher's signal, the partners will begin to move in a clockwise direction around and back to their starting positions. As an extra challenge, partners can extend one leg back and repeat the task, and/or partners can release one hand and repeat the task.

Wheel Activity (Statics)

In groups of three, students will stand beside each other facing the same direction. The middle student will spread his/her legs and extend arms to the sides. The two outside students will place their "inside feet" near the middle student's feet, grasp hands, then lean outward to the sides. The group will hold this balance for 3 seconds. As an extra challenge, the outside students could be asked to twirl a hula hoop with their free arms.

Developmental Level Three (Grade Five – Six)

Skipping Activity 1: Alternate Step (Locomotion)

Students will follow the following sequence:
1. jump over the skipping rope with the right foot (jump)
2. hop on the same foot (rebound)
3. jump over the skipping rope with left foot (jump)
4. hop on the same foot (rebound)
5. pass the skipping rope overhead and repeat

Skipping Activity 2: Jumping over One "Long" Rope (Locomotion)

Two students will hold a long skipping rope approximately 2 feet off the ground (the height can vary according to the group's ability). Skipping activities may include:
1. high jumping (consider safety here, e.g., floor surface and use of mats)
2. jumping and making shapes in the air
3. jumping and turning in the air
4. jumping and giving a high-five to a partner in the air
5. crossing the rope with a cartwheel movement
6. follow-the-leader activities

Rolls and Cartwheels (Rotations)

Beginning from different starting positions (Statics) such as crouched, lying, standing, etc., have students perform:
• consecutive rolls (e.g., log, backward)
• cartwheel progressions

When students are demonstrating a high comfort level, have them perform a cartwheel beside a partner (performing one, too).

Mission...POSSIBLE!

Your mission is to build part of an obstacle course that allows your classmates to experience Laban's Movement Concepts through Dominant Movement Patterns. You may use whatever equipment you feel you need. Consider the following when building (and testing):

Laban's Movement Concepts (LMC):
• Body (give/receive force, bear weight, gesture)
• Space (pathways, levels, personal and general space, directions)
• Effort (timing, weight, flow)
• Relationship (With what? With whom?)

DMPs (no swings due to time and equipment):
• Landings: feet, elevated, hands, combinations
• Statics (balances): individual exploration, paired, group
• Locomotion: skip, hop, gallop, leap, jump, animal walks
• Springs: hoop springing (in and out spring; out and back hop), jump turns, heel slaps, heel clicks, tuck jumps, frog jumps, mule kicks, side heel clicks, walk throughs, jump throughs
• Rotations: log roll, egg roll, shoulder, forward, backward, shoulder, backwards roll

Decide on a theme (unifying) and choose 2 DMPs and 2 LMCs that are the learning focus.

DMP #1 _____   DMP #2 _____

LMC #1 _____   LMC #2 _____

Dimension: Individual Activities

Purpose: Individual activities provide students with opportunities to work individually on activities that require minimal equipment. In support of specific curricular outcomes, such as to "perform locomotor skills through a variety of activities" (Alberta Learning, 2000), students will be exposed to learning activities that challenge them to enhance their levels of coordination, power, and strength. While developing a deeper understanding of their body awareness, spatial awareness, and quality of movement, individual activities expose students to a variety of activities.

Including individual activities in quality physical education programming enhances the breadth and variety, and serves several purposes, such as:

• Supporting fundamental movement skill (FMS) development

• Enhancing levels of strength, agility, balance, flexibility, endurance

• Developing a deeper level of understanding of perseverance

• Enhancing levels of fitness and coordination

• Developing an awareness toward being physically active without the need for others

• Enhancing self-confidence through striving to reach personal bests and goal-setting

A number of teaching considerations for Individual Activities are presented in Table 4.11.

Table 4.11 Teaching Considerations for Individual Activities	
Communication	• Explain to students the variety of individual activities that will be taught (for understanding of providing "variety") • It is essential that students do not compare their performance levels to their peers • Ensure every student feels safe, comfortable, and willing to participate in a variety of individual activities
Instruction	• Consider student knowledge and skill level • Plan accordingly to help students obtain the intended learning outcomes • Inform students of the specific learning outcomes expected from participation • Plan developmentally appropriate activities • Ensure that students have proper equipment (individual work = added equipment) • Consider safety always • Consider using the "Station Approach" (minimal equipment, multiple learning opportunities) • Consider supervision, as several activities will be going on at any given moment • Challenge students to better their own previous performances • Consider including goal-setting for students to record improvements • Provide variety for student learning (Fishburne, 2005; PHE Canada, 2015)
Differentiation	• Consider modifications for students with special needs • Consider students' cultural backgrounds when planning various activities • Attend to the variety of developmental levels of all students • Create a safe learning environment in which all students understand that it is intended to enhance an array of their individual skills as opposed to simply being a time to work with little effort • Ensure every student is safe, comfortable, and willing to participate in a variety of individual activities

Activity Examples

The following section describes a variety of activities appropriate for the Individual Activities dimension. The activities are divided into the three developmental levels present in elementary schools (Fishburne, 2005), and cover a variety of fundamental movement skills.

To modify a type of activity across the three developmental levels, adjustments must be made to support the learning needs of students in different grade levels. Examples to show how a variety of individual activities can be modified follow:

Developmental Level One: Kindergarten – Grade Two

Juggling: Introduce students to what juggling is, and have them use one (or two) beanbags (or small balls, scarves) to throw up and down with one hand and catch it with the same hand. Then have them catch it with the opposite hand.

Developmental Level Two: Grade Three – Four

Juggling: After experiencing a variety of ways to throw and catch (for juggling purposes), have students include three objects (e.g., balls, scarves, beanbags) and have them practice juggling by throwing with one hand and catching with the opposite hand.

Developmental Level Three: Grade Five – Six

Juggling: Have students include three objects (balls, scarves, beanbags...or one of each) and get them to practice juggling by throwing with one hand and catching with the opposite hand. As they are juggling, have them try to walk around. Students could juggle in pairs. For example, while facing each other, have them throw with the left hand and catch with the right hand (two objects).

Developmental Level One (Kindergarten – Grade Two)

Shuttle Relay (Running)

In the gymnasium, have students run short distances. During relay-type activities, have students run the length of the gymnasium and give a high-five to another runner who will go in the opposite direction. Once the runners reach the other side of the gymnasium, have them go to the end of the "short" line. And, so on...the shuttle relay can include running two lengths and then shouting across the gymnasium for "next" to go! When teaching running activities, it should be noted that students should not be interested in competing as opposed to working to their individual best levels.

One- and Two-Foot Jumps

On the playground, have students participate in one-foot and two-foot jumps. When teaching jumping activities, students should be asked to jump high, low, far, and/or short distances. While developing their skills in jumping, students should begin to understand there are different purposes for different types of jumps, etc. Teachers can demonstrate proper ways of jumping for different purposes. For example, jumping skills can include long and high jumps (i.e., track and field focus) or simply bunny hops, also known as Balance and Stability Skills (Francis et al., 2011) for balance, strength, and bone development. The jumping activities can be done individually (individual spots) or in partners (a partner jumps, while the other measures or provides simple feedback about height, etc.).

Throwing

In the gymnasium, have students practice and develop their short-distance throwing skills. In partners, the students can throw a small rhino skin-type ball to each other. Depending on the students' skill levels, modify the throwing distances to ensure success is possible (e.g., the ball can be thrown in the air to the partner). Students will benefit from watching their teacher perform short-distance throws.

Developmental Level Two (Grade Three – Four)

Improving the Eye-Hand (Juggling)

Have students juggle using three objects (balls, scarves, beanbags...or one of each) by throwing with one hand and catching with the opposite hand. As the students juggle, ask them to try to walk around the space in the gymnasium.

Alternative: Have the students juggle in pairs. For example, while facing each other, have them throw with the left hand and catch with the right hand (two objects).

Tai Chi (Movement Art)

Through the use of a video displayed on the gymnasium wall, have students participate in Tai Chi from a professional instructor. Have students spread out and perform the various activities led by the professional (via video). The teacher can also engage in the activity. This will be a good role modeling opportunity.

Alternative: A second strategy to teaching Tai Chi is to have a professional come to the school and lead the activity in front of all the students. Of course, if you have some background experience teaching Tai Chi, there is no need to have another person lead the activity.

Sing-a-longs (Skipping)

Hand each group of four a long skipping rope . Have students play different skipping (and singing) games. Two of the group members will hold and swing the rope, while the other two enter the "rope zone" to try and skip while singing a song. The goal is to stay skipping for a minute or so. Have the group members change roles every few minutes. As students develop their small group skipping skills, have them come up with innovative and creative new activities.

Developmental Level Three (Grade Five – Six)

Circuit Activity

Have students design their own circuit program. After having learned what makes a fitness-type program effective (e.g., cardiovascular, muscular endurance), the students can design a short 10-15 minute circuit that includes running, jumping, and strength (e.g., push-up) activities that can occur in a relatively small space around the playground. Activities can be push-ups, sprints, jumps for height, etc. Have students design their circuit, try it, and explain it to a partner.

Track and Field Events

With a Run, Jump, Throw (Athletics Canada) theme, have the students participate in a modified Track and Field event. The event can include long jump, running relays, throwing a ball for distance, etc. As with all activities, safety considerations must be planned for and included in all these activities.

Alternative: Have the students create a Track and Field event for the class, and then for the whole school maintaining a focus on individual best performances as opposed to a competitive-focus.

Cup Stacking

Have students practice and develop their eye-hand coordination through cup stacking. Students can participate in a variety of cup stacking activities such as stationary, partners, groups, locomotion (e.g., travel to the table with cups on them, stack one cup, and then travel back to the line), while doing push-ups, etc.

Challenges for Meeting All Five Dimensions

Even though teachers may have good intentions for providing quality physical education programming in elementary schools, several challenges may arise that hinder lesson delivery across the five dimensions. Such challenges are described in Table 4.12.

Table 4.12 Challenges for Lesson Delivery	
Resources	**Issue:** You would like to teach badminton, but you have no resources to assist in your planning. • Contact your school's physical education consultant or a provincial physical education council to learn about available resources (e.g., online clips, books) that may assist and fit your school's budget
Equipment	**Issue:** Your school's equipment inventory is low and/or is not in good shape. • Contact local physical education organizations to discover any schools, organizations that may be getting rid of their supply, or to find out about businesses that sell equipment that will fit your school's equipment budget **Issue:** Your equipment is being handled improperly (e.g., volleyball nets). • Have a discussion with your colleagues about the importance of equipment maintenance and how equipment impacts quality physical education programming
Volunteers	**Issue:** You are having difficulty with finding enough volunteers for a field trip. • Contact a local university; pre-service teachers are always looking for volunteer opportunities (which also provides pre-service teachers with experiences for their resumes)

Concluding Thoughts

Elementary school physical education is a critical part of the educational experience for students. Providing students with breadth and variety across all five dimensions is essential to the development of the whole child (Fishburne, 2005). Breadth refers to alternative environments, dance, games, types of gymnastics, and individual activities. Variety refers to the array of activities offered to students within the five dimensions. It is essential that students are exposed to a variety of activities so that all students have the opportunity to develop to their full potential. When teaching, teachers must attend to the students' developmental levels. Building a quality physical education program requires a great deal of attention to the content being taught. Table 4.13 identifies possible activities for Quality Physical Education Programming.

Checking for Understanding
I Can...
- Explain the rationale behind the physical education content
- Explain what breadth and variety refer to in physical education programming
- Share the benefits for student learning when breath and variety are offered in physical education programming
- State five dimensions of activity that are common in physical education programming across Canada
- Describe a variety of activities within the five dimensions
- Modify/extend activities to meet developmental levels

APPENDIX A

Table 4.13 Possible Activities for Quality Physical Education				
Alternative Environment Activities	**Dance Activities**	**Games Activities**	**Gymnastics Activities**	**Individual Activities**
Aquatics Swimming Water polo **In Gymnasium** Shufflecurl Archery **Outdoor Pursuits** Orienteering Skiing Cycling **Water Based** Canoeing Kayaking	**Contemporary** Line Partner Hip-hop **Cultural** Folk Square First Nations round dance **Rhythmic/ Creative** Clapping Singing Aerobic	**Territory** Floor hockey Soccer Handball **Fielding** Baseball Kickball Softball **Target** Curling Golf Bocce **Net/Wall** Tennis Volleyball Badminton	**Rhythmic** Balls Scarves Jump ropes **Educational** Forward rolls Lunges Balances Cartwheels	**Track and Field** Running Jumping Throwing **Manipulative** Juggling Jump rope Cup stacking **Movement Arts** Tai chi Yoga **Fitness** Zumba Yoga
				modified from Alberta Learning (2000)

APPENDIX B
GOVERNMENT SOURCES

Alberta Learning. (2000). Physical Education Kindergarten to Grade 12. Edmonton, Alberta: Alberta Education, 1.

British Columbia. (2016). BC's New Curriculum. Retrieved from https://curriculum.gov.bc.ca/ curriculum.

Manitoba Education and Training. (2000). Kindergarten to Senior 4 Physical Education/Health Education: Manitoba Curriculum Framework of Outcomes for Active Healthy Lifestyles. Winnipeg, Manitoba: Manitoba Education and Training, 3.

Ontario Ministry of Education. (2010). The Ontario Curriculum, Grades 1-8: Health and Physical Education. Toronto, Ontario: Ministry of Education, 3.

Prince Edward Island Department of Education and Early Childhood Development. (2011). Prince Edward Island Physical Education Curriculum Grades K-6. Summerside, Prince Edward Island: Prince Edward Island Department of Education and Early Childhood Development, 3.

Saskatchewan Ministry of Education. (2009). Physical Education 6. Regina, Saskatchewan: Ministry of Education, 5.

Saskatchewan Ministry of Education. (2010). Physical Education 1. Regina, Saskatchewan: Ministry of Education, 5.

Chapter 5

Teaching Physical Education

Students learn what we teach and do not learn what we do not teach…

Rink, 1999

Introduction: Creating Learning Opportunities in Physical Education

Schools are environments where students are provided with related learning experiences that challenge their current understanding in order to create new knowledge and set the foundations for future learning. Therefore, as Rink (1999) suggests, it is critically important for teachers to understand that students are likely to learn what they are taught but will not necessarily learn what is not taught to them. The key for teachers is to create and effectively present intentional learning opportunities. Teachers who select intentional learning opportunities and present them in an effective manner to students are more likely to achieve the learning outcomes that they set for their students. It is hoped that, by the end of this chapter, you will:

- Understand that learning is of an individual nature
- Appreciate the academic value of physical education programming
- Know the techniques to teach effective physical education lessons
- Understand the continuum of teaching styles and its application to teaching physical education
- Know how to create a positive, well-managed learning environment

Understanding Learning

Knowledge about learning styles and how best to create opportunities for learning can help teachers become more effective in their teaching practices and to realize that no single teaching method or strategy suits all learners. However, this is a complex issue for teachers as students can receive and process information in very different ways (Fishburne, 2005). Each student will have a preferred style of learning. For example, some students excel with highly structured, teacher-directed learning opportunities, while others prefer unstructured informal settings. Some students prefer visual stimuli, whereas others might prefer a more tactile experience gained through the use of manipulatives or being engaged in a participatory activity. Additionally, some students prefer learning opportunities that are of a more individualized nature, whereas others might prefer a shared learning experience found when working with partners or in a group situation. There is no limit to the types of preference; each student has a personal and unique learning style.

Unfortunately, identifying each student's preferred learning style and creating learning opportunities to meet each student's needs can be a difficult task for a teacher. The difficulty arises as a student's preferred learning style may change depending on the context and/

or subject area. However, even though a teacher might not have an accurate or complete assessment of each child's preferred learning style, just knowing that there will be differences in learning styles in any group of students underscores the necessity of creating a variety of conducive learning opportunities for students.

The breadth and variety of curricular outcomes of physical education programming, the characteristics of children, and the knowledge of how children learn all impact the teaching of physical education. Teachers cannot expect to have the same learning outcomes and expectations for all students. Differences in each student's maturation level, potential ability, learning style, and interests requires a teacher to design and employ teaching strategies that cater to more individualized and personalized forms of learning. Individualized instruction in physical education teaching acknowledges a process that adjusts learning opportunities to the student.

> When a teacher considers the individual, this places the student, rather than the subject area, at the centre of the curriculum decision making and teaching.

When teaching physical education, teachers can provide for individualized learning opportunities through two main approaches. First is the issue of time to complete a task. For example, if three students with varying levels of ability were to be asked to move along the top of a bench, each child would be allowed to complete the task in their own time. This is in contrast to a student only being provided a set time which, if the child does not possess the ability to accomplish the movement in the stipulated time, is an exercise in futility. The second approach is to vary the task. Allowing each child the choice of how to move along the length of the bench in any way possible would be varying the task. If a teacher can vary the time provided and the tasks asked of students, individualized learning opportunities can be provided.

Physical Education as an Academic Subject and Expectations of Learning

The benefits of student participation in quality physical education programming are far reaching and well documented (Hickson, 2009). Therefore, sharing the underlying benefits of a quality physical education program with students, other school staff members, and parents can help to influence the opinions that others have of the subject and dispel many of the stereotypical views of physical education as a place devoid of learning and rigour. Schwartz and Bouchard (2005) outlined these benefits and the corresponding research validation. They cite research that supports such benefits as improved academic achievement, likelihood of being active outside of school hours, and improved self-esteem. Therefore, understanding the role and importance of physical education learning opportunities for students is critical for teachers. By developing such an understanding, teachers can begin to create learning environments that help students and promote physically active lifestyles.

As many educational jurisdictions refer to *lifelong active living* as a goal of their physical education curriculum (see Table 4.1, Chapter 4), it is expected that physical education programming can promote a positive attitude toward being physically active and increase participation rates not only in childhood but also later in adulthood.

> Creating student learning opportunities needs to be foremost in a teacher's planning, lesson delivery, and student assessment and evaluation.

A well-structured physical education program can enhance and improve the movement proficiency and self-concept of students, thereby promoting the chances for lifelong involvement in physical activity and, hopefully, better health. Just keeping students occupied with a smorgasbord of unrelated activities or as Placek (1983) refers to as, *busy, happy*, and *good*, does not support the learning required for the development of physical literacy. If children are expected to receive learning opportunities in their physical education lessons, teachers need to acknowledge it as a true area of academic learning, and they must teach for knowledge acquisition and understanding. By taking this approach, physical education learning opportunities will maintain their rightful place in schools and the daily lives of students. It is only then that students will receive the instruction and support that they need to gain the associated health benefits from being physical active and to support their individual journeys of *physical literacy.*

Educational objectives need to be met in order to assist students in achieving specified learning outcomes. Teaching students to be competent and to excel in their physical performance should be an aim of all teachers of physical education. This should be no different to when teaching mathematics or language arts, where there is a desire to improve competency in numeracy or literacy. The acquisition of knowledge, skills, and attitudes are necessary and key components of any physical education program. The utilization of teaching practices that have student learning opportunities as a central consideration and basic tenet will help to accomplish this goal.

Physical Education, More than 'Just Activity'

Recent trends in educational planning have addressed the issue of the rising occurrence of obesity in children and youth by mandating that schools provide daily physical activity experiences. For example, in Canada, several Provinces (Alberta, British Columbia, and Ontario) have stipulated that schools are expected to engage students in physical activity for set daily time requirements. This move has also been followed in other countries outside of North America, such as Australia (Hickson, 2010)

However, providing opportunities for physical activity in a gymnasium or on a school field does not guarantee educational learning. Similarly, providing opportunities for daily reading (DEAR, USSR, etc.) does not guarantee that a student will meet the educational outcomes of a language arts curriculum. Although providing students with opportunities to be physically active is important, it is also necessary to teach students about such things as body management and awareness, motor skills, fitness, and health. PHE Canada does suggest that it is critical that physical activity programming must not replace physical education programming and states that quality physical education experiences are a fundamental right of every child (PHE Canada, 2015).

> *Physical education programs must move beyond the simplistic view of a time for students to expend excess energy, to a program that is curriculum driven and provides students with the knowledge, skills, and attitudes to lead healthy, active lifestyles.*

Although there can be confusion regarding the similarities, differences, and interplay between physical education and physical activity, the distinction between physical education and physical activity programming needs to be clearly understood by teachers. The implications of any misinterpretation have the potential to negatively impact the way physical education is perceived and delivered. In support of this, Fishburne and Hickson (2005) stated the importance of physical activity is without question, but physical activity in itself does not create a *physically educated person*, this is the role of physical education.

Understanding and appreciating the role of physical education is vitally important in supporting students to choose healthy, active lifestyles. Physical education programming can help students to gain the knowledge, skills, and attitudes to want to be active individuals. This desire to be active and lead a healthy lifestyle is often referred to as physical literacy. As illustrated in Chapter 3, developing physical literacy is a critically important outcome of physical education programming. Whitehead (2010) defined physical literacy as having "...the motivation, confidence, physical competence, knowledge and understanding to value and take responsibility for engaging in physical activities for life" Therefore, taking the first steps toward understanding that physical education programming is far more than just activity experiences and that it has a distinct role in student development and the willingness to choose a healthy, active lifestyle, is a foundational element to physical education programming and teaching.

The Teacher

If students are to develop physical literacy throughout their lives, which includes the development and maintenance of active healthy lifestyles, they must be educated toward this goal. Hence, teachers need to acquire a thorough knowledge of teaching strategies and techniques that will best facilitate physical literacy, know the strengths and weaknesses of different teaching styles and methods, and know and be able to adopt key teaching behaviours that will result in effective instruction. As such, the essential duties of the teacher when teaching physical education, as with all subjects, are to provide learning tasks that are within each child's reach (e.g., developmentally appropriate activities), and to give continuous encouragement (e.g., positive, specific feedback) and assistance throughout the learning process.

> It is important to recognize that specific learning outcomes may require the utilization of different pedagogical approaches.

It is important for teachers to understand that many skills and movement concepts of physical education cannot be learned through one teaching model, strategy, or method. Each new learning situation must be tailored to the varying degrees of interest, individual learning styles, and skill found throughout the whole class of learners. There is no ideal style of teaching, no single set of concepts or learning principles, and no best motivational technique that will guarantee success for all children in all situations. This can be described as the 'art' of teaching. It is essential, therefore, that a teacher be familiar with a variety of teaching strategies and techniques, and also know when to apply these techniques and strategies.

Reflection Corner...
In regards to the physical education experiences that you had as a student:
- *Was student learning at the forefront of your experience?*
- *What kinds of learning opportunities did you experience?*
- *Did all the students receive the same learning experiences?*
- *Did some students receive different learning experiences?*
- *Do you think that you were able to develop your physical literacy?*
- *What were some of the strengths and weaknesses of the kind of programming and teaching that you experienced?*

The following sections of this chapter will consider the role and responsibilities of a teacher through three main themes: Effective Teaching, Class Management, and Instructional Delivery. The discussion will be based upon both research understanding and best practices, and provide direction on how to most effectively meet the learning needs of students in physical education classes. See Figure 5.1.

Teaching Effectively

Although it is difficult to precisely define how teachers can be effective in their teaching, Rink (1996) stated that the identification of effective teaching techniques and behaviours is necessary if teachers are to become better at what they do, and if a knowledge base is to be developed in order to educate pre-service teachers. Hickson and Fishburne (2001) further stated that, as teachers have the primary goal of creating learning opportunities for students, it is essential they engage in effective teaching practices that facilitate student learning. Through classroom investigation, researchers have been able to determine effective research-based teaching practices that are related to positive learning outcomes (Borich, 1996). This understanding has led to the use of the term *effective teaching* when discussing teachers and the techniques used to enhance student learning. The essence of effective teaching is that teachers are viewed as teaching effectively when students are learning and achieving intended learning outcomes. These learning outcomes have been discussed in Chapter 4.

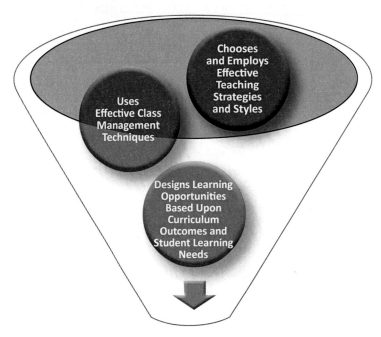

The Role of the Teacher

Figure 5.1 The Role of the Teacher

Research Understanding

Although teaching has been a focus of attention for many years, even centuries, research on teaching is still a relatively new field of inquiry. Also, when research studies have been conducted, many different designs and methods have been used in attempts to pinpoint the differences between effective and ineffective teaching (Bellon et al., 1992). Initially, studies tended to be focused on teachers and their characteristics and actions, not on the learning environment, in an attempt to identify effectiveness (Medley, 1987).

Historically, in the early 1900s, the initial idea of an effective teacher was a judgement primarily based on the "goodness" of a person. Honesty, generosity, friendliness, dedication, and consideration were all regarded to be vital components of an effective teacher. These personal qualities needed to be demonstrated in an authoritarian, disciplined, and organized classroom (Borich, 1996). This definition of an effective teacher, Borich contended, clearly lacked any objective standards of performance. To understand if teaching was truly effective, researchers realized they needed to not only consider teacher characteristics and qualities, but they also needed to consider students.

Classroom-Based Effective Teaching Research
Key Teaching Behaviours
Lesson clarity
Instructional variety
Teacher task orientation
Engagement in the learning process
Student success rate

Helping Behaviours
Using student ideas & contributions
Structuring
Questioning
Probing
Teacher affect
Borich, 1996

Research in the 1960s began to shift the focus from the personal characteristics of teachers to teacher and student behaviours. These kinds of studies also saw researchers, for the first time, beginning to visit classrooms to gather information to specifically study teacher and student interactions. Instruments were developed to measure these interactions: the frequency of interaction, types of questions, and response rates. These instruments were employed in research studies in the belief that effective teaching behaviours could be identified and, once identified, could be taught to teachers (Bellon et al., 1992). The 1970s brought about a significant improvement in research methodology. A variety of observation systems were used to identify both teacher and student behaviour. This methodological approach was important in helping to determine what students and teachers were actually doing during lessons. However, it did not result in any further understanding of the characteristics associated with effective teaching (Mawer, 1995).

During the 1980s, research was conducted to identify the facets of classroom teaching that promoted an effective learning environment for children. Much of what we do know about effective teaching comes from this research base. These well-conducted classroom research studies attempted to identify what teachers do to produce student learning.

In a comprehensive review of research studies that showed an impact on student achievement and learning, Borich (1996) summarized effective teaching methods, and outlined *five key teaching behaviours* that were supported by research: lesson clarity; instructional variety; teacher task orientation; engagement in the learning process; and student success rate. Borich also found that five other behaviours were also related to effective teaching. He identified this second group of teaching behaviours as *helping behaviours*, as the research identifying these behaviours is not as extensive. Their presence is thought to *support* and *help* the five key teaching behaviours.

Being an effective teacher is a critical goal for all educators to aim for and to achieve (Hickson & Fishburne, 2001). However, because teachers want to improve their practice in order to achieve a positive impact on student learning, it is possible to promote teaching behaviours, strategies, or ideas that are not built upon knowledge created from research findings. Teachers can develop *craft knowledge*, that is, their own perceptions of what they believe is effective teaching based on personal experiences honing their teaching craft. Although it is possible for teachers to reflect on new strategies and ideas and to compare these against their craft knowledge, teachers can, without the knowledge or the understanding of underlying assumptions and principles, still accept new approaches that are not supported by research-based evidence. This can result in strategies being incorporated into teaching that have not been researched and found to be effective. Depending on the depth and accuracy of a teacher's craft knowledge, and the appropriateness of the new strategy being adopted, student learning can be negatively affected. Therefore, craft knowledge needs to be balanced with the understanding of research in order to ensure effective practice that supports student learning is adopted.

Effective Teaching in Physical Education

The majority of the research on effective teaching has been conducted in the classroom environment, concentrating on more traditional subject areas such as mathematics and language arts. Consequently, only a relatively small amount of information has been gathered in the area of physical education, and knowledge of what is effective physical education teaching and how it supports student-learning outcomes, is somewhat limited. The understanding that has been established on effective teaching in physical education emanates from research that occurred from the 1980s through to the 1990s. In a review of physical education teaching research, Silverman (1991) suggested the following characteristics for the effective teaching of motor skills:

- the planning for class management and student learning
- the anticipation of situations and contingency plans
- the awareness of individual student skill differences and use of the information in planning and monitoring
- the acquisition of information to plan
- the knowledge of a repertoire of teaching styles and when to use them
- the accuracy and focus of explanation and demonstration
- the provision for adequate student practice time
- the maximization of appropriate student practice and engagement
- the minimization of inappropriate student practice and engagement
- and the minimization of pupil waiting

However, Silverman's review has come under criticism by other researchers. For example, one of the criticisms from Dodds and Placek (1991) was that the "...list also focuses on what teachers do, ignoring both the specific student outcomes that accrue as a result and intended teacher goals relevant to a given teaching situation" (p. 367).

Rink (1993) also reviewed the research on effective teaching and identified seven distinct teacher characteristics associated with effective instruction in the physical education realm. She identified the following teacher characteristics:

- the identification of intended outcomes for learning
- the planning of learning experiences to accomplish these outcomes
- the presentation of tasks in a clear manner
- the organization and management of the learning environment
- the monitoring of the environment
- the development of the lesson content based on student responses
- the evaluation of the effectiveness of instructional/curricular process

Mawer (1995), in a review of research and viewpoints on effective teaching of physical education, suggested that the following characteristics are indicative of effective teaching:
- the planning of work effectively
- the good presentation of new material
- the organization and management of the learning experiences and students

- the active involvement of the teacher in teaching students
- the provision of a supportive and positive learning environment
- the acquisition of a repertoire of teaching styles
- the ability to teach for the facilitation of student understanding of concepts and lesson content

When considering the relevance of each of these sets of characteristics, it is important for a teacher to consider the similarities that emerge. Strikingly, the similarities are not only between those researchers concerned with the teaching of physical education but also classroom-based research too. The characteristics

suggested by Silverman (1991), Rink (1993) and Mawer (1995) all bear some similarity to Borich's (1996) work. Several factors such as lesson clarity, structure, involving student ideas, and instructional variety have a commonality among the lists. Therefore, it is critical for teachers to appreciate that much of what is considered as being effective in the classroom, is equally important when also teaching in the gymnasium or on the playing field.

However, research has identified a disconnect between what is considered to be effective teaching and what teachers perceive to be effective in their teaching. This is disconcerting since, if student learning is a goal of teaching, it is reasonable to expect that teachers should view student learning as being of prime importance. As Fishburne and Hickson (2005) suggested, teachers of physical education have the responsibility to change or continue to use those characteristics and skills that promote student learning. Unfortunately, there is considerable research evidence to suggest that this is not necessarily the case for some teachers and their teaching of physical education (e.g., Borys & Fishburne, 1986; Fishburne & Borys, 1987; Hickson & Fishburne, 2002; Placek, 1983; Schempp, 1983; 1985). Each study confirmed that teachers in physical education lessons considered their teaching to be effective when students were participating (busy), with minimal misbehaviour (good), while providing enjoyment (happy). In essence, teachers were more concerned about student behaviour than the transmission of knowledge.

Perhaps the most disturbing issue were the findings from Hickson and Fishburne (2002) which compared the perceptions of successful physical education teaching to other curriculum areas. Their findings confirmed the *busy, happy,* and *good* trend in physical education, but also found that when considering successful teaching in other curriculum areas, the same pre-service and experienced teachers rated student learning as the highest indicator of successful teaching in these subject areas. This lack of understanding that learning must be a critical component in physical education teaching is a most troublesome and concerning disconnect!

The following charts identify effective teaching techniques that can be utilized when teaching physical education and provide activity examples to understand what such a technique looks like in practice.

Effective Teaching Techniques for Physical Education with Activity Examples

Lesson Structure	
Reasoning	**Activity Example**
• Structuring helps students organize where the lesson content fits into their learning experiences. It involves explaining why the lesson content is being covered and where this fits into learning experiences. This helps to make learning opportunities more meaningful. • Explaining why practice is necessary and how practice connects with the next activity. Without this structure, students often do not understand the reason for practicing physical activities. • There is also the need for routine, which establishes the environment in which students learn. Classroom structure and routine involve organizing equipment and facilities, establishing routine procedures, and many other day-to-day operational procedures.	"The last two classes we have been practicing balancing and different kinds of rolling. Today, we are going to continue that practice, but looking at how we can join these movements together to make a movement sentence." "Don't forget to practice your dance routine steps tonight at home, and invite your parents to join in too! This will help for our tasks in class tomorrow. "When you hear me say 'STOP,' everyone should freeze and place the equipment on the floor beside them."

Providing Variety	
Reasoning	**Activity Example**
• Instructional variety is the variability or flexibility of delivery during a lesson. Variety is an essential component in the instructional process to accommodate children's personal and unique learning styles. Teachers need to plan for variety with learning in mind.	"For your game, decide with your group what ball you would like to use." "The station is set up for you to practice your gymnastics routine. You may experiment using the equipment to best suit your movements."

Monitor Time-On-Task	
Reasoning	**Activity Example**
• Time-on-task is the amount of learning time devoted to the task. Time-on-task indicates the level of student engagement and is a very important learning variable. Teachers must monitor for engagement and plan to achieve maximum time-on-task.	"You will notice that the stations are set up so that there is no start and end place. You can begin your practicing anywhere. So that means I should see lots of movement and very little waiting."

Provide for Success with each Learning Opportunity	
Reasoning	**Activity Example**
• Success is when a student understands and correctly completes activities. In physical education, it is important that teachers only move on to the next practice when a student has correctly completed the first activity. Therefore, a teacher must organize and plan instruction that will yield moderate to high success rates for all students. • Success is linked to intrinsic motivation. Without intrinsic motivation, there is little chance that children will develop active lifestyles. Therefore, student success is a vital component in effective teaching. • Teachers need to maximize student success rate. Planning developmentally appropriate activities to match ability levels will assist in providing success. Students should be challenged to be creative, to problem-solve, and to go beyond their current levels of performance.	"The climbing wall has a series of coloured flags. For your first try, choose an easier green route that you feel comfortable following. Next time, try the red!" "You performed your forward roll well, with a good body shape. Now, can you experiment with your legs to see how else you can perform the same roll, but create a different body shape with your legs?" "Your ball throw for distance had lots of power, which is why the ball rolled so far. Now, how can you get the ball to travel further before it bounces?" "Choose the jump rope that works best for you. Work with the rope on your jumping routine."

Communicate Effectively	
Reasoning	**Activity Example**
• Effective communication between the teacher and a student or group of students is a continuous, two-way process of exchanging knowledge, skills, ideas, and feelings. • Teachers need to be able to communicate what is to be learned, how it should be learned, and what quality of performance is expected from each student. • Use positive rather than negative reinforcement. • Remember to use nonverbal cues effectively such as facial expressions and body alignment. When verbal instruction or praise is accompanied by a smile or a positive body gesture, a more positive and effective signal is conveyed.	"As we put away the equipment, we need to ensure that we place the equipment in the right locations, be careful of others, and always remember our rule about how many people to be in the equipment room at a time." "As you dribble the soccer ball, try using all parts of your feet to control the ball, and remember to keep your head up to look for space to move in to." "In your journals, I would like you to write about what you find most enjoyable about physical education classes and what you find the most uncomfortable."

Use Student Ideas and Contributions

Reasoning	Activity Example
• When student ideas are used, the content material becomes connected to previous learning experiences and contributes toward more meaningful learning. • Students become part of the learning enterprise, have a degree of ownership, and are motivated because they contribute to the learning endeavor.	"Now, by using the same music, create your own dance steps and movements." "In pairs, record the details of your game and make sure that you save it to the "Games" file on the class computer. We will use your games for our upcoming unit in February."

Effective Questioning

Reasoning	Activity Example
• In a typical elementary school classroom, 70-80% of questions would be considered low-level questions requiring a simple recall of facts, while only 20-30% requires the higher level thought processes of clarifying, expanding, generalizing, and making inferences. A low-level question would be to ask a Grade 5 student a simple game rule, whereas, a higher-level question would be to ask for a strategy for scoring. • Teachers need to consider how they phrase their questions, as different questions can elicit different kinds of responses. • By using probing style questions teachers can clarify, reframe, and redirect learning.	"In what ways is juggling a bean bag different from when we were juggling scarves." "What are the safety rules when we are getting ready for our skating lesson? What could happen if someone doesn't follow these rules?" "When we are in groups, what kinds of things do you think I am looking and listening for?" "What is the most effective way to move the ball forward with your team-mates? How can you make sure the other team does not have a chance to steal the ball?"

Positive Personal Characteristics

Reasoning	Activity Example
•If a teacher possesses positive personal characteristics, the likelihood is that the lesson will be enjoyable and educational. • Characteristics such as being enthusiastic, having a sense of humor, demonstrating a passion for learning, valuing health and wellness, displaying nonverbal qualities (e.g., facial expression, gestures, eye contact, role modeling) are all recognized as being important in effective teaching.	"Oh dear, I forgot to follow through with my strike there. That wasn't a good example to show you! Was it?" "I just love coming to the gymnasium each day, it makes me feel all energized and ready to learn! How about you?"

Adjust the Learning Environment	
Reasoning	**Activity Example**
• Adjusting the learning environment allows a teacher to meet the developmental level of the students, supports the successful completion of activities, and maintains student motivation. • Four variables under the teacher's control are REPS: 　○ Rules 　○ Equipment (type and amount) 　○ Participants (number) 　○ Space	"We tried playing with goals that were quite big and that caused difficulty for the goalkeepers. Let's make the goals a little smaller, so that it challenges us in our shooting and also helps our goalkeepers practice their skills, too." "Now, try the same movement again, but with a partner this time, and this time I want you to try to add two more steps after the turn."

Goal Setting	
Reasoning	**Activity Example**
• When students set personal and attainable goals, they usually achieve more than when the teacher simply instructs the child to "try the best you can." • Externally controlled goals have been shown to weaken intrinsic motivation, whereas, self-determined goals have been shown to enhance it. • Involving children in goal-setting decisions motivates them because they now have a personal responsibility to try to achieve the goals they set for themselves. • Personal Activity Logs (PALs) can be used to support individual goal-setting.	"Before we start, consider the task you are doing and set a target to reach when I say 'GO!'" "As you move to your stations, discuss with your group members what you want to accomplish today with your group balances." "For homework tonight, identify the different activities you are committing to participate in next week. This will be a goal that you are setting yourself to reach."

Cooperative Learning	
Reasoning	**Activity Example**
Placing children in group situations where the goal of learning together is fostered can have positive effects on both learning and motivation. Research studies have demonstrated that cooperative learning techniques lead to superior academic achievement, high motivation, and enhancement of social skills. To be effective, cooperative learning must include two elements: a group goal and individual accountability.	"As a pair, decide how you can balance with only two body parts touching the floor." "Remember, I want you to focus on the way you attempt the task rather than just the completion." "As a group, your task is to move each piece of equipment to the home base, but each person must be involved in holding the equipment. No hands or arms can be used."

Motivation...Intrinsic and, with caution, Extrinsic	
Reasoning	**Activity Example**
• Intrinsic motivation is motivation that is internally perceived by the student that encourages goal achievement. • Enjoyment and competency impact intrinsic motivation. Therefore, children must develop competencies through developmentally appropriate activities that generate success and enjoyment. • Extrinsic motivation refers to activities or behaviour external to the student that encourages goal achievement. • This form of motivation is not as desirable as the child's intrinsic motivation for performing an act or movement. If students are to develop active lifestyles that are to be continued over the entire life span, then intrinsic motivation will be essential as it is unlikely that extrinsic motivators will be available later in life to maintain this desirable outcome. • However, extrinsic motivators are very useful when a student or class is not personally motivated. They should be thought of as effective techniques to start the process to foster, encourage, and nurture intrinsic motivation. • Achievement charts, points, badges, and awards for performance would be considered extrinsic motivators. • However, they can have inherent issues or problems. If such charts or points are based on time or number of repetitions, etc., low achievers are guaranteed to be viewed as failing. Recognition should be on the basis of individual improvement.	"Decide on your personal activity goal this week, and work toward that goal daily. Remember that it is important that you want to reach your goal, so make it something that you really want to do and know that you will work toward achieving." "When recording the number of repetitions that you achieve, try to remember that we are looking for improvement each week. Getting more than someone else is not important, but striving to do one more attempt than you personally achieved last week is." "Think to yourself, 'I can do it!' Positive thinking is much better than thinking how hard something might be. Know that you have met lots of other challenges previously and this is just another one that you can reach." "In our small-sided games today, in addition to a point being awarded for the scoring of a goal, I will be giving out extra points for teamwork, assists, good passing, sporting behaviour, and general citizenship. So, keep in mind, I am not only looking for a great play or goal, but also those other things that make you a good teammate."

What does Effective Teaching Achieve?

Unfortunately, for some students, physical education experiences have not always been enjoyable. This is something that must be changed. All too often in the past, physical education experiences have been dominated by a *winner takes all* kind of attitude, where a low-skilled student lacking confidence would be excluded in favour of a highly skilled athletic student. For many students, physical education classes were painful and, at times, humiliating experiences. Physical literacy was not promoted; many students were reluctant participants in classes.

As teachers, we have a great deal of influence on such learning experiences and need to address such negativity. Remember, physical education is the ONLY place where we can guarantee all children with learn to be active for life – physical education is for all students! Therefore, teachers need to develop effective teaching repertoires that support each and every student to enhance learning opportunities and meet intended learning outcomes. If teachers are able to do this, students will be engaged in meaningful learning that assists in the development of knowledge, skills, and attitudes that support a healthy, active lifestyle. Not only will students enjoy their physical education experiences, they will have the greatest chance to develop their physical literacy.

Teaching Styles

Elementary school teachers are often "generalist" trained, meaning that their instructional responsibilities encompass all the curricula subject areas. Research has indicated that this, unfortunately, can result in some teachers not feeling confident about their teaching of physical education (Jenkinson & Benson, 2010). Such teachers often state concerns with their lack of training, minimal knowledge of developmentally appropriate lessons, and deficiencies in understanding how to plan for the overall program, which act as major obstacles blocking a generalist teacher's success when teaching physical education (Morgan & Hansen, 2008). However, Lu and De Lisio (2009) suggested that it should be recognized that elementary generalists can be excellent teachers of physical education and enjoy many benefits that specialists do not.

Summary of Teaching Styles Research

Research has consistently indicated that the choice of teaching style can have a critical effect on children's learning (Fishburne, 2005; Metzler, 2011; Mosston & Ashworth, 1986, Pangrazi & Beighle, 2013). However, teachers, and ultimately students, can benefit when they develop higher levels of knowledge concerning how to teach physical education effectively (Bradford & Hickson, 2014). Overall, there is no general agreement as to what constitutes an approach, a style, a model, or a method of teaching (Fishburne, 2005). As they are all, in essence, ways of guiding and controlling the learning experiences of children, this text considers the terms approach, model, and style of teaching as being the same thing.

Teachers constantly formulate ideas and make decisions on how to direct or guide students while providing learning opportunities. The decisions that teachers make regarding how content will be taught during a lesson influences their teaching behaviours. Consequently, the decisions children make during the learning process impacts their learning behaviour. This continuous interaction forms the teacher-learner process. Consequently, a teaching style involves both the teacher and the learner (Bradford & Hickson, 2014).

Understanding and using a variety of teaching styles can benefit teachers. Having a repertoire of styles and knowing how and when to use them to facilitate children's learning can promote an effective learning environment (Mawer, 1995; Pangrazi & Beighle, 2013). Different teaching styles have distinctive purposes in the learning environment. When teachers can call on several different styles during a lesson, their ability to meet children's learning needs should increase. Developing an understanding of what each teaching style may achieve in terms of students' learning can help reach curricular objectives and accomplish assessment requirements. Teachers who are aware of the strengths and weaknesses of different teaching styles will have a greater ability to reach objectives in the learning environment (Fishburne, 2005; Mosston & Ashworth, 1994; Pangrazi & Beighle, 2013). Therefore, recognizing, appreciating, and implementing different styles can help teachers deliver more effective programs.

Relative to how much control teachers wish or need to retain during a lesson, different styles promote different types of learning (Fishburne, 2005). When teachers recognize, choose, and instruct utilizing an appropriate teaching style, they are more likely to be effective in providing learning opportunities that benefit students (Bradford & Hickson, 2014). For example, in physical education, students are more likely to benefit from instruction that has them attempting to reproduce demonstrations of specific skills from a teacher-centered teaching style. However, if the learning outcome is the acquisition of problem-solving skills in a cooperative learning setting, a more student-centered teaching style is required (Mawer, 1999; Metzler, 2011). Teachers can create conducive learning environments when they employ different teaching styles according to the requirements of the student, the particular learning environment, the chosen activity, and the chosen learning outcomes.

In addition to increasing student learning, teachers who use a variety of teaching styles can benefit students in other ways. For example, specific teaching styles and techniques can assist in diffusing students' levels of anxiety (LaBilloisa & Lagacé-Séguin, 2009). Students with high levels of anxiety perform best in a teacher-controlled learning environment, while less anxious students perform best in a student-controlled learning environment. Therefore, when teachers utilize a variety of teaching styles, there are considerable benefits to be gained (Bradford & Hickson, 2014).

Working from Mosston's seminal work concerning the Spectrum of Teaching Styles (Mosston & Ashworth, 1994), teaching methods fall under one of three general teaching styles. These teaching styles and their corresponding methods all have value and worth for the teacher of physical education. No one style is more effective; the choice of style and method relies on what is being taught and how the teacher wishes to create the learning opportunity.

Observational Learning (Modeling): Physical education literature has emphasized the powerful medium of observational learning due to its recognized influence on learning. Much of Bandura's (1977) work concerning modeling promotes this traditional approach to teaching. With demonstration being a particular effective way to illustrate correct performance in physical education, Bandura's work resonates with many physical educators who support the notion that teachers need to be effective in their modeling and explanation. One criticism of the role model demonstration is that demonstrations do not engage students in "insightful" learning. The demonstration provides the "answer" or "solution" to the problem. Hence, student do not solve the problem for themselves, but merely copy the solution provided by the teacher (demonstrator).

Constructivist Learning (Discovery): In more recent years, a move toward constructivist learning has become more accepted amongst educators. This approach is based on the premise that learners should build (construct) knowledge for themselves. Contemporary views on learning promote this constructivist approach that emphasizes discovery learning, where students are encouraged to create their own solutions to problems and gain insights for themselves. This is believed to be more meaningful to the student because self-discovery promotes stronger connections with prior learning and fosters creativity.

Clearly, teaching styles that promote discovery learning offer exciting learning opportunities. The Movement Education approach advocated through the work of Rudolf Laban (see Chapter 3) promotes the constructivist views of learning. The merits of the constructivist approach are obvious, but although the teacher might refrain from offering a demonstration (solution), the student rarely operates in isolation and constantly views other students' performances (demonstrations) and, in doing so, may view "incorrect" demonstrations and use these as the models for their learning. Another issue facing the constructivist approach is motor skill specificity. The principle of skill specificity states that many physical activities require specific motor skills. It is quite possible that students might not create (construct) the specific motor skill during their discovery learning opportunities. If students are to develop and maintain an active lifestyle, they need to develop the required competencies. For example, a student who cannot swim will not go swimming and is unlikely to go rafting or even boating. The biomechanically efficient swimming strokes of front crawl and breast stroke are most effectively taught through demonstration and direct instruction; it is much more difficult to teach these specific strokes through discovery learning approaches.

Modeling or Constructivism? Some teachers advocate the merits of constructivism over modeling, while others offer the opposite point of view. However, perhaps the best view is that both offer value to the teacher and can be accommodated in the physical education setting. At times, teachers will stress the direct style of teaching; in other situations, the nature of learning will require the more exploratory methods of the combined or indirect teaching styles.

The Teaching Style Continuum

An array of authors has identified several styles of teaching available to teachers of physical education (e.g. Fishburne, 2005; Grasha, 1996; Mawer, 1999; Metzler, 2011; Pangrazi & Beighle, 2013). Although there are areas of commonality among the teaching styles identified, there are also differences between each author's views. However, despite the contrast, the main area of commonality between the different teaching style classifications presented by each author is the presence of a continuum of experience that ranges from teacher-controlled to student-controlled. Fishburne (2005) perhaps best summarized this understanding with the identification of a continuum that included three general teaching styles. Each style differed according to the amount of freedom and responsibility afforded to the learner. They are referred to as the direct, combined, and indirect teaching styles and lie on a non-hierarchical continuum with the combined teaching style located in the middle of the direct and indirect styles.

Different Teaching Styles Promote Different Types of Learning

The three general teaching styles differ on the basis of decision making and are based on the degree of freedom or choice given to the students in a particular learning task.

Direct Teaching Style	Combined Teaching Style	Indirect Teaching Style
Example	Example	Example
During a dance lesson, all the students follow the direction of foot steps and body movements given by the teacher. The teacher decides on the music to be used, determines the pacing of the activity, and assesses performance.	In a games lesson, the teacher places the students in to groups of four and provides each group with two hoops a ball, and four cones. Each group can create their own game and choose the rules for their game.	In the creation of a gymnastics sequence, the student chooses the movements, any equipment to be used, and the assessment of performance. The teacher supports or guides the student and poses ideas and suggestions through open ended questions.

Figure 5.2 Teaching Styles (based on Fishburne, 2005)

With the direct style, teacher decisions dominate, whereas, with the indirect style, students make their own decisions about many aspects of their learning (see Figure 5.2). As the three teaching styles lie on a continuum, it is non-hierarchical and ranges from teacher-centred experiences (direct) to student-centred experiences (indirect) (Bradford & Hickson, 2014).

Direct Teaching Style – *Teacher Directed Learning*

Direct styles of teaching are classified as teacher-centered because of the way the teacher handles various aspects of the learning process. Specifically, this style of teaching incorporates a high degree of teacher decision-making. As stated previously, research has demonstrated that direct methods of teaching are among the most effective ways of teaching specific skills. Two of the most common features associated with the direct teaching style are commands that students need to follow and the provision of tasks that students need to focus upon. In both of these circumstances, teachers decide what objectives are to be accomplished, what the content will be, how children should perform, and how the children's performance should be evaluated. Therefore, direct teaching relies heavily on the teacher's decisions, knowledge, and objectives.

Benefits and Challenges of utilizing the Direct Teaching Style: The primary characteristic of the direct style of teaching is that the teacher makes all the decisions in the learning experience for students. The teacher arranges the class in lines or in a circle, chooses the activity, and prescribes how and where each child will practice the movement. For example, when teaching a specific game skill, the teacher could organize the class in a specific semicircle formation so each child can view the skill demonstration, highlight the essential aspect that all children should observe, and then provide opportunities and time to practice.

The direct teaching style is the most effective and efficient way to teach a specific movement skill, a safety procedure, or the rules of an activity. When student level of skill is low (e.g., when a student is first learning how to perform a headstand in gymnastics), the direct teaching style is appropriate for illustrating, clarifying, and practicing various aspects of the skill or movement. This style can also be used to regain control and direction when class attention is low or if behaviour expectations are not being met. Also, as all students are completing the same activity, student assessment and evaluation is likely to be easier.

However, the direct teaching style also has challenges. Student participation in choosing the activity and how it should be practiced in the most teacher controlled ways is extremely limited and, at best, only provides minimal opportunities to recognize individual differences in levels of ability and learning. Also, opportunities for student attainment of self-responsibility, creative thinking, and problem-solving skills are not enhanced by utilizing the direct teaching style.

Combined Teaching Style – *Teacher and Student Shared Directed Learning*

The combined teaching style merges elements of the direct and indirect styles of teaching. As such, it allows for a sharing of the teaching process between the teacher and student. It offers an opportunity, within certain limitations, for students to create and discover solutions to the activity tasks set. This style of teaching often results in students working at their own pace and being provided with opportunities to make their own decisions on how to complete a task.

When utilizing the combined teaching style, the teacher provides students with some freedom to perform an activity or task in their own way and at their own pace. However, the teacher will limit the experience in some way. For example, a teacher might pose the challenge for students to create a gymnastics sequence that involves two balance positions, but explicitly direct that one balance must have three points of contact with the floor and the other have two points of contact. While the teacher choses the number of points of contact with the floor in each balance, the students can choose the type of balance and which body parts contact the floor.

Benefits and Challenges of utilizing the Combined Teaching Style: Due to the versatility of the combined teaching style, it is able to be used widely across the physical education program. Specifically, it allows the teacher to give some direction without restricting a student's creativity and the freedom of interpretation allows for children's physical differences and varying interests. Often, phrasing such as "...can you find another way of...?", "...can you add something different...?", or "...is it possible to...?" is heard when teachers utilize the combined teaching style.

While the strength of the combined teaching style is that it draws from the benefits that both the direct and indirect teaching styles afford, it also assumes many of the challenges that each style also presents. For example, while it allows for teacher direction in specific skill learning, it does not afford the teacher the opportunity to take complete control of the learning experience and request students to reproduce what is being demonstrated or taught. Also, although it does allow for student choice, it does not provide the degree of autonomy that the indirect teaching style provides to students to truly promote such things as student self-responsibility or creativity.

Indirect Teaching Style – *Student Directed Learning*

The indirect teaching style is an approach to teaching that allows students far greater autonomy and freedom in the choice of an activity, how it should be performed or practiced, and, at times, how it should be evaluated. This style requires the teacher to shift from being a director of the learning experience to becoming more of a guide or facilitator.

Benefits and Challenges of utilizing the Indirect Teaching Style:

Utilizing the indirect teaching style dramatically changes the role of students in the learning process; they are required to assume a level of responsibility for their learning experiences and become self-directed and use creative and problem-solving skills. For example, the teacher might simply present a general direction or challenge, such as "Using small equipment, create a sequence." or "Work on your balances." While students are encouraged to use their creative thinking to respond to such a task, it also allows all children to move at their own levels of ability and understanding.

However, similar to the other teaching styles, with these benefits also comes challenges. For example, issues such as class management, specific skill learning, and safety are not easily attended to when utilizing the indirect teaching style. Therefore, especially due to the important issue of student safety in the physical education setting, the use and ultimate success of this style often depends on a gradual shift by the teacher from the direct teaching style to indirect. By doing so, students gradually learn to be self-directed learners who show care and concern for their own safety as well as for the other children in the class.

Most Appropriate Teaching Styles for Learning Opportunities

As previously outlined, the choice of teaching style in physical education can have an impact on student learning. Some learning outcomes are best achieved through one particular style, whereas, different outcomes may require the use of another style. The strength of having a choice of teaching style is that the uniqueness of each style can offer students with a more accommodating learning environment.

Choice of Style of Teaching is based upon...
- The environment the lesson is occurring in
- The learning needs of the student(s)
- The activity or task
- The learning outcome(s)
- The equipment being used

In choosing the most appropriate style of teaching, the teacher should consider a number of important factors. The environment, student learning needs, the specific activity or task, learning outcomes, and equipment choice, all impact this decision. For example, when teaching a specific skill, the direct teaching style is most effective. To learn the correct foot plant, trunk inclination, and arm action properly, students require opportunities to imitate the teacher's correct techniques, as opposed to creating and discovering their own. Likewise, teaching at a swimming pool requires a completely different set of considerations due to the high level of safety required. In this case, the environment would highly influence the style of teaching that the teacher would employ. Whereas, in a creative dance setting, the teacher would need to utilize the indirect teaching style to ensure that students are able to apply creative thought to their learning and begin to develop their problem-solving skills when determining how best to align their movements to stimuli. However, it is important to note that the issue of teacher comfort and preference is not considered as a basis for the choice of style of teaching in a particular learning situation. Rather, the choice is driven from a learning perspective.

Flexibility of choice is important for teachers to remember. Teachers are encouraged to move from one teaching style to another if such a change is needed to support student learning. For example, teachers can move along the continuum and change their style of teaching even within a single lesson. They might also employ one style with a single child due to the learning needs of the particular student but utilize a different style with the rest of the class. By using an array of teaching styles, teachers can positively impact the learning opportunities for students. It is most likely to be detrimental to students for a teacher to employ only one teaching style throughout their teaching of physical education classes. As Bradford and Hickson (2014) contended, teachers who appropriately employ all three styles of teaching throughout their instructional practice are most likely to be able to meet the learning needs of the students in their classes to meet the intended learning outcomes.

Creating a Positive Learning Environment

Creating a positive environment that supports optimal learning opportunities for students is a very important aim for teachers. Arguably, it is likely the most critical feature of the daily teaching responsibilities. However, effective teaching and student learning opportunities cannot occur in a lesson that is not managed appropriately. In such a case, teachers will have difficulty teaching and students will learn far less than they should (Marzano, 2003). However, when a teacher is able to create a positive learning environment that is well-managed, teaching and learning can be optimized. Of course, all elementary school teachers, regardless of the subject area being taught would agree with this statement. Therefore, lessons in the gymnasium or on the playing field also need to be positive learning environments.

> **Reflection Corner...**
>
> Which style would you use when teaching...?
> • An introductory gymnastics lesson?
> • A cooperative game?
> • A fitness circuit?
> • Learning the underarm throw?
> • An archery lesson?
> • Creative dance?
> Why?

Summary of Class Management Research

Often referred to as "classroom management," Marzano (2003) contended that managing the learning environment has been a major concern of any teacher since the establishment of teachers and classes. Parkay, Stanford, Vailancourt, Stephens, and Harris (2010) further suggested that, particularly for new teachers, management issues are the primary concern.

In his review of a number of large scale classroom-based studies and through meta-analysis findings, Marzano (2003) suggested that creating a positive learning environment requires a teacher to be committed to implementing such things as the creation of rules and procedures, employing disciplinary interventions, developing the teacher-student relationship, and approaching teaching with a specific mental set that incorporates "with-it-ness" and objectivity. Parkay et al. (2010) concluded that sound management is aligned with effective teaching practices and that positive leadership from the teacher and preventative planning are central to achieving a managed learning environment.

Fishburne (2005) suggested discipline and class management, although related, are not the same. He clearly identified discipline as a process of helping students adjust to a particular situation and develop self-control, whereas classroom management is a more encompassing consideration of the whole classroom environment organization and practice. However, he stated that most class management and student discipline issues can be traced back to the teacher, the learning task, or the student.

Types of Misbehaviour

Although there are occasions of extreme behaviour in schools, the vast majority of issues that strain the learning environment are ones that teachers deal with in virtually every class and at every grade level. However, due to their common nature, it is of critical importance that teachers attend to them as they can erode the learning experiences for all the students in a class, can cause much frustration and angst for a teacher, and may potentially impact issues of safety.

Behaviour issues occur in virtually every grade level in the elementary school. Due to the necessity of teachers to promote both learning and safety in physical education lessons, teachers must be aware of behaviours that can potentially impact a positive learning environment. See Table 5.1.

Techniques to Handle Misbehaviour

Teachers quickly become aware that, no matter how hard they try to be effective teachers by planning and teaching appropriate activities, inevitably there will be a behaviour issue to solve. It is important to realize that there is no single answer to any one issue arising from the various types of behaviour issues described earlier. A number of acceptable practices and suggestions can be used to deal with individuals or groups who have displayed unacceptable behaviour. The following are potential solutions for teachers to consider:

Whole Child Perspective: Always try to consider the whole child, including behaviour in other classes, as well as available information about the home environment. If the student has a consistent pattern and type of misbehaviour, such as attention-seeking, the solution is to try to find the cause. Also, when there are similar issues with other teachers, check with them to ensure you are all reasonably consistent in your approach to this student's misbehaviour, or if a particular solution has been found by another teacher.

Table 5.1 Behaviour Examples in the Physical Education Setting	
Issue	**Example in the Physical Education Setting**
Talking out of turn	The most common example of this is when a student talks to peers while the teacher is explaining or performing a demonstration. Such a case interferes with learning. Another example is one or more students talking too loud or too much, or both, while engaged in physical activity. In such a case, apart from the impact on learning, the student may not be fully focused on the task at hand which could be a potential safety concern, the safety of others may be impacted due to the distraction, or the teacher may not be able to hear someone call for assistance or help due to the increased noise level.
Not paying attention	This type of behaviour takes many forms, such as looking at something else, daydreaming, or bothering another student while you are providing activity explanations or performing a demonstration. This might result in important points for learning and performance improvement not being heard or safety issues being missed.
Attention seeking	The most common form of attention-seeking is showing off or bothering other classmates. In physical education lessons, and particularly when a lesson involves equipment, behaviours such as showing off or bothering someone else, can often result in injury to the student and/or others.
Dishonesty	Dishonesty often manifests itself in the physical education lesson through the violation of rules In games or activities, lying about performance, or not following expectations. This kind of dishonesty can often result in frustration and upset amongst the student's peers. From a social development and relationship building perspective, this can be highly detrimental.
Overaggressive behaviour	Many of the physical activities in a physical education class require students to be aggressive - but in a positive sense and at an appropriate level. However, appropriate aggressiveness should not be confused with the type of aggressive behaviour that can cause upset or injury to the student or others. This can often be seen in game situations where students are overly competitive and participate in such a manner that frustrates others and possibly result in injuries.
Defiance	In this type of behaviour, the student openly refuses to obey rules or directions. Risk of injury to the student or other participants can result from this kind of behaviour; this can especially be the case when the activity involves the use of equipment.

Nonverbal Communication: If a student, or a group of students, displays unacceptable behaviour, the teacher should display a "quietly aggressive waiting stance." This stance might consist of frowning, shaking your head, or generally giving the appearance that you disapprove of the behaviour. This is a powerful form of nonverbal communication that adds to the verbal explanation that the behaviour is unacceptable. When different modes of communication are in unison, more effective communication occurs. Shouting or yelling across the gymnasium is not an effective approach in this circumstance. At times, a teacher's proximity close to the "trouble spot" is sufficient to eliminate the issue. If it is solved, quickly move on to another part of the lesson, rather than giving the misbehaving students more time than they deserve. Nonverbal signals are powerful forms of communication. An effective teacher can point a finger, give a nod of the head at a disruptive student, pause and make eye contact, or move closer to the student, and cause a change in student behaviour without having to stop the flow of teaching. Such actions can change behaviour without "calling out" the student and causing embarrassment.

Time-Out: If a student is displaying misbehaviour and will not heed your advice, removal from the activity may be necessary, particularly if safety is being compromised. Often times, a bench may be utilized for such a time-out spot. However, teachers should remember that time-out periods should not be for long periods of time. After several minutes, young students in particular, might have forgotten the reason why they are sitting out. Therefore, effective teachers create a process such as a "Time Out Card" that provides prompts informing the student to reflect on why they are there and work on a solution to ensure a positive return to the learning environment. At all times, the student must be kept in sight and under the teacher's supervision.

Student Accountability: Rather than having long discussions with students about behaviour in the gymnasium, a teacher can meet with a student at recess, lunch, or after school. This allows both the teacher and the student the opportunity to think through the situation. Such individual discussions can provide the time to find out what the cause of the behaviour may be and to solve it in a calm atmosphere. It also provides the opportunity to develop a better understanding of the student and the issue, and, equally important, to build a greater rapport. Students should be held responsible for their behaviour. A student returning from a time-out should make a commitment to prevent a repeat of the misbehaviour. Just returning to activity without a commitment to change is not appropriate. This form of goal-setting provides added motivation for the student to meet socially acceptable standards of behaviour. A teacher may consider some kind of positive reinforcement for compliance to change. Verbal acknowledgements, a note in a journal, or personally assisting with equipment storage are all examples of such reinforcements that often work well with elementary school students.

Physical Activity as Punishment

It is critically important that teachers do not use physical activity as a punishment in physical education or other classes.

Doing so can:

• Create feelings of negativity toward being active

• Cause students to equate exercise to doing something wrong

• Counters attempts to create a desire and willingness in students to be active

---

Loss of Privilege: One type of consequence for misbehaviour is a loss of privilege. For example, if a student cheats or misbehaves in an activity, the student can be denied the privilege of playing in the activity for a period of time. Instead, the student can assist with activity organization or structure. However, loss of privilege should not include denial of other subject areas. A student should not be denied art, for example, for poor behaviour in physical education. Nor should a student be denied physical education for poor behaviour in other subject areas.

At all times, teachers will be more effective in dealing with misbehaviour when they are prepared to consistently provide students with direct, clear statements of an issue and display a firm insistence on appropriate behaviour. These two important factors allow students to understand that there are boundaries to their behaviour and teacher expectations need to be acknowledged and adhered to. It is important to note that teachers need to steer clear of some unacceptable practices that have been used in the past which are not appropriate in present day classes. Namely, (1) ridiculing students, (2) punishing the whole class or a group of students for the misbehaviour of one student, (3) having the student perform an exercise as a form of punishment, and (4) forcing an apology. Care should be taken not to revert to these techniques, regardless of the pressures of the day or the severity of the misbehaviour.

Special Considerations for Managing the Physical Education Environment

It is important to appreciate and understand that the physical education setting is unique in many ways. The presence of student movement, excitement, novel environments, equipment, noise, issues of safety and teacher sight-lines serve to heighten the need for the teacher to ensure that the lesson is a managed, positive learning experience.

Student Movement: An effectively taught physical education lesson will involve all the students in a class participating in physical activity. Long lines and waiting turns are not part of such a lesson. Students need to be aware of their own movements as well as the movements of others. Therefore, with all students actively participating in activity, the teacher must be constantly observing the students, their use of equipment, and ensuring that all actions are as expected. Therefore, managing such expectations is critically important not only from a learning perspective, but also from a safety perspective.

Excitement: Physical education classes can be a time when students become very excited about their participation, the activity they are involved in, and/or being able to work closely with friends and peers. These are all important things for a teacher to foster to create a

positive learning environment that students want to be a part of. This level of excitement can, if allowed, increase to a point where the learning environment is compromised from both a learning and safety aspect. Typically, when students become overly excited, they are less likely to listen or pay attention to the expectations of participation. Therefore, it is critical that teachers are attentive to this and are aware that they might need to take an active role

in ensuring that the level of student excitement does not impede learning, and specifically, create an unsafe environment.

Equipment: Whereas other subject areas often employ various forms of manipulatives and equipment, the typical equipment used in physical education tends to be larger, can be used to climb upon, and can also be thrown about the teaching area. This does, indeed, make the physical education class most unique. Consequently, it requires teachers to be constantly scanning the learning environment to ensure that expectations of participation are being followed. If expectations are not being followed, it is the responsibility of the teacher to make the necessary changes to the situation. Although not necessarily common, it is possible for a student to use an activity in physical education or the equipment involved in the activity to hurt someone else. Therefore, teachers need to be most cognizant of overaggressive participation and students using an activity or equipment inappropriately to single out another student.

Noise: Although the physical education class is often a place where talk and general noise is much more common and appropriate than in a regular classroom environment, non-meaningful noise is something that teachers must be conscious of. Unwarranted talk can mean that important learning points are missed or safety warnings are not heard. Particularly, this can be the case when students are excited and eagerly anticipating an activity and engage in discussion without listening to instructions. Effective teachers who work to create well-managed, positive learning environments will often ask for students to recall major teaching points or safety issues prior to sending the class on to the activity portion of the lesson.

Of particular note should be the issue of laughter. Although laughter often accompanies enjoyment, teachers need to be aware when laughter is part of ridicule or humiliation at the expense of a student. Laughter at a student's performance can lead to participant embarrassment and may negatively impact future participation. In many ways, this can be perceived to be a form of bullying and should be immediately dealt with by the teacher.

Issues of Safety: As the physical education setting requires student movement, the propensity for an accident to occur increases significantly compared to the more sedate nature of classroom teaching. Therefore, the issue of safety is something that must be attended to by teachers of physical education. This must be in the form of considering student safety in the activity choice, the upkeep, state, and appropriateness of the equipment selected to be used by the teacher and/or students, and whether the environment that the students are performing the activity in is safe. As it is expected that teachers are creating nurturing, positive learning environments, safety must always be part of this consideration.

Teacher Sight-Lines: The constant movement of students and the use of equipment can result in teachers having difficulty to be able to adequately view the entire teaching area. However, to ensure that students are participating in the manner expected and that student participation is safe, it is vital that teachers maintain sight-lines that enable appropriate supervision. Therefore, it is recommended that teachers operate with the following thoughts – Get In, Get Out and Back to the Wall. When teachers are minimally in the centre of the teaching area by moving toward and then retreating to a more periphery position, this maximizes the amount of time that students are participating within the teacher's field of vision. In a similar vein, by establishing a habit of only having the wall behind them, teachers can ensure that students are constantly within their vision. These two thoughts can assist the teacher in maintaining appropriate sight-lines, and being in the position to ensure the learning environment is safe and well-managed.

Techniques to Improve and Maintain a Well-Managed and Positive Learning Environment

- **Be a role model:** Set a good example of self-control and concern for others.
- **Be consistent:** Establish reasonable rules of behaviour and have students follow them.
- **Be fair to all students:** Do not have favourites.
- **Be a good teacher, not a pal:** The two are not the same.
- **Treat every student as an individual and with respect:** All students should be valued for their true worth and dignity.
- **Make changes when necessary:** Alter your instructional program when there are significant increases in behavioural issues.
- **Be friendly but firm:** Attempt to display such an attitude in daily experiences with students.
- **Be prepared and planned:** Have strategies to deal with behaviour issues. A teacher who is not well-prepared usually "reacts" to situations, and this may not produce the desired outcome.
- **Remain calm:** Take a deep breath before dealing with issues. Emotional responses should be avoided, since they often are not linked to planned strategies and can result in both teacher and students being upset after the interaction.
- **Carefully plan teaching situations:** Effective teaching does not usually occur fortuitously. Well-planned lessons that are interesting and enjoyable engage students. Effective classroom management involves planning.

A variety of teaching strategies and techniques can be used to create an effective and positive learning environment where all students experience success at their own level of development. For example, utilizing different styles and methods of instruction caters to students' unique styles of learning. Further, effective teachers demonstrate key teaching behaviours, exhibit desirable teaching qualities, are able to motivate students, and maintain well-managed instructional activities.

Effective Teaching Practices

1. During your practicum, talk to your mentor teacher to get permission to record a 15-minute segment of one of your physical education lessons. Later, observe your actions and critically analyze your teaching performance for instructional clarity and effectiveness. View the teaching segment with the sound muted to analyze effectiveness of nonverbal cue use, too.

2. Visit a school and observe a physical education lesson. Identify the methods used to maintain and promote appropriate student behaviour. Identify the methods used to motivate students, identifying both extrinsic and intrinsic motivators. Check for smooth transitions between activities, student engagement in the activities, and time-on-task.

A critically important, and sometimes overlooked, characteristic of creating a positive learning environment in physical education is the issue of student emotional safety. Particularly in the past, all too often, some students had negative experiences in physical education. What should have been enjoyable learning experiences were certainly not nearly so. This is something that must not be continued. Ensuring that all students are taught in an emotionally safe environment is critical throughout our schools, including our gymnasia and playing fields. The picking of teams by captains, exclusionary activities or teacher language, and the making fun of the physical performance of someone, are some examples of issues that teachers need to be constantly aware of and attend to at all times. Not doing so is unacceptable.

Conclusion

Throughout this chapter we have discussed the different aspects to consider when teaching physical education. It is important to appreciate that this information is based on research understanding of best practices and how to effectively teach physical education content matter to students. This understanding forms the basis for the next chapter of this textbook which introduces you to how to effectively plan and assess for physical education teaching.

Checking for Understanding

I Can...
- Appreciate and explain why physical education should be considered an important part of the academic programming of a student's school experience.
- Identify the techniques to teach effective physical education lessons.
- Describe the continuum of teaching styles and its application to teaching physical education.
- Identify the reasons why we need to create a positive, well-managed physical education learning environment, and I know how to do so.

Chapter 6

Supporting the Instructional Process

Students who spend more time in good practice learn more.

Rink (2010)

Key Objectives

High quality instruction is a process that involves not only the actions taken while delivering a lesson, but also the thinking and decision-making that occurs prior to and after the lesson. This includes such issues as the planning for and assessment of the learning experiences within the physical education program. It is hoped that, by the end of this chapter, you will:

- Understand the critical importance of planning, and the different types of plans
- Appreciate the role of assessment and know the different ways student learning can be assessed in physical education
- Understand the practicalities of scheduling a physical education program, including facility use
- Recognize the critical importance of establishing a safe learning environment

Planning for Learning

Planning for physical education programming occurs on different levels, ranging from a general view of the program through to the identification of specific learning activities and teaching strategies. Teachers make interrelated long-, mid-, and short-range plans to ensure that curricular outcomes are met and that student learning is promoted.

Unfortunately, planning in physical education is not always evident. When teachers fail to plan, important issues for learning, or rather lack of learning, can start to emerge. For example, opportunities to create meaningful learning experiences in a sequential and well planned progression can be missed, and so students can end up receiving the same activities year after year; activities that lack progression and variety, causing students to lose interest and motivation to be physically active. Whereas, teachers who plan are able to compare and share their intended learning experiences with others in order to ensure sequential activities with well-planned progressions are in place, thus creating a positive learning experience for students, one that supports the development of physical literacy.

Types of Plans

Long-Range Planning: Creating long-range plans helps a teacher to stay organized and provides an overview of when curricular outcomes are to be addressed. Of all the types of planning documents that teachers create, a Year Plan is the most general. Normally, a physical education Year Plan provides a month-by-month outline of the activities chosen, the general and specific learning outcomes to be covered, the assessment strategies to be utilized, and the facilities needed to conduct the program.

With physical education, a *Year Plan* needs to consider a number of factors that are both similar and also different from how we plan in other subject areas. Similar to other subject areas, learning activities need to build upon prior knowledge, meaning that careful thought needs to be given to sequential learning opportunities which are chosen to reflect and meet the requirements of curriculum documents. Also, assessment strategies need to be linked to the expected outcomes and the teaching strategies employed. However, there are stark differences for physical education, too, that teachers need to consider. For example, physical education programming needs to provide a breadth and variety of activities. Therefore, teachers need to consider revisiting the major dimensions of the program (e.g., alternative environment activities, dance, games, gymnastics, and individual activities) several times throughout the year so that students are exposed to a number of different activities within each activity dimension. Overall, throughout the school year, there should be a balance of time spent in each of the activity dimensions; approximately 7-8 weeks devoted to each. The idea of having 6-week long units of learning devoted entirely to soccer or basketball is not conducive to developing physical literacy and enhancing student willingness to be active daily.

Another unique element of creating a *Year Plan* for physical education is the necessity to consider local weather conditions to know when to plan for outdoor activities, off-site facility bookings and accompanying transportation needs, and gymnasium access during various times of the year, etc. Considering such issues at the *Year Plan* stage is advisable to create a program experience that supports student learning.

The initial steps of creating a *Year Plan* are to ensure alignment with the relevant curriculum document. At this stage, it is critically important that teachers consider both the general and specific learning outcomes identified in the curriculum documents. From there, a teacher needs to identify which kinds of activities can best achieve these learning outcomes and also consider their placement throughout the *Year Plan*. As a teacher decides on the activity areas to be covered, distinct units of learning are identified. By doing so, teachers can see if the Year Plan covers all the required general and specific learning outcomes. Checking the Year Plan frequently throughout the year is important in order to keep track of progression toward meeting the yearly curricular aims. For example, if a teacher wishes to promote cooperation and playground style game activities, it may be worthwhile for the teacher to plan to include such experiences early in the school year and then provide further opportunities throughout the year. Following this plan, the teacher can provide learning opportunities to students that can be practiced, reinforced, and developed throughout the school year.

A year plan should be regarded as a document to ensure that students receive an overall program that is developmentally appropriate; one that provides appropriate progressions for effective learning throughout the whole of the elementary school experience. In the same way as teachers collaborate to ensure that certain novels are introduced at particular grade levels in a school to lessen the chance of repetition and to promote a developmental approach with correct progressions for the overall school language arts program, it is important that teachers also share their physical education Year Plans to ensure that students are not receiving the same activities and learning experiences year after year. An example of this is the repetition of teaching the lay-up shot in basketball lessons year after year. Undoubtedly, many of us experienced such needless repetition. See Figure 6.1 for an example of a *Year Plan*.

Year Plans are expansive and general in nature. For example, Year Plans:
- Focus on an overview of learning opportunities across the whole school year
- Provide a general picture of how the curriculum will be introduced
- Focus the teacher on identifying when general and specific curriculum outcomes will be addressed
- Provide opportunities to sequence learning
- Identify the types of assessment strategies to be used throughout the year to ensure that a variety of measures are used
- Consider the most beneficial time of the year to plan outdoor activities dependent on good weather or the kind of indoor activities that are best planned when the typical Canadian inclement weather results in activities mainly being taught in the gymnasium
- Identify times when specialized equipment is needed or off-school sites are to be accessed

Grade: _____

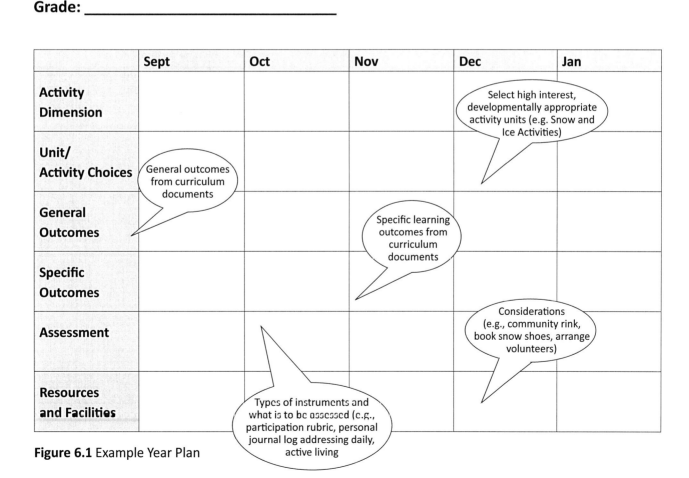

Figure 6.1 Example Year Plan

Mid-Range Planning: *Unit Plans* are a key feature of mid-range planning. Generally, a *Unit Plan* is a group of lessons related to a theme or an activity. Units do not have to always be taught on successive days. The plan identifies the number of lessons, but not necessarily where it is exactly positioned within the overall program. Therefore, a teacher could have a number of units occurring at the same time, alternating class time between units. However, in elementary schools, most often teachers choose to have only a single unit occurring at any one time.

Organizing the instructional program into units enables the teacher to focus on the same activity for a period of time. In most cases, elementary school teachers have units that consist of between 5 – 10 lessons. In terms of time, this would equate to units being 1-2 weeks in length.

Creating and following an intentional plan of instruction has some distinct benefits to both the teacher and the students. First, a *Unit Plan* enables a particular theme or set of activities to be explored over a period of time which allows for scaffolding of learning, reviewing, and extension. Therefore, students have the benefit of having more time to acquire physical skills and learn how to apply them. Second, by having a series of lessons on a similar theme or activity, less time needs to be spent on managerial or organizational matters. After establishing expected routines, a teacher can spend more lesson time on the teaching and learning process. Third, when a *Unit Plan* is created, student learning is planned for with logical and meaningful progression in mind. Such an approach enables the students and the teacher to note improvement in understanding and performance.

Before creating a *Unit Plan*, a teacher should consult the previously established Year Plan to determine what prior learning has already occurred and what is expected to be known for later learning. That way, the teacher can ensure sequential learning is accounted and planned for and that the unit plan supports student acquisition of learning outcomes.

Unit Plans have a greater level of specificity than Year Plans. For example, *Unit Plans*:

- Align with and address provincial curriculum documents
- Identify specific learning outcomes
- Focus on a particular activity dimension
- Outline progressions
- Detail specific learning activities and teaching strategies
- Identify equipment needs
- Recognize potential safety issues
- Outline the possible assessment strategies to be used to determine if students meet the expected learning outcomes

See Figure 6.2 for an example of a *Unit Plan*.

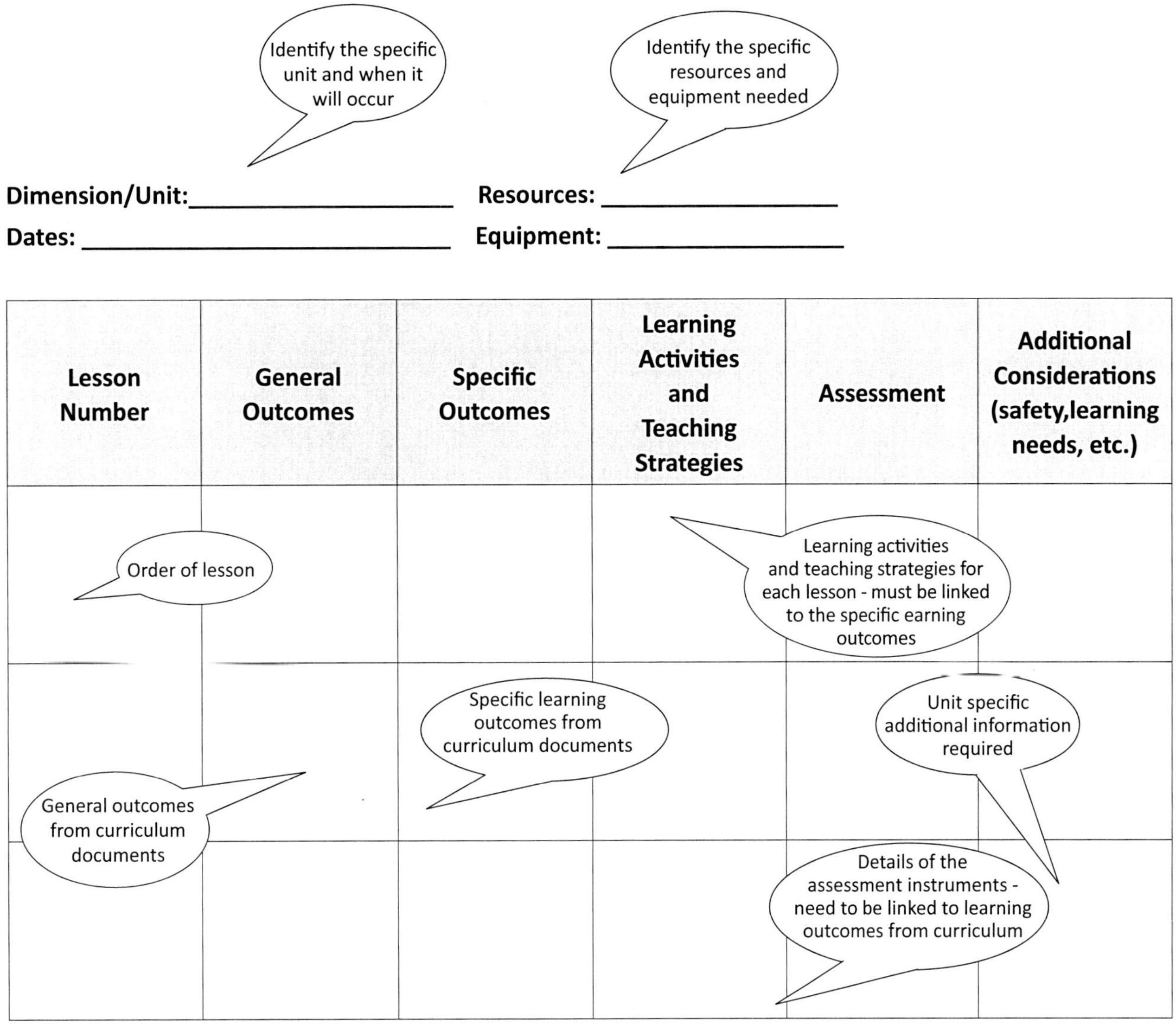

Dimension/Unit:_____   Resources: _____

Dates: _____   Equipment: _____

Lesson Number	General Outcomes	Specific Outcomes	Learning Activities and Teaching Strategies	Assessment	Additional Considerations (safety, learning needs, etc.)

Figure 6.2 Example Unit Plan

Short-Range Planning: Short-range planning consists of *Lesson Plans*. Although Lesson Plans are often considered to be individual entities, they should truly be considered as part of a series of connected lessons that make up the content of a *Unit Plan*. Therefore, the creation of a *Lesson Plan* needs to take into consideration the overall outcomes identified in the *Year Plan* along with those learning outcomes more specifically addressed in the corresponding *Unit Plan*.

Lesson Plans are detailed accounts of what the teacher expects to transpire during a set period of time. Often, in the case of elementary school physical education programming, lessons tend to range from 30 – 45 minutes in length. The level of detail included in a Lesson Plan is extensive, especially for a beginning teacher, as it provides a *road map* for successful lesson delivery and student achievement of the specific learning outcomes.

The important features of a *Lesson Plan* can be seen in Figure 6.3. However, the learning outcomes, the activities and teaching strategies to meet these outcomes, and the manner in which student learning is to be assessed, all feature prominently. It is important for a teacher to understand that the strength of a *Lesson Plan* lies in creating opportunities for intentional learning and, as such, is a vital component of being an effective teacher. *Lesson Plans:*

- Address provincial curriculum documents
- Identify specific learning outcomes and align and describe, in detail, the specific learning activities and teaching strategies to achieve student learning
- Describe, in detail, how the lesson will proceed from start to finish
- Identify exact equipment needs – including number of items, location of equipment, set up and take down of equipment, etc.
- Provide details of how instruction for inclusion of all students is to be met
- Describe steps to be taken to mitigate potential safety issues
- Provide the assessment strategies that are to be used to determine if students achieved the expected learning outcomes
- Provide an opportunity for teachers to reflect on the successes of the lesson and any future consideration

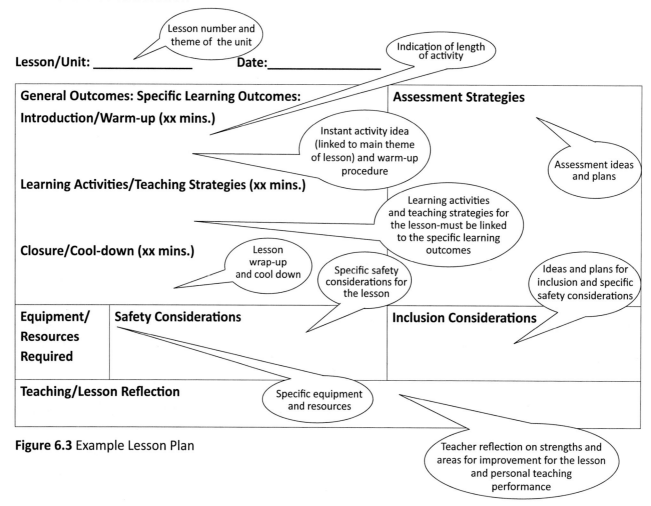

Figure 6.3 Example Lesson Plan

The Benefits of Planning

Armstrong, Henson, and Savage (2015) stated that when teachers are well-planned it provides many benefits for both the teacher and students. For example, there tends to be less behavioural issues during lessons and students are more likely to be engaged in meaningful learning experiences. Preparing planned instruction that is matched to learner needs requires time and understanding on the part of the teacher. Stimulating and engaging lesson and activity ideas require teachers to know and understand the physical education program requirements and the learners in their classes. Critically, if done well, plans can assist a teacher in creating learning opportunities for students to achieve curriculum outcomes, and provide opportunities for students to develop their physical literacy.

Assessment

Teachers in schools are faced with a vast amount of documentation from provincial and local school authorities that consistently make reference to such things as learning outcomes, competencies, and performance standards. This has resulted in pressures for teachers to assess student performance against expectations of learning. The provincial curriculum or program of studies is one such document. Once teachers begin to consider what they intend students to learn, equal thought must be placed on how will they know if students have learned what they have intended. This is the critical role of assessment.

Purposes of Assessment

At the school level, it is vitally important that teachers are able to link their planning, instruction, and assessment. The intentional creation of such a link improves the opportunities for successful learning for students (Wood, 2003). Traditional practice has not emphasized such a link between these stages of the instructional process. In the past, the development of curriculum and the construction of assessment strategies were separate and distinct from each other. Whereas, today, planning, instruction, and assessment are correctly viewed as an integral partnership.

Assessment in Physical Education

Alberta Education (2000) stated that assessment practices should be conducted in a manner that promotes, encourages, and supports ongoing learning and contributes to the overall development of students. To do so, teacher assessment of student learning should be a continuous, collaborative, and comprehensive process that includes clearly identified and communicated criteria. In short, the 4Cs! See Figure 6.4.

Continuous: Based on general and specific curriculum outcomes, assessment encourages student learning through on-going assessment that occurs frequently rather than isolated performances. Such assessment practices focus on both the process of learning and the final product of performance.

Collaborative: Collaborative assessment encourages students to become partners in understanding of and being responsible for their own learning. This can help students to develop positive attitudes toward an active, healthy lifestyle and the development of physical literacy. It also allows for the involvement of and the sharing of information to educational partners to create an overall awareness of program outcomes and expected performance criteria of student learning.

Comprehensive: A program built upon developmental appropriateness and taught in a developmentally appropriate manner, can consider all facets of learning from a student perspective, focus on strengths, and encourage further learning.

Clearly Communicated Criteria: Performance criteria should be understandable to all. Students should know what they are expected to understand and perform and be able to articulate this to others. Students can also be involved in identifying and/or creating the criteria for assessment.

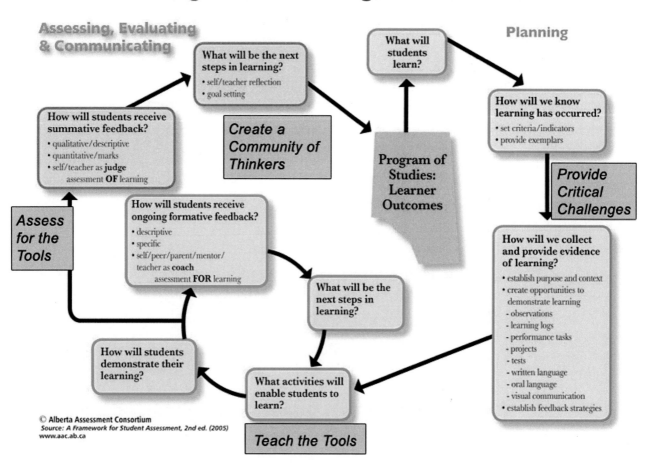

Figure 6.4 Student Assessment

Types of Assessment

Assessment can take the form of being:

- Qualitative or quantitative
- Formative or summative
- Norm-referenced or criterion-referenced

However, the most accurate profiles of student performance are based on the findings gathered from assessment in a variety of contexts, and by utilizing many different strategies. This is due to different assessment strategies providing different information; what is suitable for one purpose may not be suitable for another. Therefore, teachers need to acknowledge this and provide students with many ways to demonstrate their learning. If they do, such assessment can truly become a learning activity that enables students to reveal what they know and can do, and provides students with information about their performance to guide for future improvement.

Assessment Strategies in Physical Education

Personal Observation: Activity/performance is visually assessed – can be on an individual or whole class basis

Exit Slips: Short responses to demonstrate general understanding of learning from lesson

Developmental Benchmarks: Fitness tests, etc.

Checklists: Two-point scales. Normally Yes/No, little specific information or quality of performance

Analytic Rating Scales: 3 or more-point scale, provides more information than a checklist

Rubrics: Designed as a continuum of quality, accompanying narrative describes performance at a particular level

Personal Activity Logs (PALs): Log books that indicate such things as knowledge, interest, and performance levels

Portfolios: Variety of records of personal work and performance

---

Examples of Assessment in Physical Education

Although, as mentioned previously, teachers have an array of assessment strategies that they can use to evaluate student attainment of learning outcomes, observation techniques, checklists, rating scales, and rubrics tend to be most frequently used. The following is a brief overview of these assessment strategies and an example of their construction.

Observation Techniques: Teachers use observation in conjunction with many of their assessment strategies. However, it is not simply the watching of the environment. Teachers need to know what they are observing, who in particular they are observing, and how they can record what they observe. For example, some teachers create a simple chart for the taking of anecdotal notes that can be added to each lesson. This chart can take the form of a number of cells for all the recording of observations of all the students or an individual chart for each child. Table 6.1 and 6.2 provide examples of each type of chart:

Table 6.1 Observation Chart Example – All Students				
Moves safely and is aware of the space of others				
Raj　　　　Oct. 3 Worked well in the gym today, shares space well.	Rikki　　　Oct. 3 Took a while to understand personal space of others, but got there!	Rachel　　Oct. 3 Did not want to share space with others, kept to self.	Rob　　　　Oct. 3 Hurt his hand in first 5 minutes. Becoming a habit? Need to check!	Name: Date:
Name: Date:	Name: Date:	Name: Date:	Name: Date:	Name: Date:

Table 6.2 Observation Chart – Individual Student				
Moves safely and is aware of the space of others				
Raj　　　　Sept. 7 Already shows signs of knowing safety rules quite well.	Raj　　　　Oct. 3 Took a while to understand personal space of others, but got there!	Raj　　　Nov. 10 Shares the space well with others. Plays safely.	Raj　　　Jan. 8th Was able to verbalize the difference between personal and general space.	Name: Date:
Name: Date:	Name: Date:	Name: Date:	Name: Date:	Name: Date:

Observation techniques, when undertaken appropriately, are very helpful in keeping the teacher constantly aware of performance levels of their students and can be most useful to provide immediate feedback to students.

Checklists: Checklists are quite simplistic in nature. They consist of a 2-point scale with the teacher indicating whether a student has achieved or not achieved the established criteria. Often they incorporate language such as YES/NO, DEVELOPING/NOT YET, ABLE TO, NOT ABLE TO, etc. They are very easy to use as long as the teacher has clearly identified exactly what is being assessed. They are also time expedient, but a down side is that they offer little in the way of detailed information. See Table 6.3 for an example of a checklist:

Table 6.3 Checklist Example			
Moves safely and is aware of the space of others			
Name	**Date**	**Developing**	**Not Yet**
Nina	Nov. 2	✓	
Nate	Nov. 2		✓
Niera	Nov. 3	✓	

Rating Scales: Rating scales can be viewed as a more detailed and extensive type of checklist. However, in the case of rating scales, there are more scale points and include the opportunity to provide a teacher with more detailed information on the quality and extent of learning being displayed by the student. When creating a rating scale, the teacher must identify the learning outcome and then decide on how many scale points to use to be able to appropriately describe student performance. Scale points should be distinguishable and easily interpreted. The minimum number of scale points is three, with no highest number. However, we would suggest that five scale points would likely be the highest to use. There is contention that teachers should use an even number of scale points rather than an odd number. This is due to the suggestion that oftentimes, we pick the central scale point. Whereas, an even number of scale points ensures that the teacher must choose to indicate whether the student is performing more to one particular side of the scale. See Tables 6.4 and 6.5 for examples.

Table 6.4 Rating Scale (3-point) Example

Moves safely and is aware of the space of others				
Name	Date	Demonstrates consistently	Demonstrates sometimes	Demonstrates rarely
Bill	Nov 2		✓	
Brianna	Nov 3			✓
Batima	Nov 3		✓	

Table 6.5 Rating Scale (4-point) Example

Moves safely and is aware of the space of others					
Name	Date	Demonstrates consistently	Demonstrates most of the time	Demonstrates sometimes	Demonstrates rarely
Bill	Nov 2			✓	
Brianna	Nov 3				✓
Batima	Nov 3			✓	

Rubrics: Rubrics have become a very popular assessment strategy for teachers. In many ways, they can be viewed as a more detailed rating scale. Through their use, teachers attempt to provide detailed communication on the achievement of learning expectations to students. Generally, a rubric describes the expectations of performance by identifying the necessary criteria and providing descriptors of level of quality that usually range from poor to excellent. If used well, rubrics can help explain expectations of performance to students, allow them to understand what is needed for improvement, and know what their performance has been assessed at. Thereby, rubrics can provide feedback to students for and of learning. See Table 6.6 for an example.

Table 6.6 Rubric Example

Moves safely and is aware of the space of others					
Name:		**Date:**			
	Exemplary **4**	**Accomplished** **3**	**Developing** **2**	**Beginning** **1**	**Score**
Moves in a safe manner in the gym	Does not need to be reminded and always moves in a safe manner	Is aware and demonstrates safe movements	Is becoming aware of how to move safely	Is seldom aware of how to move safely	
Is aware of own personal space	Always aware of personal space	Is aware of own personal space	Is becoming aware of own personal space	Is seldom aware of own personal space	
Is aware of and respects general space	Always aware of general space and is able to describe why the need to respect general space	Is aware and respects general space	Is becoming aware of general space	Is seldom aware of general space	
Is aware of and respects the personal space of others	Always aware of and respects the personal space of others and is able to describe why the need to respect the personal space of others	Is aware and respects the personal space of others	Is becoming aware of the personal space of others	Is seldom aware of the personal space of others	

Beyond Student Assessment

It is important for teachers to remember that the overall assessment process does not start and stop with the student. While the assessment of student learning in physical education is critically important, teachers must also take the time to assess all facets of their teaching and the environment they teach in.

A multitude of assessment techniques can be used to gather information on these issues, such as peer feedback, visual and audio recordings of teaching, student feedback, safety check-points, etc. When teachers effectively assess the program they have planned, their instructional delivery, and the equipment and facility they are intending to use, and make the appropriate changes to whatever they determine needs changing to support student learning, students will likely receive a learning experience that supports the attainment of learning goals.

Beyond Student Assessment Examples

Program Content and Delivery

Is the order of units allowing for progression in learning?

Over the year, has the program covered expected learning outcomes?

Teaching

Are lesson plans effective in meeting student learning needs?

Consider monitoring off-task behaviours, effective teaching strategies, etc.

Facilities

Consider potential safety issues

Is the area and/or facility set-up in a developmentally appropriate manner?

Equipment

Is the equipment in good repair and safe to use?

Is the equipment developmentally appropriate?

Summary

Teachers must fully understand what they are assessing and why. Linking assessment to intending learning assists the teacher to support on-going student learning. A most crucial part of the communication process of assessment, is ensuring there is a shared understanding between the person providing the information and the person receiving it. Research has shown that the greater the role that students are given in the overall assessment process, the richer the information that is shared and the greater the potential impact on future student learning.

> *Assessment must be FAIR, APPROPRIATE, and HONEST*

Program Scheduling

The Practicalities of Scheduling a Physical Education Program

Ideally, teachers should be aiming to have their students involved in physical education classes on a daily basis. Unfortunately, all too often the reality is that this is not achieved on a consistent basis. Therefore, a good start would be for teachers to be proactive in scheduling daily physical education classes at the start of the school year. That way, they will be making a commitment. However, at times schools are faced with the difficulty of too many classes and not enough time slots available in the gymnasium. It is this particular hurdle that causes some teachers to make the decision to schedule less physical education classes. We contend that a good approach for a school to take at the start of the year is that all teachers have the choice of two or three time slots. This will provide everyone the opportunity to be able to choose their favourite times and all classes will have an equal number of scheduled times that the gymnasium is available to them. From there, teachers can choose another time slot, etc. until all the time slots have been chosen.

If a teacher is still faced with physical education only scheduled four times a week, some creative solutions can be adopted. Perhaps on the non-scheduled day there is outside or off-site facilities that can be utilized. At times, classrooms can be used for activity such as resistance band work or yoga stretches. Perhaps, two classes can share a time slot, with one class using the gymnasium one week, the other class the next. Please note, we do not promote the idea of multiple classes utilizing the gymnasium at the same time as this presents many instructional challenges, raises questions of developmental appropriateness, can negatively impact opportunities for student learning activities, and can increase safety concerns. Working to ensure students have the opportunity to be active in physical education daily is something that all elementary teachers should aim for.

During the school year, there are normally several time blocks when the gymnasium is unavailable. Such times might coincide with spring or winter concerts, science or art fairs, or even community use. However, this should not be a reason for the physical education program to come to a halt. With foresight, teachers can plan to utilize outside or off-site facilities. For example, a winter unit activity of tobogganing, ice skating, and snow shoeing would enable a teacher to still provide a quality physical education program during a time when the gymnasium is used for a Winter Concert.

Facility Considerations

Equipment: Storing, accessing, and maintaining equipment is always a challenge in schools. This can be especially so when a large number of teachers are all using the same equipment inventory. Therefore, many schools will identify a teacher who takes overall responsibility of ensuring that the equipment is in good repair and that the equipment room is kept in an orderly manner. However, it is every teacher's responsibility to store equipment properly in the appropriate location and in a manner that supports ease of access and safety. It is far too easy for inappropriately stored equipment to become a safety issue. Many teachers establish clear procedures for the collection and storing of equipment. This not only helps to promote safety but, very importantly, also saves wasted time and promotes student self-responsibility.

Facility and Space: Unfortunately, at times, physical education environments can be somewhat daunting for some teachers. Thoughts of noise, constant student movement, equipment being jumped on and over, balls flying through the air, and even worries of accidents and injury can impact a teacher's confidence to teach a quality physical education program. However, we would suggest that the gymnasium is a far more controlled area than the playground at recess where sight lines, teacher-student ratios, and proximity all place the teacher in a much greater arena of risk.

It is imperative that teachers remember when they are teaching in physical education facilities and spaces that they will need to adopt practices that are different from those they regularly use in their classrooms. For example, they will likely need to check that the gymnasium floor is free of anything that may cause harm to the students such as a water spill or small stones from the soles of shoes. Such things can cause injury to students jumping and rolling in a gymnastics lesson. Observation of all learners is key in a physical education lesson. This can be remarkably different from a classroom-based lesson where often teachers can be seen working with a small group of students and only occasionally look up at the rest of the class or circulate the room. The physical education environment demands a different level of observation and supervision. Due to the kind of activities, multitude of equipment, and constant movement of students, teachers must maintain their sight lines at all times. Teachers must practice keeping their back to the wall not to the students, and when needing to move in to the centre of the teaching environment, always remember to quickly move back to the outside again – get in and get out. When outside of the gymnasium, sight lines are still important, but so too is maintaining verbal contact. Therefore, teachers should consider limiting the space available to students in order to maintain visual and verbal contact.

Safety in Physical Education

Necessity of Safety

When teaching physical education, it is critical for teachers to review and adhere to their respective provincial safety guidelines document. These documents can normally be found on provincial curriculum websites and are often referenced as support documents. However, they are, in our view, of equal importance as the curriculum documents. The safety guidelines documents provide a minimum standard of care for students at school when engaged in physical activity.

At all times, it is important for teachers to explain that the physical education learning environment is a safe place to learn, both physically and emotionally. Therefore, not only the choice of activity and equipment to be used needs to be constantly considered, but also that students are not embarrassed or ridiculed. All these factors can lead to an unwillingness to participate, something that is certainly not the aim of a quality physical education experience. Student safety, and physical and emotional considerations, must be at the forefront of teacher attention and if a student does not demonstrate the willingness to follow safety guidelines, the teacher must address the situation for the safety of the student and all others in the learning environment.

While physical safety is often in the foremost of our thinking, emotional safety of students is something that teachers need to be particularly aware of. This can be difficult though as emotional safety cannot always be seen or easily detected. Therefore, teachers should be constantly looking for such things as:
  • Subtle signs of student discomfort or unhappiness
  • Whispering or giggling behind the backs of other students
  • Teasing or joking at the expense of others
  • Students being left out of groups

The emotional safety of students is critical in physical education teaching. Too often, in the past, this has been, at best forgotten, if not ignored. It is our experiences that, when discussing with pre-service teachers their physical education experiences as school children,

the lack of emotional safety is often raised as a reason for disliking physical education and becoming discouraged from participating in physical activity.

Safety across Physical Education Programming
Although there are many common safety considerations that need to be taken into account for most physical education lessons, such as equipment being in good repair, it is important for teachers to remember that the variety of activity dimensions present in physical education programming require, at times, specific safety considerations.

Alternative Environment Activities: Unique to the teaching of alternative environment activities is that students may be allowed to enter specific areas where they may be unsupervised for some time (e.g., ski hills). Hence, the necessity for teachers to adhere to the adult to student ratios required by district and provincial safety regulations for student safety. It is of critical importance that teachers help educate volunteers on how to observe and what to look for, and how to identify foreseeable risks in order to avoid them.

Dance Activities: When teaching dance activities, students are often asked to move to different types of stimuli such as musical selections. Although many dance lessons incorporate generic style safety considerations such as the floor being free of all debris, jewelry removed, etc., given the creative an d performance-based nature of dance, it is important for teachers to maintain a learning environment that is not only a physically safe place but, most importantly, also emotionally safe. In other words, students are free to take risks and try new things and also free from the threat of ridicule, which could lead to unwillingness to participate.

Games Activities: Unique to teaching games activities is that specific students are likely to come to class with more background knowledge, expertise, and/or experience than others. Hence, it is important for teachers to provide opportunities for all students to reach a level of success, at the same time as ensuring that each student understands how to cooperate and compete in a safe way. This means that all students need to demonstrate behaviours that encourage and support others. Students being overly aggressive, using equipment dangerously, or playing in a manner that could potentially hurt another physically or emotionally is something teachers should be aware of.

Gymnastics Activities: Teaching gymnastics activities safely requires careful and thoughtful consideration from the teacher. The choice of activity, the equipment to be used, and the amount of background knowledge, expertise, and/or experience of the students are all important safety considerations. Ensuring that students are challenged and exposed to developmentally appropriate activities in gymnastics is of critical importance. To promote safety, many teachers utilize a station approach when teaching this dimension. Stations can help to promote safety as the arrangement of the activities can provide students with controlled, safe areas to practice and learn. Gymnastics safety guidelines are normally well-detailed in provincial safety documents. It is important that teachers consult such documentation to ensure their lessons not only meet the provincial requirements, but also maintain a safe learning environment.

Individual Activities: As suggested by the name, individual activities most often involve the application of fundamental movement skills in activities that are held in environments where students participate individually. Hence, teachers need to be aware of different equipment being used and also that students may be performing very different movements or actions at any given time. This requires a heightened level of observation at all times. Similar to gymnastics, many teachers utilize a station approach when teaching this dimension, as such a choice can help to promote safety as the arrangement of the activities can provide the students with controlled, safe areas to practice and learn. It is also important for teachers to provide opportunities for all students to understand how to properly perform the activities. For example, teaching proper ways to long jump or hold a yoga-stretching pose will help enhance learning and promote a safe learning environment.

Assessment of Safety

It is imperative that teachers consider safety during the planning process. Provincial safety documents should be accessed for information when considering long- and mid-range plans, and strictly adhered to and followed when developing short-range plans and teaching individual lessons. When a teacher is always conscious of safety and teaches with safety in mind, students are likely to be exposed to quality physical education experiences and environments that allow them to be challenged while they learn.

In Alberta, the 2013 provincial safety guidelines document was produced primarily by the Alberta Centre for Injury Control & Research, together with several other educational and recreational partner organizations. The document states that teachers need to ensure they are not engaging students in activities that will likely expose them to unreasonable risk of injury and the teacher to legal liability for negligence. Also, in an attempt to support teachers in being safe, the document indicates that teachers should be able to respond positively to four key questions. If teachers can demonstrate they are following identified precautions, they will be providing the necessary standard of care to students to protect them from unreasonable risk of injury. In other words, such teachers will create teaching/learning environments that are unlikely to be found negligent.

The Four Key Questions are:

- Are the chosen activities suitable to the age, cognitive and physical condition, and abilities of the student(s)?
- Have the students been progressively taught how to perform the activity properly and instructed how to avoid the dangers inherent in the activity? Do teacher plans indicate this?
- Is the equipment being utilized in the activities adequate and suitably arranged?
- Is the chosen activity being supervised properly for the inherent risk involved?

Alberta Centre for Injury Control & Research, 2013

Concluding Thoughts

Quality physical education experiences do not just happen. They require a dedication to thinking and decision-making that occurs prior to, during, and after lessons. Teachers must understand the importance of planning, assessment, and safety in order to create conducive learning experiences for students that will help develop physical literacy.

Checking for Understanding

I can...

- Describe why planning is important to the instructional process
- Distinguish between long-, mid-, and short-range plans, and know how to use such documents to create a quality physical education program
- Appreciate the role of assessment in the instructional process, and know the different ways student learning can be assessed in physical education lessons
- Understand the practicalities of scheduling a physical education program and facility use
- Recognize the critical importance of establishing a safe learning environment

Chapter 7

Teaching for All – Diversity and Inclusion in Physical Education

If the right to education for all is to become a reality, we must ensure that all learners have access to quality education that meets basic learning needs and enriches lives.

UNESCO, 2016

Introduction

All teachers will be faced with issues of diversity and inclusion during their careers. It is a fact of life that in most elementary schools, teachers will encounter new situations and uncertainties around diversity and inclusion. These complex phenomena evolving in education are also growing occurrence in the physical education environment. This chapter will introduce you to the following:

- Physical education programming that is diverse and inclusive
- The need for change in physical education
- Embracing *teaching for all*
- Understanding strength-based and holistic approaches to instruction
- Supporting and planning *teaching for all*
- Understanding the student, environment, teaching and activities: SETA
- The role of individualized planning
- Effective strategies
- Measuring success and the benefits of including all children in physical education

An Overview of Diversity and Inclusion

Due to the rich and complex nature of diversity and inclusion, standard definitions are hard to establish. The many discussions and evolving nature of these terms demonstrates their importance and how critical it is to understand how to plan, teach, and manage diversity and inclusion in elementary school physical educa tion programming. UNESCO (2005), in defining inclusion, suggested that it is "...a dynamic approach of responding positively to pupil diversity and of seeing individual differences not as problems, but as opportunities for enriching learning" (p. 12). Teachers are responsible for attending to and addressing the needs of all learners, and to minimize any exclusionary practices and feelings in schools (UNESCO, 2015). This process involves "...changes and modifications in content, approaches, structures and strategies, with a common vision which covers all children of the appropriate age range and a conviction that it is the responsibility of the regular system to educate all children" (UNESCO, 2005, p. 13). Physical education can be the environment where diversity and inclusion are celebrated and where students feel welcome in a unique classroom community. Therefore, for the purposes of learning to teach physical education, in this chapter we will use the phrase ***teaching for all*** when considering how to include all learners while respecting and embracing the diversity present in your class.

In order to *teach for all* in physical education, we must consider the range of possibilities to develop and deliver programs for diversity and inclusion for all students. *Teaching for all*, as a physical education teacher, means we ensure that every student has access to high quality physical education experiences. A quality physical education program "...implies creating an environment...in which children are both able and enabled to learn. Such an environment must be inclusive of children, effective with children, friendly and welcoming to children, healthy and protective for children..." (UNESCO, 2005, p. 10). Also refer back to Figure 1.2 - PE drives inclusion in Chapter 1.

Many of today's classrooms/schools contain a richness of diversity among the student populations. Educators are challenged with supporting the varied needs, interests, and backgrounds of their students to ensure they are attending to the whole child, meeting ministry, board, and curricular standards, and societal expectations. It is essential that teachers recognize that students' daily lives and backgrounds have an impact on school life; what occurs outside of school strongly influences students in the classroom. The multifaceted nature of our classrooms engages teachers and students with many diversities such as: socioeconomic status, class, race, culture, ethnicity, gender, sexual orientation, language, ability, skill, bodies, religion, beliefs, values, age, experience and perspectives.

The Need for Change in Physical Education

The way physical education has sometimes been taught in the past has resulted in negative stereotypes that have hindered the importance and mission of this curricular subject (Williams, 1992, 1994, 1996). Unfortunately, at times low-skilled performers and specific genders have been made to feel unwelcome, alienated, disengaged, or marginalized (Forsberg & Chorney, 2014). At times, physical education experiences have been described as masculine, fitness oriented, or for the elitist (Fishburne, 2005; Kirk, 2010). Physical education might not be every student's favourite subject; some students will not always enjoy every activity, game, or movement dimension taught in the physical education program. The historical representation of physical education – and the negative stereotypes portrayed – is not a program that supports *teaching for all*. A quality physical education program is taught by a teacher who strives to not only empower students, but motivate them to engage in lifelong movement. A physical education program that is *teaching for all* is "...committed to creating safe, equitable, learning spaces that inspire students to move because they can, not because they should or have to..." (Tischler, 2014, xiv). A teacher of physical education views the student first and creates a welcoming environment built through relationships and communication; this empowering teacher embraces diversity to include all in the physical education experience.

We challenge you to think about diversity and inclusion in this new way. Set aside assumptions; direct energy to a new way of planning, organizing, and instructing; and remember your teaching impacts every single one of the students in your classes. Quality physical education programming is about providing students with educative experiences (see Dewey, Chapter 2) that they carry beyond the school doors to a healthy active lifestyle. Consider the reality that your students will be leaving your classroom to confront new adventures outside of school. If we begin to open up the conversation with our students to learn about *them* and if we open ourselves up to new experiences, then we have begun to establish a holistic program developed for *all* students with their perspectives included. Furthermore, it is essential we set out to create a positive learning environment for all students to prepare them for the adventures they will encounter day-to-day and in the future; creating a positive learning environment begins by getting to know those students in front of you, to provide a safe space for all.

Reflection Corner...

From your personal experiences of physical education, have the choices of activities and learning experiences:

- Met the diverse nature of the school community?
- Been inclusive of all?
- Been exclusive of some? Who?

Embracing Diversity and Inclusion: Teaching for All

" The woods would be very quiet if no birds sang there except those who sang best"

Henry van Dyke

Understanding *teaching for all* begins with developing an awareness of the complex and dynamic environments in today's classrooms. Facilitating physical education to enable the elements of *teaching for all* starts with the teacher becoming an ally – begin by getting to know your students (Halas, McRae, & Petherick, 2012). First and foremost, successful teaching for all in physical education promotes and develops a community; a community that embraces difference with openness and appreciates opportunities to explore and learn about others. We are moving beyond the token gestures to demonstrate diversity such as only including cultural dances, having a Parasport or modified games day, or gender specific activities. This shift is to enable a safe space for the intersecting identities present in your class and to open up supportive lines of communication for all students.

In physical education, it is important to positively recognize individual differences and uniqueness. Teachers should aim to establish acceptance and respect therefore helping students build social relationships, which support the forming of a cohesive and collaborative community. Physical education teachers must support students by being aware of and implementing resources, provide positive encouragement, and use humour when appropriate (Halas, McRae & Petherick, 2012). Physical education can have a positive influence on the whole-child, including the physical, emotional/social, cognitive, and spiritual possibilities – to fulfil these potential possibilities, teachers must be enlightened by each student's background and differences to provide meaningful opportunities for all.

"It has long been recognized that physical education...can be used as a vehicle to promote the social inclusion of marginalized populations, and to contribute towards better understanding among communities."
UNESCO, 2013, p. 38

Although many recent developments in education and society have demonstrated the importance of recognizing diversity (UNESCO, 2005; UNESCO, 2015), the inclusion of students with differing learning requirements has long been established as a teacher responsibility in education. We need to support and follow the directives provided by school boards and administration to be certain all students who require appropriate and individualized programs receive them. By doing this, classrooms can be enriched and will become a "...platform for learning mutual understanding and respect for difference..." (Vickerman & Hayes, 2014, p. 53). *All* students should have access to a curriculum that is relevant and meaningful regardless of ability or uniqueness.

Teaching for All is about Valuing Each and Every Student

As a physical education teacher, you must remember that every student is an essential part of the whole environment and one size does NOT fit all.

Students are on a continuum of learning. Empowering students to feel included and accepted in a program requires teachers to encourage the importance of student voice. Listening to students' stories and experiences allows teachers to respond to varied needs and to be collaborative. This student-teacher collaboration is critical and necessary to create effective pedagogical approaches and to successfully plan curriculum and instructional strategies for a program that supports *teaching for all.*

At times, students with disabilities have been excluded from participating in physical education programs and segregated to other settings. Some cultural or religious groups have also been segregated due to different beliefs about participation in activities such as dance or swimming. Additionally, controversies about biological sex, gender roles and abilities, while always a concern, are becoming increasingly divisive and contentious in schools. All of these situations can be influenced positively by *teaching for all.* Physical education is a facilitator for social interaction, physical development and functions, and an expressive subject. It is a medium for students to support each other in the processes of learning to move and moving to learn. *Teaching for all* in physical education also requires the teacher to have an open-mind, maintain a positive attitude, and be ready to adapt, modify, simplify, and extend all practices being enacted (Vickerman & Hayes 2013).

> *"Creating an education system that is truly inclusive requires all schools to identify and implement evidence-based strategies that ensure the safety, belonging and full participation of all members of the school community."*
> Alberta Education, 2016a, p. 1

Teachers have an opportunity to bring community culture and individual uniqueness into the school. This openness shifts the attitude from the negative stigma that is related with being "different," the "other," or "less than". Azzarito and Solomon (2005) believe "...physical education classrooms are not vacuums in which teachers fill students with knowledge; rather they are sites of complex knowledge building and socialization" (p. 27). It is time to shift attitudes and perspectives in physical education and advocate for a depth of knowledge and understanding to build supportive relationships empowering each individual student.

> *Students enter the school with unique stories, experiences, and backgrounds that shape their lives and impact their personhood in the physical education classroom.*

There is an increased recognition in Canada of the importance of addressing and understanding cultural differences, such as Aboriginal practices and knowledge; new immigrants and English language learners (ELL); the rights and needs of students with diverse sexual orientations, gender identities and expressions in schools; and supporting students with disabilities. For example, Alberta Education (2016b) is ensuring integration of different cultures. They suggest that teachers should strive to engage and support First Nations, Métis and Inuit cultures and communities by honouring history, cultures, languages and perspectives through their teaching practices. Dwayne Donald (2013) describes the importance of opening up to understand the stories of Aboriginal people rather than simply infusing or integrating Aboriginal perspectives in teaching practices. Aboriginal perspectives ought to be treated as an "opportunity for relational renewal and enhanced understanding" (Dwayne Donald, 2013) to learn more deeply about the various experiences, stories, and perspectives of those in the communities in which teachers work. Teachers might choose to connect with the communities and affiliated organizations to support their learning and to ensure they have up-to-date information and applicable resources for their classroom. Therefore, as teachers of physical education, we need to consider and implement strategies that address these issues.

> **Reflection Corner...**
> What might be some possible scenarios you may be faced with as a new physical education teacher who wants to honour Indigenous histories, cultures, languages, and perspectives?

Another example of addressing and understanding differences that teachers need to value and learn through other perspectives is with students with special needs. These students often have minimal opportunities to participate in both physical education classes and community physical activity programs. At times, the ability of these students is questioned and frequently underestimated when deciding on their level of participation in programming programs.

Goodwin and Watkinson (2000) suggested that students with special needs that have negative experiences in physical education are often attributed to social isolation, having their competence questioned and being limited or restricted to participation in class.

How would you address a new student coming into your class with such feelings?

In regards to students with special needs, it is important that we understand that they are at a greater risk of being inactive because of the possible assumptions and barriers to their participation in physical activity. Inactivity levels and obesity rates are on the rise for all children (ParticipAction, 2015); students with special needs are perhaps even at greater risk due to their unique needs (Hogan, McCellan, Bowman, 2000). Therefore, fitness skills are not only critical to stay healthy, but also to navigate and overcome barriers in their environment (AbilityPath.org, 2011). Learning opportunities in physical education classes invite students to practice and learn life skills that can support these challenges in everyday living tasks. Physical education is a vehicle for supporting students to lead healthy physically active lives; a program that provides social interactions, cognitive stimuli, and physical activity is important for students' overall well-being – all students.

Being a Teacher for All

Understanding Strength-Based and Holistic Approaches

When considering the curriculum and pedagogical strategies in physical education taking a strength-based approach has many advantages. This approach is recognized as a positive way to recognize individual strengths, keep the student at the centre of learning and, teach all students.

Strength-Based Approach: A strength-based approach encourages teachers to focus on developing a program and ways of instruction that will serve the whole child. This approach "...lies in the space or zone of teachers identifying what a child can or could achieve when provided with educational support and motivation" (State of Victoria, Department of Education and Early Childhood Development, 2012, p.7). To deliver an effective physical education program for students, teachers must first recognize an individual's strengths, consider their interests, and identify their talents. Highlighting students' positive attributes and abilities allows teachers and students to concurrently understand the potential, interests, abilities, and capacities of learners rather than the deficits individuals may experience.

This approach is so much more than simply describing a student's learning and development in a positive light. Teachers should certainly not neglect to identify areas for development and improvement. However, a strength-based approach involves consistent sharing of information and recognizes that students' learning is dynamic, complex, and holistic. Within this purview, students may demonstrate their learning in different ways (State of Victoria, Department of Education and Early Childhood Development, 2012). A physical education program aimed at developing students' strengths consists of positively identifying movement abilities, individualizing learning experiences for students, providing and building support networks, and focusing on the application and development of strengths (Passarelli, Hall & Anderson, 2010).

Utilizing a strength-based approach applies pedagogical strategies that focus on student choice and offer multiple opportunities. It strives to provide students with a sense of confidence and competence to support their overall well-being and therefore is very consistent with the goals of physical literacy (Chapter 3). The strength-based approach actively engages students in a positive, safe, and stimulating environment. Meaningful physical activity for all students involves engagement and participation in activity that is developmentally appropriate for each student.

> *"Start with what's present – not what's absent..."*
> State of Victoria, Department of Education and Early Childhood Development, 2012, p. 6

> *"When schools and educators begin to tap the strengths of their students and to shift thinking from deficit to strength, students may begin to realize their potential..."*
> Brownlee, Rawana, & MacArthur, 2012, p. 9

McCashen (2004) outlines five characteristics essential to consider when implementing a strength-based approach:

- **Respect** for the unique or common attributes including individuals: worth, rights, and capacities
- **Sharing** information with others to provide proper: knowledge, resources, and decision-making for each individual
- **Collaboration** with all parties involved. Fostering inclusion through teamwork and consultation with the student, other teachers, and parents.
- **Social justice** to ensure: equity, accessibility, participation, and self-determination of each individual
- **Transparency** that involves having open lines of communication

The relationship that exists between school environments, teachers, and students is very intricate. Such complexity makes the learning environment dynamic and constantly changing. Bower, Carroll, and Ashman (2014) believe that active agents, the individuals present in a child's life such as guardians and teachers, should all be participating and involved in supporting change towards positive strength-based experiences. A strength-based approach is a collaborative process. This process promotes goal setting for students, communication among active agents, and constant reflection. Such a process must consider the physical education environment to encourage engagement in physical activity to allow students to achieve learning goals through the utilization of their strengths.

Holistic Approach and Understanding: Being holistic emphasizes understanding the whole child. This means recognizing the development of each individual separately as well as creating an environment that is supportive of differences. The physical, cognitive, and social/

emotional domains and development of each student are relevant to planning and teaching in physical education. Overall, being holistic means:

- Promoting student growth and learning
- Having pedagogical strategies that connect and engage to student lives
- Being supportive of students' varied needs
- Providing a balanced program with choice and variety minimizing barriers to participation

Physical education teachers should include activities and create environments that embrace equality and equity of all students including individual difference, such as representing and supporting LGBTQ students; the variety of cultures and religions; and students with learning challenges. A holistic approach specifically emphasizes creating conducive opportunities for students who feel or seem to be 'outsiders' to participate in physical education with meaningful and developmentally appropriate activities.

Being holistic and ensuring a strength-based approach confirms that students achieve success when learning opportunities are most suited to their needs and background. In this chapter, when discussing how to support *teaching for all*, the elements that emerge for teacher preparation and planning are the **students, environment, teaching**, and **activities** (SETA). It is important for us to remember that the student should be foremost in all of our thinking and planning. Therefore, the acronym of SETA purposefully situates the student first in the environment, which drives teaching and activity choices. As such, SETA will be used in this chapter to help incorporate the ideas of strength-based and holistic approaches in physical education.

Supporting and Planning *Teaching for All* in Physical Education

The silencing that takes place in many classrooms must be stopped,
as must the blurring over of differences.
Greene, 1993, p.219

High quality physical education programs recognize individual student needs. These needs may vary from physical abilities, cognitive function, or levels of social acceptance. All students deserve the opportunity to participate with their classmates and to be appreciated. If we assume that a student does not fit into our physical education class or that the student dislikes and cannot perform the necessary skills to participate, it is a most problematic viewpoint. Often, disruptive behaviours, a lack of motivation or participation, negativity, frustration, and poor skill performance occur because activities being administered are not developmentally appropriate. For example, students should not be subjected to specific roles constantly, such as only playing the goalie or being the scorekeeper. Students should be engaging in play, their strengths should be valued, and their participation should maintain their self-respect and dignity. We suggest that teachers consider evaluating their programs by understanding and thinking holistically to support and plan for *teaching for all* in physical education.

We would suggest that approaching *teaching for all* takes an open mind and heart; this is the role that using the SETA framework can assist us with in our teaching of physical education.

Students

Building on students' strengths and acknowledging their diverse backgrounds levels the playing field and provides a safe space in the physical education class. Halas, McCrae, and Carpenter (2013) suggested that a strength-based approach situates students as "...allies and co-learners within the program..." (p. 198). In this way, a reciprocal learning environment is created: trust, respect, and acceptance can be established. Starting with students' strengths and understanding who they are, their traditions, abilities and historical identities allows a collaborative effort towards goal setting and personal success. Some important questions that, as teachers, we need to ask about each and every student can be found in Table 7.1.

Table 7. 1 Important Questions for Teachers
Information and Attitudes:
• What are the student's strengths and interests?
• To support learning, should the student work alone, with a partner, or in a group?
• Are there curricular adaptations that need to be made?
Policy and Practices:
• What type of supports and resources are provided or needed and who will provide them?
• Have long- and short-term goals for the students and the class been considered?
• Are the activities you are teaching matching the needs of students and are they representative of everyone in the class?
• IPP applications?
Communication:
• Have you talked to the student to understand how they feel about the activities and experiences you are providing?

It can be an uncomfortable or unfamiliar environment to step into a change room in elementary school. All of the places and spaces that create the physical education learning environment should accommodate for the diversity and backgrounds of students in your class:

Scenario 1

"I am from a reserve and I never grew up in a town, and the culture that I am from for some reason (coming from northern Manitoba) we don't have, culturally, a change room like that. So, when my friends and me would go to Thompson or something and there is a change room and you see a guy all naked, that is weird for us, we don't feel comfortable." (Halas, 2011, p.13).

Scenario 2

"Students with diverse sexual orientations, gender identities and gender expressions have a right to accommodation when it comes to the use of washroom and change room facilities that are congruent with their gender identity. This applies during school time and school-related activities on and off school property (such as field trips and athletic events)" (Alberta Education, 2016a, p. 9).

Environment

To establish a welcoming space in physical education, teachers must acknowledge the complex environments and contexts that students live in. In a safe learning community, students need to believe that they can share who they are with everyone and should have a drive to learn about others in the class as well. Recognizing the difficulties some students face through such things as disability, the transition of moving to a new country, or learning a new language, it is important to connect conversation and course content to the students' daily lives. For example, how do we relate activities chosen to meet the provincial physical education curriculum, such as ice sports or winter activities, to a recent immigrant from a country with a warm climate?

The environment, including the physical space and social interactions, can account for many barriers or challenges that students experience in physical education. To create and uphold a safe and inclusive environment, the teacher must change the area so all students can participate. There could be obstacles, distractions, or accessibility issues in the places and spaces in which physical education lessons occur.

If you consider the environment in terms of physical space, it should be free from restrictions. Factors that could impact the learning in physical education are:

- Spatial area for entering and exiting the environment
- Distractions of sharing gymnasium space
- Clothing required for certain activity environments
- Sounds and lighting issues
- Spatial boundaries and equipment set up
- Physical supports or specialized equipment
- Different surfaces or facilities

Social inclusion in the environment is also an essential piece to creating a safe environment for all students. Maintaining positive attitudes, modeling appropriate behaviour, reinforcing positive interactions, and including all children in as many activities as possible can assist and facilitate social inclusion in the physical education environment (Block, 2007).

"Inclusive physical education recognizes the inherent value and strengths of each student, the need for independence and self-determination, and the right to choose."

Saskatchewan Curriculum, 2016a

Examples of curriculum outcomes: How could you teach these outcomes?

British Columbia (2016) Physical and Health Education Curriculum Grade 1: Physical Literacy – it is expected that students will know proper technique for locomotor skills (movement skills that incorporate travelling across the floor or surface)

Saskatchewan Ministry of Education (2016b) Physical Education Curriculum Grade 3: (PE3.1) "Apply a repertoire of strategies for developing components of health-related fitness, (cardiovascular endurance, flexibility, muscular endurance, and muscular strength) through movement activities during scheduled times in school, at home, and in the community"

Ontario Ministry of Education (2010) Physical and Health Education Curriculum Grade 5: Understanding Health Concepts - Personal Safety and Injury Prevention (C1.1): Students will "identify people (e.g., parents, guardians, neighbours, teachers, crossing guards, police, older students, coaches, elders) and supportive services (e.g., help lines, 9-1-1,Telehealth, public health units, student services) that can assist with injury prevention, emergencies, bullying, and abusive and violent situations" (p. 143).

Teaching

Curricular documents may not explicitly provide a guide to ensure *teaching for all* is being implemented in physical education; however, the openness to choose the approaches we utilize to teach learning outcomes and program content is in the hands of physical education teachers. The outcomes are often broad enough for instructors to implement activities that will be inclusive to all students in their class, which presents the opportunity to utilize culturally relevant, non-traditional or non-gender specific, high interest and developmentally appropriate activities that foster the inclusivity of all students.

Teachers must ensure they are also teaching culturally relevant activities to meet the curriculum outcomes. Culturally relevant activities "...are those that resonate with students' family and community identities, those to which students have access in their immediate community, and those that have the resources necessary to participate..." (McCaughtry & Centeio, 2014, p. 11). These activities are important to incorporate and learn about to engage students with their cultures and surrounding communities. They do not have to always be specific to one culture, but should provide a variety of opportunities for students to learn and explore different cultural activities that exist. One way to implement culturally relevant activities is having a focus on wellness (physical, social, intellectual, occupational, environmental, emotional, and spiritual). Wellness advocates for equal attention on the health of the mind, body, heart, and spirit (for more information refer to Chapter 8).

Wellness moves beyond the physical, cognitive and social/emotional elements in a child's life and opens up the spiritual and mind-body connections. Teachers of physical education can teach about wellness and support individuals from all backgrounds by introducing the cultural teaching of the medicine wheel (Karhioo, 2009). The medicine wheel (Wenger-Nabigon, 2010) is a symbol "to help people understand things or ideas we cannot physically see" (Hart, 1999, p. 1). It is a guide for human development on the journey of life to seek balance, healing, and growth. It helps understand our lives through Aboriginal approaches and perspectives to human development. Balance, wholeness, harmony, growth, connectedness or relationships, and healing are ways to help individuals see beyond their own traditions and open themselves to understanding others as they seek to increase personal well-being (Hart, 1999).

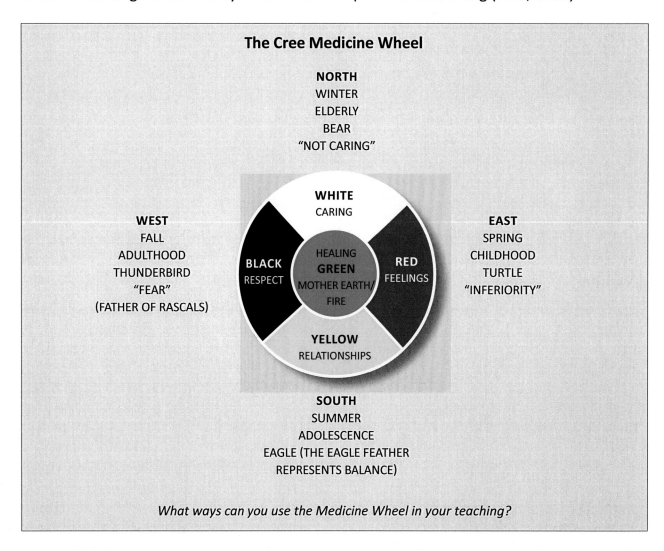

The Cree Medicine Wheel

What ways can you use the Medicine Wheel in your teaching?

It is important when *teaching for all* to reflect on the instructional strategies and teaching methods used in the physical education class. Considering changes to instruction can assist students in developing a greater understanding of the objectives and outline of a lesson.

There are many factors related to the teaching process and instruction that can support successful learning and clear instruction. Block (2007) highlighted the following instructional modifications in physical education to help all students learn, increase motivation, and have an impact on skill development. For example:

- **Teaching Style:** Direct, combined, indirect
- **Class Format and Group Size:** Small/large groups, stations, whole-class instruction
- **Pedagogical Strategies and Order of Learning:** Consider the order and how you present the materials and instruction, verbal cues, demonstrations, story boards, or picture exchange communication (PEC) systems
- **Duration of Participation and Time of the Class:** Length of activities and expected time of participation
- **Routines, Schedule, and Structure:** Consistent and clear routines for the class or layout of lesson, set the organization of instruction each day, and where you are positioning yourself to give instruction
- **Instructional Setting:** Indoors/outdoors, in the gymnasium, in the classroom before the physical education class
- **Level of Difficulty:** Control complexity of instruction, presentation of information, organization, task cards

---

Reflection Corner...

How do you ensure the physical education environment is supportive and welcoming to all students? Brainstorm ideas on how you would deal with:
- Making teams/groups
- Favouritism/ differing bodies and abilities
- Cooperation and/ or competition
- Teaching your students about diversity and inclusion

Activities

The activities you plan need to be developmentally appropriate (see Chapter 3) and also account for the range of interest and differences of students. Such an approach supports the uniqueness of each student and provides opportunities to explore new movements, be exposed to different activities they can do outside of school, and activities both you, as the physical education teacher, and students may try for the first time.

Reflection Corner...

How can you improve your physical education repertoire to include diverse cultures other than your own? Provide an example from each of the five dimensions (Chapter 4).

It is critically important that every activity in physical education be intentionally chosen to support student learning. Each should have the opportunity to participate in safe, welcoming activities. It is the teacher's responsibility to incorporate activities where students believe they are valued members of the class and, specifically, within the activities.

> **Student Voice:** *"I'm always Goal Keeper and hardly ever touch the ball. I just sit there, cold and bored, wondering why I'm there. No one seems to notice me; not the teacher, not the others; it's like I'm invisible. They just play around me, until I get in the way. I mean how am I supposed to move so quickly in my chair? There's not enough room to wheel around and by the time I get to the ball someone else has picked it up. Can't they throw it at me? It's not so bad if Clare's near me. She always passes to me if no one is standing in front of me, blocking my view, or worse still, not marking me so that I get to touch it. Should I be grateful or summat? We usually end up talking when the ball's down the other end, planning what we're gonna do after school. And then we get shouted at if we're not paying attention and the ball flies past us."*
>
> Fitzgerald & Stride, 2012, p. 289
>
> **Discussion Questions:** Now that you have been introduced to SETA, how would you ensure that students would have a different experience than above?

The Role of Individual Programming

The goal of these instructional support plans is to create meaningful and successful learning opportunities for all students, utilizing the programs of study as a starting point of instruction."
Alberta Education, 2013

Individualized programming is a requirement when addressing the learning needs of students with special needs. At times, ministries of education and school districts refer to such programming as Individual Program Plans (IPP), Individual Education Plans (IEP), or Instructional Support Plans (ISP). The essence of all of these plans is the creation of a working document or plan of action that outlines learning and teaching expectations particular to the individual student with special needs. Often, students with individualized planning have learning expectations in relation to the curriculum that are different from other students. The individualized plan should be a practical tool that outlines the modified learning expectations to support students in achieving their learning goals. They address the expectations of a student by providing accommodations and modifications for learning and instruction.

> *With regard to individualized plans, ensuring that goals and objectives are embedded within chosen activities and taught across the curriculum and environments is important to successful student learning.*
> British Columbia, 2016

The individualized plan is an effective tool for teachers to gather information about the individual student with special needs to plan and support inclusion in the class. This profile is essential for noting an individual's current strengths and levels of achievement and for addressing the specific goals for a student. The individualized plan is not at the specificity level of a daily lesson plan. It is a document that encompasses information on a student's background, potential teaching strategies, student learning goals, and resources/supports that teachers can refer to when creating their plans for learning. Therefore, individualized plans are employed to help develop appropriate learning opportunities for subject and grade specific outcomes. Unfortunately, in our experience, these plans rarely include strategies, goals or content from physical education.

> *"IPPs need to be accessible working documents to be useful for ongoing instruction and monitoring. Some teachers keep them in binders in their desks for planning lessons… teachers have access to the IPP so they can use it to plan instruction, monitor progress, and contribute to evaluating and changing goals and objectives noting observations."*
>
> Alberta Education, 2005, p. 6

Individualized Plans in Physical Education

When aiming to *teach for all*, physical education teachers can employ individualized plans to support their planning, delivery, resourcing and assessment for the inclusion of students with special needs. Therefore, individualized plans need to contain specific and broad goals, as well as short-term and long-term goals that relate to learning outcomes in the physical education class. These plans are critical to drive the planning and assessment of objectives and outcomes in the physical education curriculum for those with special needs.

As the individualized plan is created through a collaborative process involving teachers, administration, support staff, parents, and whenever possible the student, it is vitally important that this document forms the basis for all decisions regarding the expectations of learning for the student. Individualized plans assist in the strength-based and holistic understanding of the individual and needs to provide insight on SETA and based on curricular expectations. Individual plans are essential documents to ensure that teachers have a broad understanding of students with special needs entering or leaving their class; these documents should note physical, cognitive, and social/emotional attributes of students to help teachers plan physical education activities for the inclusion of the student. With this information, teachers are able to track student development and learning along with recording student progress towards set goals. Implementing individualized plans ensures that students with special needs have support and appropriate expectations set for their developmental level. The individualized plan is not an 'option' for physical education; it is an essential element for students with special needs.

Ensuring Physical Education is Part of Individualized Plans

Often when creating individualized plans, physical education specific suggestions are not documented or included. Physical education should be an important part of the plan noting instructional strategies and goal setting in relation to student strengths and challenges in the physical, social/emotional, and cognitive domains. It is also important that consideration is made of student interest, desires, likes/dislikes, and social and emotional attributes. All of this information is important for teachers to support inclusive physical education programming. Physical and Health Education (PHE) Canada stated "Physical education is an integral part of every child's education and should be included (by law)…although lack of resources may prohibit this in reality. It is important for planning and evaluation purposes that each lesson plan and task relate back to the child's IEP [/IPP] goals" (PHE Canada, 2010, p. 10). See Table 7.2.

Including Physical Education in an Individualized Plan

Table 7.2 Example Individualized Plan for Students in Physical Education	
Student Name:	School Year:
Birthdate (mm/dd/yyyy):	School Name:
Teacher:	Grade/Program:
Strengths and Interests (likes/dislikes) in relation to participation in physical activity	
Relevant Information on any Medical Condition in relation to participation in physical activity	
Student's current level of achievement in relation to participation in physical activity (is able to run, jump, and throw, does not work well in group situations, etc.)	
Necessary supports for learning (individualized equipment, support personnel direction, etc.)	
Program Goal(s) (short term & long term)	Program Goal(s) (short term & long term)
Instructional Strategies (use of peer tutor, length of activities, positioning of teacher during instruction,etc.)	
Learning Expectations and Success Indicators	
Future Review Dates	

Accommodation vs Modification: Know the Difference

An *accommodation* doesn't change the curricular expectations for a grade-level but it provides supports, teaching and assessment strategies, or considers changing equipment to be more appropriate for a student.

> **Example:** A student with cerebral palsy may be accommodated for in a game of soccer by playing "zone soccer" where students only have to navigate a particular space instead of travelling through the entire field. The learning outcomes are still the same and students can change which zone they work in but it accommodates for any mobility difficulties and still provides opportunities for successful participation.

A *modification* refers to the learning outcomes being changed; the grade-level or developmentally appropriate level for subjects is adjusted to meet a student's learning needs.

> **Example**: A student with a developmental delay may be functioning at a lower grade-level than same-aged peers. Outcomes for this student in a dance lesson could be changed to meet specific needs. The student would not necessarily be expected to perform specific dance steps in the same way as other students and they may be evaluated using a different assessment tool to ensure fair assessment of their individualized learning outcome.

Key Strategies: *Teaching for All*

Although there are many strategies a teacher can choose from to support the achievement of learning goals identified in an individualized plan, stations, peer tutors, and task cards have been recognized (Fishburne, 2005) as being particularly effective in physical education environments.

Stations

In the physical education environment, stations are places or spaces designed to help develop particular skills or movement patterns. They can be used to encourage participation of all students rather than having students sitting on the sidelines, score keeping, or being disengaged from participation in activity. Often times, the physical education class can seem to be overwhelming for teachers due to an abundance of students engaging in activities that require movement, equipment, and noise all at one time. Stations can alleviate what, at times for some teachers new to teaching physical education, seems to be too complex. They provide opportunities for more individualized participation and utilize the learning space to have multiple or progressive activities occurring at one time (Hickson, 2005).

Although stations are beneficial to all parts of the physical education program as they allow students to work on skills at their own comfort and developmental level, they are especially effective when working with individualized plans. Stations provide choice and variety so students with special needs can work at their own pace with curriculum modifications or lesson accommodations. Students are still included in the activities physically, socially, and cognitively, but meet the learning outcomes established in the individualized plan.

How to design and to use stations in your class: A station should be designed to move from simple to complex progressions of movement skills, allow for variety and choice, and support individualized plans. Figure 7.1 illustrates considerations for the SETA when utilizing stations in a physical education class.

Peer Tutors

Students with special needs often work well in pairs or smaller ratios for instructional and support purposes. Lieberman and Houston-Wilson (2002) suggested that peer tutors are often used to support and enhance the learning experience for students with special needs. Peer tutoring "...is considered the most widely known peer-assisted learning method in which specific role-taking is used" (p. 43), one peer has the role of the tutor and the other student receives assistance or guidance from the tutor (Cervantes, Lieberman, Magnesio, & Wood, 2013, p. 43). Having students act as peer tutors to assist students with special needs can be an effective way to meet learning outcomes. Specifically, they can support the improvement of physical skills, motivate and assist interaction in activities, and increase student time-on-task (Goodwin, 2001).

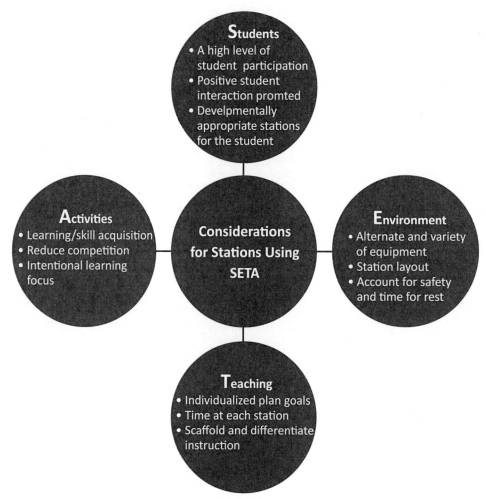

Figure 7.1 Teaching Considerations for Stations using SETA

A peer tutor is often a student selected or who has volunteered to work alongside a student with special needs. The peer tutor supports the teacher to create a safe and trusting environment for students to work and collaborate in (Cervantes, Lieberman, Magnesio, & Wood, 2013). Through direction from the teacher, the peer tutor can assist and support implementing individualized plans and developmentally appropriate activities/movement. It is important to remember that the peer tutors would also be working on their skill development, and, when necessary, take on a leadership and assistant role with instruction, demonstration, etc. for the student with special needs.

Peer tutors help provide direction for particular students, increase visual demonstrations, deliver social and communication opportunities, and encourage positive relationships or interactions and attitudes of students in the class. The role of the peer tutor may vary based on the needs of the student with special needs, the physical activity or activity dimension, and the location of the physical education class. The peer tutor's role often includes being empathetic and encouraging, providing feedback, and assuming a leadership role (Lieberman & Houston-Wilson, 2002).

There are many benefits to having peer tutors. With increasingly large class sizes and minimal support for teachers in physical education, peer tutoring is an effective tool to assist students with special needs. One-on-one instruction and a chance to practice skills with a peer foster independence for students with special needs. This also allows the teacher to check-in with multiple sets of students and different groups without having to focus all of the attention on one student; peer tutors provide support and can liaise with the teacher allowing the teacher to distribute attention across the whole class.

How to effectively utilize peer tutors in your class:
- Decide on students that would work well together and be supportive to others
- Provide peer tutor *training*, which should include: clear expectations, awareness of student interests and needs, communication techniques, instructional strategies, demonstrations and scenarios, etc.
- Encourage relationship building and social interaction
- Reinforce learning objectives and skill acquisition or progressions
- Provide feedback and maintain consistent communication with tutor and student

Task Cards

Task cards are instructional tools that are often a portable card or piece of paper that combines instructions on how to perform a skill or execute a mission with a photograph or visual to complement the instructions (Iserbyt & Byra, 2013). Task cards are used frequently in other subjects so students in PE will recognize their use and process. They supplement instruction and reinforce activities to students. They allow students to focus on a particular learning experience and they can be implemented as warm-ups, stations, circuits, individual or group work, etc. Task cards are helpful in physical education because they can be used multiple times and for various purposes such as visual supports, instructions, or demonstrations. They can also be used as a progressive and sequencing strategy such as breaking down a skill into sequential steps. Iserbyt and Byra (2013) also note, "...they can help the teacher in addressing several motor, cognitive, and social goals in a progressive way" (p. 26).

The purpose of using task cards is to promote independent study or exploration of information. They support differentiated instruction and allow for opportunities of progression at individual levels (Fishburne, 2005). The tasks can be set up differently to differentiate for students and cater to developmentally appropriate activities that may be individualized such as having different card levels or sequences students are required to follow. Task cards also encourage students to be accountable and responsible for their work and get assistance while the teacher is able to circulate throughout the learning environment (Fishburne, 2005). They can also be used for individual, pair, or small group work, which allows for leadership, tutoring opportunities, and collaboration. Using task cards as instructional tools in physical education is beneficial because students are often familiar with this instructional method from their classroom experiences. Task cards are a best practice strategy in the classroom and demonstrate effective teaching, but they are often forgotten about in physical education.

How to design and use task cards in your class:
- Pre-plan and create appropriate task cards that organize topics, themes, skills, and content progression

- Identify the equipment needed to support the learning task identified on the card.
- Ensure that cards require a level of creative input to maintain student interest
- Consider student input into design and content of task cards
- Include modified activities for the learning needs and developmental levels on each card to address the individual abilities of the students in the class

Station # 1: Kicking	Station # 2: Jumping	Station #3: Shapes
1. Choose a ball that you want to kick 2. Try using different parts of your feet to kick the ball towards the wall 3. Find 3 different ways that you like to kick the ball 4. Share with someone else what you can do	1. Choose a line on the floor or a jump rope to work with 2. How many times can you jump over the line or the jump rope without stopping 3. Are there different ways you can jump over the line or jump rope? 4. Share with someone else what you can do	1. Use your whole body to make the 1st letter of your name! 2. Can you make the 1st letter of someone else's name? 3. With a partner can you make a shape such as a square, circle or triangle?

Tables 7.3, 7.4, 7.5, 7.6, and 7.7 provide a number of examples of experiences, activities, or skills in the physical education dimensions that are important to practice and implement in order to support all students' development.

Table 7.3 Using Physical Education Dimensions to Support all Developmental Levels
Individual Activities
Examples of Movement Domain Benefits: • **Physical:** Individual needs and progressions are targeted that allow students to work at their own pace and level while establishing fundamental movement skills or fitness skills. • **Cognitive:** Explore activities that help students work on individual movements or skills. These activities can be taught to help students participate outside of school. • **Social/Emotional:** Personal goal setting and introducing students to activities that engage and interest them specifically that they can choose to participate in outside of PE class.
A specific example connecting to the Physical Domain: • Some individuals with Down Syndrome are very flexible because they experience something called low muscle tone (relaxed muscles and loose joints that can lead to poor posture and prone to injury). In this case, some individuals need to work on gross motor movements and fitness skills to ensure they don't injure themselves. • Teaching how to properly perform fitness skills and stretching (skipping, yoga, upper/lower body strength exercises, etc.) supports students' physical development. • Consider setting up individual fitness stations. At these stations, allow students to work at their own pace, focus on skills that you know will assist students' personal development (how to stretch properly without over stretching), and travel to stations to guide students with more one-on-one instruction.

Dance Education

Examples of Movement Domain Benefits:

- **Physical:** Rhythm, patterns, creative and free exploration of body actions/parts, and other fundamental movement skills.
- **Cognitive:** Explore activities that help students work on movements or skills that assist them in leading healthy active lives. These activities can be taught properly to help students participate outside of school.
- **Social/Emotional:** Interaction and collaboration with others and builds self-confidence to move in front and with others.

A specific example connecting to Social/Emotional Domain:

- Being in a social setting, a loud chaotic environment, and in close quarters with other students can be overwhelming for some students. Some individuals with high anxiety or Attention-Deficit Hyperactivity Disorder (ADHD) get distracted and act out in different ways. Being in a dance class with music on and movement to particular steps can also get students off track or create a lack of focus.

- Teaching a social dance or folk dance that starts with no music and then progresses to allow students to clap or create their own beat can help keep more students on track and engaged. This helps students with motivation, to learn the steps, to work with or beside other students, and to still maintain focus and use up energy.

- Examples of dances that could support attention and anxiety challenges are folk dances like The Jiffy Mixer (involves simple movements with basic steps like jumping, walking, moving forward and backwards: http://activeafterschool.ca/activities/jiffy-mixer-dance). These can be done in a circle keeping attention on one place or a partner. Students can have someone to follow and help them keep on time with the steps. These dances involve repetitive basic movements that allow students to interact with each other during the activity. They ensure that everyone is included in the space and encourage students to interact socially and work in small groups. They can also be done in one large group together as a class.

Educational Gymnastics

Examples of Movement Domain Benefits:

- **Physical:** Locomotion, gross motor movement, balance and stability, body/spatial awareness rotations, transferring weight, and other fundamental movement skills.
- **Cognitive:** Exploring patterns, how to manipulate objects, navigating obstacles such as benches or surfaces like mats, and combining movements together (example: how to take off and land).
- **Social/Emotional:** Collaboration with others on group sequences, individual opportunities to work on Dominant Movement Patterns for self-confidence and self-esteem

A specific example connecting to the Physical Domain:

- Students encounter many physical barriers or spatial obstacles on a daily basis. It is really important to incorporate times to practice these skills in physical education so students can navigate these issues when they come across them. A student with Cerebral Palsy may use a mobility aid or equipment for support with locomotion (e.g., orthotic devices, walkers, standers, wheelchairs, canes).
- Practicing how to navigate obstacles in an obstacle course could help all students practice travelling through the physical spaces we encounter on a daily basis such as curbs and steps, slippery or icy surfaces, being on different terrain (e.g., pavement, grass, sand). Mimicking or implementing obstacle courses in gymnastics allows individuals to experience how to navigate similar spaces properly and effectively. You could set up a few different obstacle courses for students to try out and have different types of challenges for different students.
- Students with mobility aids should try to go over, under, around, and through different pathways. They could even work towards travelling forwards, backwards, and sideways through the same course to challenge themselves and work on locomotion, balance, stability, weight transfer, and spatial awareness at the same time.

Table 7.6 Using Physical Education Dimensions to Support all Developmental Levels

Games Skills

Examples of Movement Domain Benefits:

- **Physical:** Sending, receiving, retaining, object manipulation, locomotion, and other fundamental movement skills.
- **Cognitive:** Tactics, strategies, spatial awareness, and rules of activities.
- **Social/Emotional:** Teamwork, leadership, cooperation, and learning about healthy competition.

A specific example connecting to the Cognitive Domain:

- Games in physical education often include a lot of strategies, tactics, and rules. It is important to be progressive in nature when teaching games. Start with simple rules first, then make them more complex.
- Students in your class will not all be at the same developmental level cognitively. You may have to modify strategies or rules in your activities to ensure all students are included in game-type situations. If you want to teach the rules and play a game of handball to division 2 students (grades 4-6), but you have a student with a learning disability that affects cognitive processing of oral information, you might want to consider small-sided games first and introduce a new rule once all students have got the basics down. This would require you to set up groups you know students work well with. You can provide whole class instruction, but be sure to give one-to-one or small group instruction again with a demonstration. The rules can also be written on the board for students to refer back to.
- Example: Start in pairs travelling in a space passing back and forth to a goal line or end target. Now have students pause/freeze when they have no ball, their partner's role is to travel 3 steps, and then the person in possession of the ball will make a pass to their partner– repeat this until they understand they can't move when they have the ball. Then have groups of 4 doing the same passing back and forth all in the same direction to a goal line, but the student who has the ball can't move. Now have students play keep away 2 vs. 2. Once they have that down, students then can have a target to aim at in keep away in a small space. Continue adding rules, a bigger space, more individuals, etc. until you progress up to the full game. Also continue to provide demonstrations and simple instructions.

Table 7.7 Using Physical Education Dimensions to Support all Developmental Levels

Alternative Environments

Examples of Movement Domain Benefits:

- **Physical:** Fundamental movement skills, body and spatial awareness, balance and stability, and integration with various physical environments (land, ice, snow, water, etc.).
- **Cognitive:** Safety, how to be active in the community, exploring creativity and problem-solving opportunities.
- **Social/Emotional:** Cooperation, self-awareness, and promotes engagement with senses.

A specific example connecting to the Social/Emotional Domain:

- Students with Autism may sometimes have social anxiety and navigating spaces, obstacles in the environment, conversations, and crowds can be challenging tasks. Having opportunities to explore the outdoors and different settings helps them experience and practice life skills such as interacting with others and asking someone to play at the park, finding a bathroom or asking where the bathroom is located at the local pool, or even navigating public transit.
- You could begin by taking your students outside and having them do activities that incorporate the senses. Feel, smell, see, and hear different things in the environment. Students can discuss these in pairs, draw, or write things in a journal. You could then have them focus on one sense in that environment and develop self-awareness.
- An example could be if they see the clouds are starting to change colour to become a bit darker, students could ask a peer if they know what the weather forecast is, if they know the nearest shelter in case of a storm, or describe the clouds and what they see. This type of activity allows students to engage with others, self-discover, incorporate experience cross-curricular learning, while emotionally engaging in environments and activities that they will have to navigate themselves in everyday life.

Reflection Corner...

Considering all five of the activity dimensions, what kind of changes can a teacher make to an activity to ensure teaching for all occurs? For example, think of size or height of targets in a games lesson, number of participants in a dance, the time spent at a gymnastics station, the type and variety of equipment used for a track and field lesson, etc.

Case Study

Last year, Stephanie received a contract position half way through the school year and was teaching a Grade 1 class for the first time. She had 25 students with 3 students who had substantial learning needs. One of her students was non-verbal, one had behavioural issues, and the third was a visually impaired (legally blind) student. The previous teacher told her that in PE they were working on throwing and catching skills. Seeing as this was where the previous teacher left off, this is where she was going to start.

How would you approach teaching this PE class?

1. What type of lessons or activities would you develop and implement to work on throwing and catching skills?
2. What types of accommodations and modifications might you need to make or consider?
3. While thinking about SETA, discuss the steps to planning and supporting for inclusion in your class.
4. What observations or notes could you make to put in an individualized plan for the teacher working with these students next year?

Measuring Success

Some ideas for criteria on how you can measure successful inclusion in your physical education program and class include:

- Individualized plan goals and outcomes
- A change in performance to indicate that skill level improvement and learning occurred
- Level of participation
- Extent of integration with and from other students
- Participation of child in other programs – intramurals, community programs
- Beneficial experiences for all class members
- Understanding and acceptance
- Happiness, enjoyment during class – smiles!

Conclusion

Teaching for all means planning for, supporting, and celebrating the diversity and uniqueness of each student in your physical education class. It is our professional and personal responsibility to provide opportunities for all students to achieve success and feel welcome in our teaching environments. Physical education is about teaching to the students and strengths for a holistic program that develops the physical, social/emotional, and cognitive domains of each student.

Throughout this chapter, the importance of *teaching for all* has been emphasized. It is hoped that an understanding of how teachers can create such an environment has been established.

Checking for Understanding

I can:

- Understand the necessity for and embracing *teaching for all* in my physical education class
- Focus on students' strengths
- Create a holistic PE program considering the students, environment, teaching practices, and activities (SETA)
- Teach activities that encourage participation by all and attend to the varied needs of students in my physical education class
- Support my students and plan strategies that teach to the curriculum and consider diversity and inclusion in the physical education environment
- Develop an individualized plan for students in my physical education class
- Measure the success and recognize the benefits of including all students in my physical education class

Chapter 8

Health Literacy and Comprehensive School Health

To keep the body in good health is a duty...otherwise we shall not be able to keep our mind strong and clear.
Buddha

Introduction: Why Should Schools Focus on Student Health?

A school's core mission is to teach students academic knowledge, cognitive and physical skill development. However, it has become understood that schools cannot achieve this if their students are not healthy (Story et al., 2009). Health and education are interdependent. Individuals who are well educated have better health and well-being (Bradley & Greene, 2013) and those who have better health have high academic achievement (Suhrche & de Paz Nieves, 2011). This suggests that schools also need to teach the knowledge and skills needed to promote their own emotional, mental, and physical health (Bonell et al., 2014). But how can educators, administrators, and other school officials plan for quality health programming? How can health be promoted within an educational environment? The purpose of this chapter is to introduce the concept of health literacy and examine ways to effectively promote health within school settings. By the end of this chapter, we hope you will:

- Understand the concept of health literacy and the issues faced in Canada
- Realize the need for and value of health education and curriculum implementation in schools
- Be introduced to the Comprehensive School Health framework
- Understand how Comprehensive School Health programming can be implemented into existing school practices including physical education

Health Literacy

According to the Canadian Public Health Agency of Canada (2016), health literacy is a way in which an individual can access, comprehend, evaluate, and communicate information to disseminate, sustain, and improve health in settings throughout life. Similarly, the Canadian Council on Learning (2007) suggested that health literacy refers to the degree that individuals can access and use health information for healthy decision-making and to maintain their basic health. In agreement, Berg, Hickson, and Fishburne (2010) also contended that when a person has developed a sound foundation of health literacy they will have the skills to gather, understand, and act upon information and knowledge to improve their health and well-being.

What are the Benefits of Health Literacy?

Similar to physical literacy, the knowledge, skills, and attitudes gained through the development of health literacy can benefit children and youth throughout the life course. It can assist them to thrive and navigate their pathway in a world that seems to constantly present new challenges. Importantly, it can also lead them to not only adopt healthy active lifestyles for themselves, but also promote the advantages of healthy living to their peers and others around them (OPHEA, 2010).

The effective implementation of programming that develops health literacy assists children and youth to be exposed to not only the immediate effects of healthy decision-making, but also the potential of a lifetime of increased well-being. One might further contend that the development of health literacy can actually empower children and youth and provide them with the skills to take control of their well-being. As the children and youth of today will become the adult backbone of our communities of tomorrow, developing health literacy can help to create healthy communities in the future.

Another important benefit of health literacy is the impact it can have on the overall education of children and youth. At all ages, there is evidence that health and learning are closely intertwined. Research has illustrated that the higher a person's attained level of education is, the better the person's health (Canadian Council on Learning, 2007). The Canadian Council on Learning also suggested that researchers and policy-makers in the health and education fields regard health literacy as a critical link to address health disparities between different population groups. As well, health literacy is a sound predictor of overall population health. Health literacy can provide keys to future success for children and youth. When provided with effective learning strategies, children and youth can understand the linkages between what they learn and what they experience in their day-to-day lives. Change can then begin to occur in their decisions and promote actions to follow a healthy, active lifestyle.

Why is Health Education Important?

Issues in Canada

Over the past century, common diseases that led to disability or early death have been virtually eliminated. However, despite advances in the treatment of childhood disease, new challenges have risen. The number of overweight and obese children in Canada has reached epidemic levels. At the same time, evidence indicates that significant numbers of young people are experiencing mental health issues. Evidence also suggests the prevalence of diseases such as Type II diabetes, cancer, and heart disease will reach levels previously unheard of if left unchecked. Berg, Hickson, Bradford, and Fishburne (2017) provide the following overview of risk behaviours children and youth in Canada are facing.

Physical Inactivity
- Between 1980 and 2005, the Canadian rates of obesity in children and youth tripled (Tjepkema & Shield, 2005)
- Children and youth between 11-15 years old in Canada spend each day an average of 2 hours and 24 minutes playing sedentary video games (Public Health Agency of Canada, 2015)

- Since 2011, the ParticipACTION report card indicates that very few children and youth in Canada receive at least 60 minutes of moderate to vigorous intensity physical activity each day (ParticipACTION, 2016)

Nutrition

- Sugar sweetened beverage consumption is believed to contribute significantly to the development of obesity and has been associated with increased risk of coronary heart disease (De Koning, Vasanti, Malik et al., 2012; Woodward Loeps, Cao, & Ritchie, 2011)
- 1 in 5 children in Canada have an energy intake that exceeds their energy needs (Health Canada, 2012)
- According to the Heart and Stroke Foundation, schools can support a healthy, balanced diet for students by improving both food literacy and access to appropriate food choices (Heart & Stroke Foundation, 2016)

Mental Health

- The total number of 12-19 year old in Canada at risk for developing depression is a staggering 3.2 million (Canadian Mental Health Association, 2016)
- Surpassed only by injuries, mental disorders in youth are ranked as the second highest hospital care expenditure in Canada (Canadian Mental Health Association, 2016)
- Approximately 5% of male youth and 12% of female youth have experienced a major depressive episode (Canadian Mental Health Association, 2016)

Sleep Deprivation

- Sleep is an important component of healthy development and necessary for overall health (ParticipACTION, 2016)
- Sleep deprivation is common in contemporary society with children and youth sleeping less than those previously (ParticipACTION, 2016)
- 12% of 5-13 year olds have difficulty staying awake during normal waking hours (Statistics Canada, 2012-2013)

Substance Abuse

- Positive family relationships, school connectedness, and the presence of caring adults in the community can serve as emotional support and role models in preventing early onset of substance use (Public Health Agency of Canada, 2015)
- Although there is evidence of a decline in cigarette smoking among adolescents, there is a concern with wide spread availability of e-cigarettes and whether this will erase the gains made in tobacco prevention (Public Health Agency of Canada, 2015)
- Although not frequent, the use of over-the-counter medications has become more common among adolescents (Public Health Agency of Canada, 2015)

Injury

- 46% of boys and 38% of girls in grade 6 report that they sustained an injury requiring medical treatment, and 19% of boys and 16% of girls in grade 6 also report sustaining one or more injuries requiring significant medical treatment (cast, stitches, surgery, overnight hospital stay) (Public Health Agency of Canada, 2015)

- Only 44% of boys and 45% of girls in grade 8 report wearing a bicycle helmet when cycling (Public Health Agency of Canada, 2015)
- 40% of all head injuries in children and youth treated in emergency departments are sustained during sport and recreation activities (Canadian Centre for Ethics in Sport, 2016)

Bullying

- Bullying puts young people at immediate and long term risk for emotional, behavioural, and relationship issues (Public Health Agency of Canada, 2015)
- Any participation in bullying increases risk of suicidal thoughts in youth (Statistics Canada, 2015)
- The prevalence of youth being victimized at least twice a week has increased significantly from 2006 to 2014 (Public Health Agency of Canada, 2015)

Developing an effective approach for the delivery of health programming that improves health literacy in children and youth should be a high priority for Canada. It is essential that opportunities be provided to children and youth to develop the knowledge, skills, and attitudes to develop healthy lifestyles (Berg et al., 2017).

The Health Curriculum

Across Canada, health education curriculum documents vary. Four provinces (British Columbia, Manitoba, Ontario, Quebec) have combined health with their physical education programming, while the other six have distinct, separate health education programs. Regardless of a combined *health and physical education* program or a 'stand-alone' *health education* curriculum, the aims and goals, curricular elements, and suggested activities and ideas for the health curriculum outcomes within each province are similar across the country. Generally, students are expected to develop and understand the skills and competencies necessary to improve health, make informed decisions based on health-related knowledge, and apply the knowledge and decision-making to improve personal health as well as the health and well-being of others.

Teaching 'Tips' for Health Education

In order to assist teachers with the different types of learning styles among children and

youth, a variety of instructional strategies are available. Differentiation can help achieve desired learning outcomes associated with the health and wellness education of children and youth. Therefore, it is important that teachers recognize the strengths and weaknesses of different strategies to select appropriate tasks and create effective learning environments. Berg et al. (2017) have identified the following instructional strategies to assist in the delivery of health and wellness education.

- **Creating and developing cooperative learning environments**

  Promotes understanding and respect for self and others
  Encourages responsibility and recognition of choices and actions

- **Creating discussion circles**

  Provides a forum for expressing and exploring ideas and thoughts
  Allows for discussion in a controlled setting

- **Fostering independent learning**

  Allows for the exploration of topical issues of interest
  Takes learning from the classroom to the home and beyond

- **Providing opportunities for journal writing**

  Allows for the expression of thoughts, opinions, and reflections in a private manner
  Promotes opportunities for teachers to guide thinking or present ideas for thought

- **Role playing**

  Provides opportunities to practice and act out new skills in a safe environment
  Enables students to recognize potential solutions to issues

- **Utilizing peer educators**

  At times, peers are more effective in the delivery of material than adults.
  Provide leadership opportunities for the peer educators

- **Using technology**

  Allows students to gather information from a variety of sources
  Promotes learning experiences that may not be readily available in day-to-day situations.

- **Student presentations**

  Allows students to gather and demonstrate their understanding on a wide variety of topics
  Allows for personal interest or chosen topics to be pursued

- **Accessing expertise**

  Allows for well-qualified community resource people to be invited to present to students
  Supplements school-based programming

- **Field trips**

  Brings relevancy to school-based learning
  Connects school and community

Adapted from Berg et al. (2017)

Comprehensive School Health (CSH)

Research evidence has identified the most effective way to impact health and wellness behaviours in children and youth, which is through school programming that is comprehensive in nature (Joint Consortium for School Health, 2010). As a result, the agreed upon view is that a 'comprehensive' approach to health is needed. This has led to the adoption of the term *Comprehensive School Health* (CSH). It is widely accepted that CSH supports student learning while, simultaneously, addresses school health in a planned, integrated, and holistic manner

(Berg et al., 2017). It is not just about what happens in the classroom. Rather, it encompasses the whole school community, school environment, and school policy with actions that provide a strong foundation for comprehensive school health. The Pan-Canadian Joint Consortium for School Health (JCSH) represents the interest of Health and Education provincial government ministries across Canada and, in describing CSH, has categorized the components into the 'pillars' of: Social and Physical Environment, Teaching and Learning, Healthy School Policy, and Partnerships and Services. Figure 8.1 provides an overview of those four pillars:

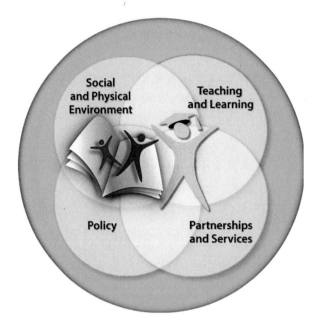

Figure 8.1 Pillars of Comprehensive School Health (JCSH, 2010)

Social and Physical Environment includes the quality of the relationships among and between staff and students in the school, the emotional well-being of students and the influence of relationships with families and the wider community. The physical environment includes the buildings, grounds, play space, and equipment in and surrounding the school, and basic amenities such as sanitation and air cleanliness.

Teaching and Learning refers to the resources, activities, and provincial/territorial curriculum where students gain age-appropriate knowledge and experiences while helping build the skills necessary to become health literate.

Healthy School Policy addresses the management practices, decision-making processes, rules, procedures, and policies at all levels that promote health and well-being, and shape a respectful, welcoming, and caring school environment.

Partnerships and Services are considered to be the connections between the school and students' families and the supportive working relationships within schools (staff and students), between schools, and between schools and other community organizations and representative groups. The importance of health, education, and other sectors working together to advance school health is recognized along with community and school-based services that support and promote student and staff health and well-being (Adapted from JCSH, 2010).

Harmonized action in all four pillars of the CSH framework will support students to be healthy, productive members of society who realize their full potential as learners (JCSH, 2010). Table 8.1 displays examples of actions within each pillar of the CSH framework, to show practical use of how the model has been implemented into Canadian schools.

Table 8.1 Examples of Actions Within CSH Pillars	
CSH Pillar	**Example Actions**
Social and Physical Environment	• Create a positive learning environment within physical education classes that teaches students about fair play, equity, respect for diversity, sensitivity for individual requirements and needs, leadership role opportunities, and to be socially responsible citizens. • Incorporate a variety of physical environments in physical education lessons, such as: outdoor space, fields, trails, schoolyard, and playgrounds.
Teaching and Learning	• Provide a health education program that promotes commitment to healthy choices and behaviours and allows for health promotion discussions in the classroom. Listen and validate student perspectives and incorporate culturally relevant themes. • Provide a quality daily physical education program that ensures all students have the opportunity to develop the knowledge, skills, and habits needed to lead an active, healthy lifestyle. • Utilize cross-curricular learning, by incorporating physical activity and health education in all subject areas.
Partnership and Services	• Work together with, and establish relationships between, health and education sectors. • In planning and organizing physical education and health education programs, schools should establish partnerships with community organizations and facilities to provide students with additional experiences and opportunities for physical activity and healthy living. • Explore partnerships with a local restaurant or food supplier to look at offering healthy meals at a reduced cost to students.

Comprehensive School Health
- Recognizes that healthy young people learn better and achieve more
- Understands that schools can directly influence students' health and behaviours
- Encourages healthy lifestyle choices, and promotes students' health and well-being
- Incorporates health into all aspects of school and learning
- Links health and education issues and systems
- Needs the participation and support of families and the community at large

JCSH, 2010

Congruent Frameworks

Many provinces/territories across Canada use other titles for CSH (e.g., Health Promoting Schools, Healthy Schools, Healthy School Communities) and the components of the framework may have been given different labels and expressed in different ways (Bassett-Gunter, Yessis, Manske, & Gleddie, 2015). This is because many organizations work with schools to support and implement health promotion and have developed their own versions that meet the needs of their particular geographical context (Gleddie, 2010). Regardless of the framework's title or component's labels, each framework relies on a multi-component approach to establish a healthy school community by bringing together a wide range of activities to address school health and student well-being. These strategies for health promotion share the connecting thread of a whole-school approach and recognition that all aspects of the life of the school

JCSH	PHE Canada	Word Health Organization
Social and Physical Environment Teaching and Learning Healthy School Policy Partnerships and Services	Education: Supporting a culture of learning for all school community members including wellness related programs for students and health promotion learning opportunities for teachers, staff and parents. Everyone: Collaborating in a meaningful way with the people involved in the everyday life of the school and equal and inclusive opportunities for everyone to make healthy choices. Environment: Fostering a safe social and physical environment in the school, home and community, implementing policies that enable healthy active lifestyles and cultivating a place where everyone knows they belong. Evidence: Collaboratively identifying goals, planning for action and gathering information to indicate the effectiveness of actions to support healthy active lifestyles throughout the school community	Foster health and learning with all the measures at its disposal. Engages health and education officials, teachers, teachers' unions, students, parents, health providers and community leaders in efforts to make the school a healthy place. Strives to provide a healthy environment, school health education, and school health services along with school/community projects and outreach; health promotion programs for staff; nutrition and food safety programs; opportunities for physical education and recreation; and programs for counseling, social support and mental health promotion. Implements policies and practices that respect an individual's well-being and dignity, provide multiple opportunities for success and acknowledge good efforts and intentions as well as personal achievements. Strives to improve the health of school personnel, families and community members as well as pupils; and works with community leaders to help them understand how the community contributes to or undermines, health and education.

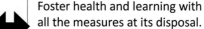

Figure 8.2 CSH frameworks

community are potentially important in the promotion of health. Consider the previous three interpretations of the CSH framework (Figure 8.2, adapted from Gleddie, 2010). The first box is the CSH framework from the JCSH. The second box describes the four components of the Health Promoting Schools framework adopted by PHE Canada. The third box contains the elements of HPS as interpreted by the World Health Organization.

As you will notice, the frameworks are essentially the same with basic elements and guiding principles of a CSH framework spanning across all three frameworks. It is important to note, none of these frameworks are wrong, they represent the use of different language and the flexibility of the model (Gleddie, 2010).

Reflection Corner...

CSH Framework in Canada

Three interpretations of the CSH framework were briefly reviewed.

- What similarities are present across all three frameworks?
- What are some of the differences?
- Why is it important to be able to adapt and alter the CSH framework?

Why Do We Need CSH?

Schools are uniquely positioned to promote health and impact short- and long-term knowledge and behaviours of young people (WHO, 1997). Students spend approximately half their waking hours in schools and no other institution has as much continuous and intensive contact with students during the first decades of life. Since school programs have near universal enrolment and are delivered at no or little cost to families, students from diverse ethnic and socioeconomic backgrounds can be reached (Cale & Harris, 2013; Story, 1999; Story, Nanney, & Schwartz, 2009). In addition, schools are equipped with the facilities (e.g., gymnasiums, playing fields), programs (e.g., physical education, health education), and the necessary personnel (e.g., subject area lead teachers, school counselor) to effectively promote health and/or prevent health issues (Story, 1999).

Physical education and health education provide opportunities for students to learn about how to lead an active, healthy lifestyle, but knowledge gained in curricular programs can either be reinforced and supported or undermined by what happens outside the classroom walls. For example, students could learn about the benefits of engaging in physical activity, but this may be counteracted by the lack of opportunities available to them within their school. Student behaviour change requires a more comprehensive approach that involves teachers, parents, and community stakeholders and includes supportive policies, programs, and environments (Veugelers & Fritzgerald, 2005; Veugelers & Schwartz, 2010). CSH strives to provide a link between health and education outcomes, emphasizing a partnership between the health and education sectors, engagement of young people, their families, and their communities, and the need to tailor initiatives to the strengths and needs of the respective school environments.

CSH in Canada: The Evidence

There is research evidence to support the notion that CSH frameworks have a positive impact on student health and education outcomes (Murray, Low, Hollis, Cross, & Davis, 2007; Veugelers & Swartz, 2010; Kriemer et al., 2011; Pardo et al., 2013). Canadian schools have used the CSH framework to focus on health issues of physical inactivity, eating behaviours, obesity, mental health, bullying, and substance abuse. For example, Action Schools! BC is a CSH program in British Columbia aimed to improve the physical activity and eating behaviours of children and youth. Students attending schools addressing Action Schools! BC showed increases in physical activity levels, fruit and vegetable consumption, and variety, and cardiovascular fitness (Naylor, Macdonald, Warburton, Reed, & McKay, 2008; Reed, Warburton, Macdonald, Naylor, and McKay, 2008). In a similar manner, the Alberta Project Promoting active Living and healthy Eating (APPLE Schools) has shown that students who attend APPLE Schools were more physically active, ate more fruits and vegetables, consumed fewer calories, and were less likely to be obese (Fung et al., 2012). Additionally, the CSH framework has demonstrated effectiveness in sustaining physical activity levels as students progress through their school years. For example, Action Schools! BC, which is an elementary school program, had a positive influence on high school students' physical activity behaviours. Students who attended Action Schools! BC in elementary or middle school, when compared to students who did not attend an Action Schools! BC, reported more physical activity minutes/day in grade 10 (McLean, 2012). This provides support for the long-term influence of a CSH framework by demonstrating that opportunity for students to experience a physically active school culture during their elementary years influences their physical activity behaviours in high school (McLean, 2012). It is essential to recognize the importance of continuing CSH programs at the high school level (Sulz & Gibbons, 2016) to maintain the improvements in physical activity levels, particularly during the adolescent years when activity levels typically decline (Hyde, Maher, & Elavsky, 2013; Long et al., 2013).

Fundamental Principals of the CSH Approach

Keeping in mind the complexity of a school community (Keshavarz, Nutbeam, Rowling, & Khavarpour, 2010; Veugelers & Schwartz, 2010) and the ability of the CSH framework to be adapted and tailored to a school's specific needs, it is important to consider several common key principles necessary for a successful CSH program. Bassett-Gunter et al. (2015) discussed five fundamental principles of a healthy school community approach:

- **Whole School Approach:** A whole school approach is important as many factors and influences impact student health behaviours including, the school (e.g., policy, curricula, playgrounds), home (e.g., family), and community (e.g., physical infrastructure, programming) environments. The involvement and cohesion of key members within these environments are needed to employ the CSH framework. This includes: school principals, teachers, students, parents, and other members of the school community.

- **Education and Health Synergy:** Within a CSH framework, education and health are both integral in the implementation of policies, practices, and actions to support healthy school communities. This highlights the importance of the cooperation and collaboration between health and education sectors to ease the implementation of a CSH framework. At times, health and education sectors have incongruent priorities creating tension and lack of cooperation. In order to achieve effective implementation, sectors must work together through joint planning and coordination policies and resources (e.g., funding, time). In doing so, both health and education can achieve optimal outcomes, reduce duplication of efforts to enhance student well-being, and decrease gaps in existing policies and practices.

- **Leadership Team/Champion**: An individual champion or a team of individuals to help guide and develop capacity for a CSH framework is essential to successful implementation. Some provinces and jurisdictions employ dedicated staff within schools to act as champions for CSH framework and others may engage a team of individuals to aid in facilitating the actions of a CSH framework. The leader or team should be individuals who strongly value a healthy school community approach and should include teaching and non-teaching staff, students, parents, and community partners from stakeholder groups.

- **Assessment, Planning, and Evaluation:** An effective CSH framework requires thoughtful planning and careful assessment of the existing school community and the identification of priority issues. To do so, school communities should assess current healthy school practices, policies, goals, structures, resources, processes, personnel, and the needs of students and staff. The development of a specific well thought-out action plan involves all stakeholders (i.e., administrators, teachers, staff, students, and community members), and should address the identified priority issues, using actions related to the four pillars of CSH.

- **Planning for Sustainability:** A CSH program is intended to be implemented over a long period of time and, as such, requires strategies to achieve sustainability. Strategies to achieve this sustainability include: creating policies at the school and district levels establishing and securing long-term commitment from sponsoring agencies, and schools should allow adequate time for changes to occur, recognize progress, and celebrate success.

Creating a CSH Program in Your School

Because there is no single right way to use the CSH framework, it will look different from school to school and the activities associated with a CSH approach will vary widely. However, process is extremely important. Below are six critical steps to help implement a CSH approach. These steps are intended as a broad implementation guideline, keeping in mind the CSH framework is adaptable to local demographics, available resources, predominant issues, community assets, and available supports (Gleddie, 2010).

Steps to Implementation (adapted from albertahealthservices.ca):

1. **Prepare:** Building a CSH program involves gaining support of school community members, identifying a health champion and/or creating a collaborative team who will develop a shared understanding of what it means to be a healthy school community.

2. **Create a Shared Vision:** Creating a shared vision involves developing a common understanding of what makes your school a *healthy school*. The vision should be created with the input of all those involved in the school community: staff, students, parents, and community members.

3. **Determine the Priority Issues:** Completing an assessment of the school community will help you to determine priority issues and to identify opportunities for improving student health and learning. The JCSH Healthy School Planner is an online tool to assess the school health environment (http://healthyschoolplanner.uwaterloo.ca)

4. **Develop an Action Plan:** Developing a clear and realistic action plan will keep the school health team focused on addressing the high priority issues identified in the school health assessment.

5. **Implement and Monitor:** Implementing the action plan begins following all of the planning in the previous steps. The school health team will want to monitor activities to ensure that what was planned is achieved on time and has the intended impact.

6. **Reflect, Evaluate, and Celebrate:** Reflecting on your work and conducting the evaluation activities described in your action plan will provide feedback to the school health team and school community about all that has been achieved. Celebrate your accomplishments!

Students Have an Integral Role in CSH Programs

- Involving students in the development of CSH programs will allow for greater alignment between student needs and preferences and program activities
- Students, who believe their preferences are considered in the program design, demonstrate higher participation in the new program
- Students should be contributing members of the School Committee responsible for developing and implementing the CSH program
- Teachers can support students' role on the School Committee by incorporating student voice into the Action Plan and allowing students to take leadership roles in the development and implementation of CSH initiatives

Gibbons & Naylor, 2007; Sulz, Gibbons, Naylor, & Wharf Higgins, 2016

Conclusion

Throughout this chapter we have discussed the benefits of health education and the importance of placing value on health education as a subject area. We have also discussed how health education goes beyond the classroom setting and that a CSH program is essential in building health literate students. As you reflect on this chapter, consider how you, as an educator, can champion a CSH approach. As well, how you can be a positive advocate for health education, so that we can have a society full of health literate children and youth.

Checking for Understanding

I Can:

- State 3 different benefits of health education for students
- Explain how the concept of health literacy is important for educators and students
- Share the value of health education as an essential part of children and youth's schooling
- Explain what CSH is and how it goes beyond health and physical education in the classroom
- State and explain the 6 steps to implementing a CSH program

---

Case Study: Implementing a CSH Program

A teacher who enjoys teaching physical education would like to start a CSH program at their school. The teacher begins to reach out to people to help with the program. This group of people will be the School Committee in charge of planning, developing, and implementing the new CSH program. This committee includes: 3 teachers, the school principal, cafeteria staff, and 2 community members. The committee has their first meeting, begins to brainstorm and discuss their vision and possible actions, and completes the Healthy School Planner.

- What are the next steps the teacher and the team should take in creating a successful CSH program at their school?
- Who else should be included on the School Committee?
- How could the teacher support a CSH model within their physical education lessons?
- What do you consider to be some of the challenges the physical education teacher and the team will face in developing and implementing a CSH program at their school?

Chapter 9
Daily Physical Activity and the School Community

The goal of Daily Physical Activity is to enhance students' physical activity levels, and is based on the belief that healthy students are more equipped to learn.

Alberta Education, 2016

Introduction

Daily Physical Activity (DPA) can offer students opportunities to participate in physical activity during the school day. Although DPA is not intended to replace physical education programming, it can promote development in several areas such as social inclusion, personal fitness, and cooperation (Fishburne & Hickson, 2005). It is important for teachers to have a deep understanding of both DPA and physical education in order to be able to clearly distinguish them from each other. Hence, it is vital that teachers understand ways to offer DPA within the school day (e.g., effective activities), while still maintaining a quality learning environment during physical education time.

Our hope is that, by the end of this chapter, you will:
- Understand the rationale behind DPA
- Understand the benefits of DPA
- Recognize and understand the differences and similarities between DPA and physical education
- Become comfortable with activity ideas for successful DPA implementation
- Understand how school clubs, intramural programming, and activity theme days can support DPA and physical education
- Know some ways to reflect on DPA experiences

Importance of Physical Activity

For health benefits, it is recommended that children and youth get at least 60 minutes of moderate-to vigorous physical activity (MVPA) every day (Tremblay, et al., 2016; WHO, 2016). As the ParticipACTION (2016) Report Card has shown yearly since 2011, a low percentage of children and youth in Canada actually meet this recommendation. Therefore, questions continue to be raised about how we can create a better environment for physical activity in our schools.

Emerging research highlights the importance of physical activity for healthy brain development, which can lead to improved learning and academic outcomes. For example, children who are physically active for as little as 20 minutes daily have been found to have more active brains, greater attention in the classroom (Hillman et al., 2009), and higher standardized test results (Donnelly & Lambourne, 2011). Additionally, grade 2 and 3 students who participated in math and language learning lessons that involved physical activity experienced greater academic gains in those particular subject areas compared to students who did not participate in these types of physically active lessons (Mullender-Wijnsma et al., 2016).

Quick Facts: Physical Activity and Children and Youth in Canada
- Physical activity helps children fall asleep quicker (ParticipACTION, 2016)
- 9% of 5 – 17 year olds accumulate at least 60 minutes of moderate-to-vigorous-intensity physical activity per day (ParticipACTION, 2016)
- 3 out of 5 school-aged children in Canada (ages 5 – 17) are not physically active enough to experience optimal growth and development (British Columbia, 2016)
- 1 out of 4 children in British Columbia (ages 2 – 17) is overweight or obese (British Columbia, 2016)
- Excessive sedentary time influences brain health in a negative manner, and may even counteract the benefits normally experienced from physical activity (Voss, Carr, Clark, & Weng, 2014)
- Physical activity assists in the development of new blood vessels and neurons and with an increase in growth factors in the brain that help with the nervous system's development, maintenance, and plasticity (i.e., ability to change/adapt) (ParticipACTION, 2016)
- Children who are not physically active enough are at a higher risk of developing chronic diseases (e.g., type 2 diabetes, high blood pressure) (Government of Canada, 2016)
- Physical activity helps in the regulation of stress responses in which the brain is involved, and increases the size of parts of the brain which are associated with the learning process, and assists in the activation of neural networks that are turned on during cognitive activities (ParticipACTION, 2016)
- Increased physical activity and reduced sedentary behaviour are associated with less depression, anxiety, and psychological distress (ParticipACTION, 2016)

Why DPA?
We know that most children and youth in Canada do not engage in enough physical activity to experience the numerous health benefits (Active Healthy Kids Canada, 2014; ParticipACTION, 2016; Tremblay et al., 2011; 2016). We also know that children spend a large part of their day at school. Therefore, it makes sense that the school environment becomes a setting that is supportive of and conducive to DPA. As well, it can be argued that an overweight and obesity epidemic does exist in Canada. Currently, more than a quarter of all children are overweight or obese (PaticipACTION, 2016). Although physical activity is not a panacea for obesity reduction, it has a wealth of benefits (see Chapter 1) and can be an excellent entry point for improving the overall health and well-being for children (and adults!). Three provinces and one territory in Canada (Alberta, British Columbia, Ontario, and the Yukon) have introduced a DPA requirement into their school systems. Canada is not alone in requiring children to be active during the school day, such requirements have also been implemented in Australia (Hickson, 2010) and are being considered in other countries (e.g., United Kingdom) as they

attempt to combat issues of inactivity levels and poor health in children and youth. While mandating 20 or 30 minutes of DPA, schools within these Canadian provinces and territory are expected to ensure that every elementary school student participates in the minimum number of minutes of DPA throughout the school day.

> *Active children and youth are healthier and learn better! Unfortunately, statistics show physical inactivity and unhealthy choices are impacting our children and youth.*
> British Columbia, 2016

According to Hickson, Robinson, Berg, & Hall (2012), implementation of DPA has not been without struggle or resistance. One particular concern has been the tension between DPA and physical education programming. Hickson (2010) contended that confusion has existed among professionals in the field, as well as by media and the general public regarding the similarities, differences, and interplay between physical education and DPA, and that several documents erroneously employ the terms interchangeably. However, generally, it is accepted that DPA should supplement and add to physical education experiences, not replace it. With the correct mindset in regards to the health and wellness of children and youth, DPA should work in tandem with physical education programming. Therefore, the following section discusses the relationship between quality physical education and DPA. It is, after all, essential for teachers to have a clear understanding of these differences and similarities.

The Relationship between Physical Education and DPA

> *Physical education programming that does not provide students with the knowledge, skills, and attitudes to lead healthy, active lifestyles will not achieve the benefits that are hoped for and presumed to occur.*
> Hickson, 2010

Physical Education: Physical Education is a curricular area designed to help students develop the attitudes, knowledge, and skills necessary for participating in active, healthy living; to develop a student's physical literacy. As such, physical education programming is a critical component of the whole school experience. When physical education is taught in an effective manner, students are exposed to learning that encompasses an array of carefully planned learning experiences that offer breadth and variety (e.g., games, dance, individual activities, etc.). When engaged in a physical education learning environment, students participate in developmentally appropriate activities which include maximum participation opportunities and safety. According to Fishburne and Hickson (2005), in physical education, students with all abilities and interests are able to develop a foundation of movement skills, experiences and knowledge – that is, a language of physical movement or physical literacy that helps lead toward lifelong active, healthy living.

"Must Haves" for a Physical Education Program (Fishburne & Hickson, 2005)
- Qualified, enthusiastic teachers who are willing to be positive role models
- A minimum of 150 minutes of class instruction/week for every student
- Well-planned lessons promoting breadth and variety

- Developmentally appropriate and safe activities for every student
- Maximum participation opportunities for every student

Physical Activity: Physical activity is a movement of the body that expends energy, and is used in physical education programming as a medium for teaching curricular content and for providing enjoyable opportunities through which to practice and improve on learned skills (Fishburne & Hickson, 2005). Physical activity, therefore, is the vehicle to become physically educated and develop physical literacy; however, physical activity in itself does not create a physically educated person and physical literacy. According to Alberta Education (2006), physical activity refers to the planned and spontaneous activities that individuals participate in on a daily basis (e.g., walking, sports, gardening, running, etc.). Being physically active on a daily basis is crucial to the health and wellness of everyone in Canada, especially children. Hence, strong evidence exists that physical activity contributes to the overall well-being of all individuals. People of all ages can substantially improve their health and quality of life by including physical activity in their daily routines.

Physical Education and DPA: As discussed previously, the current low levels of physical activity in children and youth in Canada creates the necessity for teachers to consistently promote and provide opportunities for students to be physically active. Therefore, the challenge faced by teachers is the issue of how they can ensure that the experiences provided to students in physical education and DPA support and complement each other (see Table 9.1 for a summary of two programs).

Earlier in this chapter, and in several of the previous chapters, it has been explained that physical education programming needs to provide opportunities for students to develop the knowledge, skills, and attitudes to be able to successfully participate in a wide variety of physical activities, encourage students to participate in physical activity opportunities beyond the learning environment (e.g., during recess, at home, in the community), and contribute to a student's physical literacy. DPA experiences can also support this aim. Physical education programs can be used to meet DPA requirements and, when physical education experiences are not possible, a teacher can certainly continue to provide opportunities for students to be physically active through DPA experiences.

How Can DPA Look in Schools?

DPA can be successfully implemented in a number of ways. In the classroom, through school clubs, as intramural programs, and activity-themed days are a few examples that will be discussed in the following sections.

Table 9.1 The Relationship between Physical Education and DPA		
	Physical Education	**DPA**
Structure	Physical education programming involves: • Teaching for learning • Year, unit and daily planning • Intentional links to curricular outcomes for student learning • Effective teaching for student learning • Assessment of learning outcomes and program effectiveness • Reporting measures for report card completion	DPA programming involves: • Provision of DPA opportunities • Supervision of activities • Valuing and promoting physical activity opportunities • Promotion of a healthy, active lifestyle through various physical activities
Benefits	• Provides skill set for lifelong participation in health-enhancing activity • Supports personal fitness levels • Social inclusion and overall sense of belonging • Development of fundamental movement skills required in a variety of physical activities • Increased levels of self-efficacy required for active living • Enhanced levels of academic achievement • Development of physical literacy	• Opportunities to participate in health-enhancing activity • Supports personal fitness levels • Social inclusion and overall sense of belonging • Opportunities to practice fundamental movement skills required in a variety of physical activities • Lower levels of anxiety and depression • Enhanced levels of academic achievement • Supports the development of physical literacy

modified from Fishburne & Hickson (2005)

DPA in the Classroom

When planning for successful DPA implementation, it is essential for teachers to not confuse it with the teaching of physical education (see previous sections). According to Bradford, Hickson, & Berg (2015), successful DPA can occur in various school locations other than the gymnasium. DPA that is offered in the classroom, for instance, can include: dance-type; fitness-type; games-type; gymnastics-type; and/or individual-type activities. Hence, the following section illustrates a variety of activities that can be offered throughout the school day in the classroom to help meet the requirements of DPA, whilst not taking away from physical education learning time. See Table 9.2 for DPA implementation considerations.

> *Daily physical activities should vary in form and intensity levels, allow for student choice, and take student ability into consideration.*
>
> Alberta Education, 2006

Table 9.2 DPA Implementation Considerations	
Maximum Participation	• Divide students into small groups when possible • Provide a sufficient amount of equipment for student use
Safety	• Remove objects off the desks and around the activity area • Minimize running

Noise	• Promote alternative means of communicating besides talking
	    • Clapping
	    • Thumbs up sign

	modified from Bradford, Hickson, & Berg (2015)

The following activity examples have been modified from Bradford, Hickson, & Berg, 2015 and can be further modified according to the specific needs of the students or classroom environment.

GOOD HEALTHY MORNING!

Formation: Have students stand next to their desks
Equipment: No equipment required
Rules/Directions:
At the beginning of the school day, have students engage in a series of easy-to-organize activities lasting 20 – 30 seconds:
- Jogging on the spot
- Arm circles
- Hopping on one foot
- Squats
- Lunges
  - Follow each activity with a basic stretching movement (10 – 20 seconds):
    - Reach for the sky
    - Butterfly stretch (sit with bottom of feet together)
    - Knee to chest
    - Touch toes, etc.
- Repeat a different activity followed by a stretch as many times as desired

THE 10 ACTIVITIES OF FITNESS

Formation: Have the students stand next to their desks
Equipment: No equipment required
Rules/Directions:
Have the students act out the following fitness song: "On the first day of fitness, my trainer/ teacher gave to me…"
- 10 seconds of jogging on the spot
- 9 push-ups
- 8 jumping jacks/janes
- 7 toe touches
- 6 imaginary basketball shots
- 5 vertical jumps

- 4 imaginary rope jumps
- 3 wall sits (for 10 seconds each)
- 2 lunges
- 1 high-five to another student closest to them for finishing!

ANTS IN MY PANTS!

Formation: Have the students stand next to their desks
Equipment: No equipment is required
Rules/Directions:
Have the students jog on the spot while doing the following activities in order:
- Ask the students to begin by wiggling their fingers
- Wiggle their fingers and wrists
- Wiggle their fingers, wrists, and forearms
- Wiggle their fingers, wrists, forearms, and elbows
- Wiggle their fingers, wrists, forearms, elbows, and shoulders
- Wiggle their fingers, wrists, forearms, elbows, shoulders, and hips
- Wiggle their fingers, wrists, forearms, elbows, shoulders, hips, and knees
- Wiggle their fingers, wrists, forearms, elbows, shoulders, hips, knees, and head

PHYSICALLY ACTIVE ROCK, PAPER, SCISSORS

Formation: Have the students scatter throughout the classroom with a partner
Equipment: No equipment is required
Rules/Directions:
- Explain the basics of the Rock, Paper, Scissors game (rock beats scissor, scissor beats paper, paper beats rock)
- Have the partners stand facing each other and count 1...2...3, but instead of standing still, ask them to jump on 1, jump on 2, and on 3 ask them to physically make their bodies one of the following ways:
    - Rock – Crouch down into a ball
    - Paper – Stand with feet together and hands over head
    - Scissors – Cross legs and arms
- Have the partners repeat the game as a best 2 out of 3, then ask the partners to split up and find new partners to participate with

SCRIBBLE IT...JUST A LITTLE BIT!

Formation: In partners, have the students stand at their desks
Equipment: One piece of paper and pencil for each set of partners
Rules/Directions:
- Call out a physical activity, such as...
    - Jumping
    - Squats
    - Jogging on the spot
    - Jumping jacks/janes

- o Hopping on one foot
- o Knee lifts
- o Push-ups
- Students perform the activity until you call out a spelling word
- Have the students stop performing the activity, and work together to try to spell the word correctly on a piece of paper
- After 15 – 20 seconds, call out a new activity, and repeat (call out a spelling word)
- Continue until all spelling words are used
- While students cool down, share the correct spelling of the words and have the students check their work

ACTIVITY CARDS

Formation: Have the students form a circle around perimeter of the classroom
Equipment: A regular deck of playing cards
Rules/Directions:
- Provide each student with a card
- Have the students identify the symbol on the card and perform the activity that directly corresponds to that suit or symbol for 20 – 30 seconds:
  - o Club: squats
  - o Diamond: vertical jumps
  - o Heart: push-ups
  - o Spade: crunches
- Have the students return their cards to the front, and provide them with another one
- Repeat
- Consider having students choose exercises for each of the 4 suits – including strength, cardio, and flexibility-type exercises
- Using 2 sets of playing cards, limit the cards to only those numbered 5 – 10. When students choose a card, they must perform the required exercise for the number of times indicated on the card (e.g., 6 of Hearts would mean 6 push-ups)

BECOMING A FUTURE ATHLETIC CHAMPION!

Formation: Have the students stand next to their desks
Equipment: No equipment is required
Rules/Directions:
- Call out a variety of sport skills for the students to mimic for at least 10 – 15 seconds:
  - o Shooting a jump shot
  - o Fielding a ground ball
  - o Swimming the front crawl
  - o Serving a tennis ball
  - o Downhill skiing
  - o Walking on a gymnastics balance beam
  - o Throwing a football
  - o Shooting a hockey puck

Although this is not an exhaustive list of possible activities, it is hoped that it can illustrate the kinds of activities and ideas for physical activity that can be accomplished in a classroom environment. When choosing and leading activities such as the ones shared in this chapter, is it recommended that you consider the developmental level of students; so that you can make effective modifications to help the students reach success while also being challenged. Also, as with all classroom and gymnasium activities, maximum participation, enjoyment, and safety should be encouraged and followed.

Targeted DPA Scheduling

Some schools have organized DPA to occur school-wide to ensure that all students can access quality activities for the required amount of time. Examples of this type of programming include (modified from Barthel & Gleddie, 2005; Gleddie, 2006):
- Creating a 30-minute block once a week for DPA. The school splits into grade levels (1 & 2, 3 & 4, 5 & 6) and each level does something different together in a separate location (e.g., dance in the gymnasium, tag on the school grounds, yoga in the park, etc.)
- Scheduling 15 minutes each day for a school-wide walk around the grounds led by the principal
- Providing 10 minutes as part of each of 3 specific teaching blocks throughout the day that are dedicated to DPA activities. Scheduling these into the teaching timetable helps with accountability

School Clubs

School clubs are a wonderful way to encourage students to follow their interests and provides them with more exposure to a particular activity normally in a non-competitive manner. School clubs can include activities such as traditional sports (e.g., volleyball, floor hockey, badminton, etc.), dance, track and field, walking and running groups, and more. Often times, school clubs will operate for a whole term or even the entire school year. The length of time that a club is offered for student participation depends on a number of factors such as student interest, teacher availability, environment needs, etc. School clubs are normally participatory-based; therefore it is essential that all students have the opportunity to participate. Teachers should ensure that modifications can be made to activities to promote inclusive environments.

Intramural Programs

Intramural programs are normally very similar to school clubs in that they allow students to pursue an interest and provide extra opportunities for practice. However, they do tend to be more competitive in nature and involve some kind of schedule with teams playing against each other, with activities normally taking place at lunch time. Similar to school clubs, intramural activities can include traditional sports such as soccer, basketball, etc. However, although the intramural program can operate for the whole school year, often times the specific activities are changed on a frequent basis to allow for a range in student interest and to provide exposure to many activity environments. It is important that teachers ensure that any competitiveness in the intramural program is kept at a healthy and appropriate level and that students understand the parameters for participation. For example, some intramural programs often ensure that students are frequently placed on different teams to create an evenness of experience.

Although teachers are normally heavily involved in the organization and officiating of intramural activities, older students (Grade 5 and 6) can often be enlisted to assist in the process. Such experience can assist in developing leadership skills for these students. It is important to remember that, at the elementary school level, intramural programs need to be constructed in a manner that encourages all students to participate. Therefore, inclusive activity environments are a necessity and a wide range of activities should be considered.

Activity Theme Days

Activity theme days can promote physical activity and provide opportunities to be active in the school community. When students have opportunities to participate in activity days, they are usually exposed to breadth and variety as the choice of themes can offer innovative and creative types of activities. Consider how you might organize inclusive and engaging events for the school community as part of these activity theme days:

- **Seasonal:** Winter Carnival (Bon Homme du Neige!), Spring Fling, Summer Olympics, Fall into Movement

- **Cultural:** invite parents and community organizations to share traditional dances, sports and activities

- **Track and Field Day:** school-wide track and field events including traditional and modified events

- **Olympics Day:** host your own games (winter or summer theme) using modified activities based on the Olympic year and host country

- **Sports Blitz:** invite a number of local sport organizations to host stations featuring their community sport for students to try

- **The Day of Dance:** a variety of dances offered to all grades together

- **Orienteering Day:** a variety of control points to discover through the school community

- **Mathletics:** Olympic-type activities that incorporate math problem-solving

- **Jump Rope for Heart Day:** visit the Jump Rope for Heart organization for more information

When organizing activity theme days, the whole school community should be included. Ensure you invite community members to come to the school to participate and get to know the students by being part of their teams, and role modeling the importance of being physically active.

Reflection Corner...
- What are some ways you experienced school clubs, intramural programs, and/or activity theme days when you were an elementary school child?
- What elements would you keep and what would you change?

Involve Parents/Guardians and Community Organizations

Whether it is a school club event, intramural games, or an activity theme day, it is beneficial to invite the students' parents/guardians and community organization members to come out to encourage the students and show their support. This provides families and the community with wonderful opportunities to observe the students engaged in physical activity while demonstrating their willingness to be active and supportive, too.

Share DPA Information

Whether it is an upcoming school club event, the new intramural schedule, or the next activity theme day, teachers should consider sharing the important information on bulletin boards or display screens throughout the school for all to see and read. Also, these bulletin boards and display screens can be used to showcase photos of student success along with student work on their DPA experiences (e.g., PALs). Be proud of your DPA programming, and be sure to advertise all the student (and even staff) success throughout the school. In a similar manner, teachers should consider sharing this information on the school website and in school and class newsletters.

Supporting Materials

As the main expectation of DPA programming is student participation in physical activity, the following student recording tools have been developed. It is suggested that you continue to utilize recording tools such as these to help students reflect on their ongoing development, enjoyment, and increasing physical activity levels. Also, such records can be used as an accountability measure when discussing the overall effectiveness of your DPA program.

Vignette: Daily Physical Activity (DPA) in the Staff Meeting?

Tracy, an elementary teacher, was dedicated and passionate about physical education and DPA. To help her colleagues to get on board she took the following steps:
- Asked and received permission from the principal to lead 1-2 DPA activities in each staff meeting
- Developed 'DPA Bags' (mesh, string top bags) that contained all the equipment and instructions teachers required for 3-4 DPA activities in their own classrooms
- Tracy also showed teachers how some of these activities could be incorporated into quality physical education by providing curricular links and sample lesson plans

---

PHYSICAL ACTIVITY TRACKING – My Daily PAL (Physical Activity Log)

Name:_____ Date: _____

This week, I participated in the following activities:

	Home	**School**	**Community**	**Total Minutes**
Monday				
Tuesday				
Wednesday				

This week, I averaged _____ minutes of daily physical activity.

This week, my two favourite physical activities were:

1. _____
2. _____

PHYSICAL ACTIVITY GOAL-SETTING My Daily Physical Activity Goals

Name:_____ Date: _____

	My Daily Physical Activity Goals for this Week
Fitness Goals **- flexibility** **- cardiovascular endurance** **- strength**	
Other Physical Activity Goals	

I made these my DPA goals for this week because:

_____

_____

_____

Concluding Thoughts

DPA offers students a number of wonderful and diverse opportunities to engage in physical activity throughout the school day, and to practice what they have learned during their physical education programming. It is important for teachers to know the variety of ways to offer DPA within the school day (e.g., effective activities) to support health and wellness. At the same time, it is important to maintain the distinction between DPA and physical education. DPA provides the opportunity for students to develop the enjoyment of physical activity so they are better equipped to choose lifelong healthy, active lifestyles outside of the school environment.

Checking for Understanding

I Can...
- Explain the rationale behind incorporating DPA time into the school community
- Describe the differences and similarities between DPA and quality physical education
- Share the benefits of DPA
- Offer an array of activities for successful DPA implementation
- Explain the importance of including school clubs, intramural programming, and activity theme days
- Describe a variety of ways to reflect on DPA experiences

Chapter 10

Connecting Learning with other Curricular Areas

Benefits of cross-curricular connections include greater levels of student engagement, increased teacher collaboration and professional growth, and greater opportunities to differentiate learning.

Drake & Reid, 2010

Introduction

In elementary schools, teachers are commonly referred to as generalists as they are likely to teach most, if not all, subject areas. For these teachers, connecting subject areas can be an effective way to help students learn in meaningful ways. Research has found that students who are exposed to connected, or integrated, curricular areas demonstrate academic performance equal to, or better than, students who are exposed to discipline-based programs (Drake & Reid, 2010). Likewise, Rauschenbach (1996) contended that connecting subject areas is effective for "...increasing teacher collaboration and student motivation" (p. 49). For example, integrating math with physical education may assist in developing a student's ability to count by 1s, 2s, 3s, etc. through various fundamental movement skill activities such as hopping and skipping. Or, when students are asked to solve math problems, they could also be asked to demonstrate their answers by "...throwing beanbags at cells in a number grid" (Rauschenbach, 1996, p. 51).

The focus of this chapter, therefore, is to explain the rationale behind cross-curricular connections and share a variety of ways to effectively connect physical education learning outcomes to other curricular areas. When planning for cross-curricular connections, it is vitally important to ensure that intended physical education learning outcomes remain a primary focus – and are met. It is not, after all, 'true' cross-curricular learning if students are simply asked to walk to various locations while meeting an array of intended learning outcomes from another subject area such as art, science, or social studies. Remember, physical education is more than 'just' physical activity (Chapter 9)!

Our hope is that, by the end of this chapter, you will:

- Understand the rationale behind cross-curricular learning
- Recognize the benefits of connecting learning outcomes from other subject areas to physical education
- Understand the importance of 'true' cross-curricular lessons that meet the intended learning outcomes of each subject area
- Know a variety of approaches for connecting physical education with other subject areas
- Develop confidence toward making cross-curricular connections between physical education and other subject areas while maintaining a focus on student learning

What is Cross-Curricular Learning?

Cross-curricular learning, or subject integration, can generally be defined as a teaching approach that purposefully connects competencies from within or across subject areas to develop a more powerful understanding of key curricular learning outcomes. Manitoba Education and Training (2016) contends that to integrate means to coordinate, blend, or connect separate parts into a functioning, unified, and harmonious whole. Hence, cross-curricular learning occurs when various components of the curriculum are connected and related in meaningful ways by both the students and teachers (Alberta Education, 2007).

Although cross-curricular learning refers to the joining of subject areas, teachers must recognize the importance of meeting the intended learning outcomes in each subject area. According to Alberta Education (2007), cross-curricular learning is more than a clustering of learning outcomes from different subject areas. Therefore, we must emphasize that it is not a 'true' cross-curricular connection when one subject area is given a great deal of focus on intended learning outcomes, while the other subject area receives little to none. For example, just because a teacher takes a Grade 4 class outside to collect a variety of items for a science project, the lesson is not deemed a 'true' cross-curricular connection to physical education. All the students are asked to do is walk to a variety of spots to collect pine cones, rocks and leaves. Although there is certainly inclusion of physical activity in this scenario, there are no physical education learning outcomes explicitly met. However, when a teacher involves students in investigating winter habitats using snow shoes, the possibility of cross-curricular learning can be enhanced. For example, the teacher can provide an overview of snow shoeing technique, allow for practice and instruction, and then address the way animals create their winter habitats before setting the students off on their explorations in a pre-defined area. Such a learning experience intentionally covers both physical education and science learning outcomes.

> *At their best, cross-curricular connections highlight the most unique aspects of each subject and blend them, so that they reveal relationships among the subjects that would not have been understood had each subject been studied alone.*
>
> Rauschenbach, 1996

Benefits from Cross-Curricular Learning

In addition to students becoming more engaged in school and less prone to attendance and behaviour issues (Drake & Reid, 2010), there are many other student benefits from cross-curricular activities (see Table 10.1).

Table 10.1 Benefits of Cross-Curricular Learning	
Builds on Prior Knowledge/ Experiences	• Helps students, through meaningful connections among subjects, build on their diverse prior knowledge and experiences, supports their holistic perception of the world and ensures meaningful learning
Unifies Student Learning	• Enables students to develop a unified curriculum view to broaden the context of their learning beyond single subjects
Reflects Real World Situations	• Reflects the real world and the way students learn at home and in the community
Matches The Way Students Think	• Reflects how young students' brains process information (younger students take in many things and process and organize them at one time)
	modified from Alberta Education, 2007, p. 2

Making Strong Cross-Curricular Connections with Physical Education

When planning a cross-curricular lesson in physical education, it is of critical importance to identify the intended physical education learning outcomes. This part of the process is no different from planning a regular physical education lesson – the identification and choice of learning outcomes or objectives come first. Once you have identified these learning outcomes, then decide how you can bring in outcomes from other subject areas. For example, when you identify a learning outcome such as a throwing skill, think about how another subject area can be connected to the learning of a proper throw (e.g., graphing the distances of each throw [math], conducting some research on proper throwing techniques and presenting the information visually and/or orally [language arts]). In this manner, you have ensured that students' proper throwing skills are developed (i.e., intended physical education learning outcome), and that other subject area learning outcomes are connected (or brought in) to the overall lesson.

> **Reflection Corner...**
>
> How can you have your students develop their throwing skills, and graph the distances of their throws (math connection) all within a 30-minute lesson? (Hint: It does not need to happen all in the 30 minutes). What are some creative ways to make this work while still providing for maximum participation of throws?

Cross-Curricular Learning Examples

There are many ways to teach elementary school physical education while using cross-curricular connections. This section shares several ways in which physical education learning outcomes can be connected to other subject areas. In addition to these cross-curricular connections, it is hoped you can develop other ways to add to your cross-curricular teaching repertoire.

Physical Education and Art

According to Alberta Education (1985), through the four components of reflection, depiction, composition, and expression, students are provided opportunities "...for a variety of

experiences: a chance to grow and develop as an individual; to develop perceptual awareness; to learn visual arts skills and concepts; to interpret and communicate with the visual symbol; to create; to value, reflect upon and appreciate the cultural aspects of art; to relate and appreciate art in everyday life" (p. B.1). Likewise, according to the British Columbia Ministry of Education (2016), as part of Arts Education, the body and mind work cooperatively when developing artworks, and the artists experiment in a variety of ways to discover new possibilities and perspectives. The following activities support the rationale behind cross-curricular connections for student learning in both physical education and art. See Table 10.2.

Look and Move! Creative Movement based on a Composition Observation

I Can **Statement:** *I can look at a picture and travel in a variety of ways based on my thoughts of a picture's lines.*

Table 10.2 Intended Learning Outcomes		
Subject	**Alberta (General Outcomes)**	**British Columbia (Curriculum Competencies)**
Physical Education	**Activity:** Acquire skills through a variety of developmentally appropriate movement activities	**Physical Literacy:** Develop and apply a variety of fundamental movement skills in a variety of physical activities and environments
Art	**Reflection:** Respond to visual forms in nature, designed objects, and artworks	**Communicating and Documenting:** Express feelings, ideas, and experiences in creative ways

Activity Description: In the general space of the learning environment, students will be asked to perform a variety of locomotor skills (e.g., running, sliding, galloping, tip-toeing, crawling, bear walking, etc.) to illustrate the various lines observed in different art drawings made during a previous art lesson. In addition to the direction of the movements (representing the lines), students will be asked to consider movement concepts (e.g., Laban's Movement Concepts) such as spatial awareness, body awareness, effort and qualities, and relationships to others and objects. For example, a particular line in a picture may be perceived by a student as representing a *rapid line* which would require a fast running approach (or dart, sprint). And, another line could be perceived as being rough in texture requiring zig-zagging, twirling, etc.

It should be noted by the teacher that the intended learning outcomes for physical education are to develop various locomotor movements, and each student should be provided with learning opportunities to explore their movements, enhance their movement vocabulary, develop spatial awareness, etc. For art, students will develop their observation skills while looking at art components such as lines, shapes, textures, etc.

Lesson Delivery

Teacher: *"Last week, we used crayons to draw some pictures at the zoo. You were asked to draw things that you noticed at the zoo. Some of you drew leaves, trees, animals, flowers, food, and even the whole zoo. Today, those pictures will inspire us to travel around the gymnasium in different ways. So, as a class, let's examine your pictures."*

At this point of the lesson, the teacher will project one of the student's pictures on the gymnasium wall (this could be done by scanning the pictures beforehand, or through a document camera). The students will have a quick moment to view the picture, and listen to the teacher's description of the picture's lines (e.g., *"What do you notice about the lines of the flower petals? Are they curved or straight?"*).

Possible Student Response: *"They're curved!"*

Possible Teacher Response: *"Thank you. From where you're sitting, show me a curved line with your hands and fingers!"*

After a short class discussion, have the students spread out into their own space. Once in their own space, the teacher will call out a locomotor movement such as running, hopping, crawling, skipping, etc., while reminding the students they're asked to perform these movements based on the lines in the picture. After a moment or two, repeat with another picture.

Possible Adaptations: Physical Education

- Locomotor Skills
    - Place more focus on different movement concepts: space, shape, body, effort
- Cooperation
    - Have students work in partners
- Manipulative Skills
    - Have students use equipment (e.g., dribbling a ball)

Possible Adaptations: Art

- Use famous pieces of art
- Study other composition details (e.g., texture, shapes, patterns)
- Interpret feelings (e.g., mood of the lines)

Sketch and Throw: Sketching Inspired by the Overhand Throw

I Can **Statement:** *I can identify and sketch basic lines and shapes of an overhand throw as a way to perform and assess proper technique.*

Table 10.3 Intended Learning Outcomes		
Subject	**Alberta (General Outcomes)**	**British Columbia (Curriculum Competencies)**
Physical Education	**Activity:** Acquire skills through a variety of developmentally appropriate movement activities	**Physical Literacy:** Develop and apply a variety of fundamental movement skills in a variety of physical activities and environments
Art	**Depiction:** The development of imagery based on observations of the visual world	**Exploring and Creating:** Create artistic works collaboratively and as an individual using ideas inspired by imagination, inquiry, experimentation, and purposeful play

Activity Description : In partners, students will practice their overhand throwing skills. As one student practices throwing a ball against a wall, the other student will be asked to watch the thrower and record all observations by sketching the thrower's throwing pattern in five empty boxes (see Figure 10.1). The student responsible for throwing will be asked to demonstrate proper throwing technique at various speeds and also to hold positions. The second student will be asked to use observation skills to first, assess if the throwing technique is correct, and second, using sketching technique, record how the body looks during five basic positions on the paper provided. This lesson will help students think deeply about how the body moves when throwing overhand, and will provide students who are drawing the opportunity to visually discover basic lines and shapes in a familiar movement skill.

It should be noted by the teacher that the intended learning outcomes for physical education are to develop the proper overhand throwing technique. For art, students will develop their observation and drawing skills while looking at live overhand throws.

Figure 10.1 Drawing of an Overhand Throw				
Position 1	**Position 2**	**Position 3**	**Position 4**	**Position 5**

Lesson Delivery

Teacher: *"During the past few physical education lessons, we have been working on developing our overhand throw. We have discussed and practiced the positions our body moves through to send the ball to our target. Who remembers what these positions are?"*

Possible Student Response: *"Face the target, step forward, extend arm, release ball, follow through."*

Teacher: *"Today, as we continue to develop our over overhand throws, we will pay special attention to how the body looks during each position. As a new way to learn about each position, you will be using your observation skills as your partner throws a ball, and then sketch what you observe. Remember, sketching is a quick way to record your ideas, not your finished position. We also know that any images, no matter how complex it appears, can be broken down into basic shapes and lines. So, let's all take a look at the first position together."* (At this point, a student will come to the front and 'freeze' in the starting position of an overhand throw). *"Look at the starting position, watch the white board as I start to sketch what the core/trunk of the body looks like. What do you notice?"*

Possible Student Response: *"I notice you have made sure the eyes are looking toward the target!"*

Teacher: *"You will all be given a piece of paper with room for five positions to take note of. With your partner, take turns 'freezing' at each position to discuss and sketch what the body looks like."*

Possible Adaptations: Physical Education
- Manipulative Skills
    - Have students roll the ball or throw underhand

Possible Adaptations: Art
- Students are provided the throwing positions and need to glue them in order
- Students are asked to add finishing touches to enhance their drawings at a later date
- Have students draw several pictures in an overhand series and create a flip book
- Have students use a variety of art materials
- Have students use media images (e.g., from magazines) to record proper throwing positions
- Have students record each other with a camera, and then take it back to class for both to use for the drawing activity

Physical Education and Health

"Health and life skills involves learning about the habits, behaviours, interactions, and decisions related to healthy daily living and planning for the future. It is personal in nature and involves abilities based on a body of knowledge and practice that builds on personal values and beliefs within the context of family, school and community" (Alberta Education, 2002, p. 1). Likewise, the Saskatchewan Curriculum (2016a) stated, "Health education contributes to fostering improved health, while recognizing there are many factors that promote health at every stage of a child's development. Throughout this curriculum, opportunities are provided for children to attain and maintain a healthy mind, body, and spirit." The following activities support the rationale behind cross-curricular connections for student learning in both physical education and health (see Tables 10.4 and 10.5).

The Greeting Alphabet!

***I Can* Statement:** *I can develop quality greeting skills while using my body to form letters.*

Table 10.4 Intended Learning Outcomes		
Subject	**Alberta (General Outcomes)**	**Saskatchewan (Goals)**
Physical Education	**Cooperation**: Interact positively with others	**Skillful Movement:** Enhance quality of movement by understanding, developing, and transferring movement concepts, skills, tactics, and strategies to a wide range of movement activities
Health & Life Skills	**Relationship Choices:** Develop effective interpersonal skills that demonstrate responsibility, respect, and caring to establish and maintain healthy interactions	**Understanding, Skills, and Confidences:** Develop the understanding, skills, and confidences required to take action to improve health

Activity Description: In the general space, students will be asked to spread out in partners. As the teacher, you will call out a letter of the alphabet that partners must use their bodies together to represent. While the students are forming a variety of letters with a partner, ensure they are practicing their greeting skills (e.g., introduction, eye contact, correct volume, and appropriate hand shake/high five).

It should be noted by the teacher that the intended learning outcomes for physical education are to cooperatively problem-solve movement challenges with their peers. For health, students will develop interpersonal skills to enhance their own (and their peers') mental, social, physical, and emotional health.

Lesson Delivery

Teacher: *"Remember last week when we had a guest teacher tour our school? Who can remember how I greeted Mrs. Lee? Throughout your whole life, you will meet lots of people. What are some important things to remember when you greet others?*

Possible Student Responses (to lead into further discussion):

"Shake their hand!"
"Shoulders up...not down!"
"Smile!"
"Make eye contact!"
"Say their name"

Teacher: *"Today you will work with many different peers. Each time you work with someone new, please greet them using the important communication and greeting skills. After greeting your peer, your challenge will be to work together, cooperate, using your bodies to represent the letter I call out."*

At this point, divide the students into partners. Have each set of partners find a spot in the general space, and practice their greetings to one another. Once the greetings are sufficient, with further demonstration as needed, call out a letter (e.g., A. D, Z, etc.). After a few rounds, assign different partners and continue the *Greeting Alphabet*.

If needed, project the letter on the wall for all to see.

Possible Adaptations: Physical Education

- Nonlocomotor Skills
  - o Replace the letters with numbers
- Cooperation
  - o Include different cooperative learning challenges (e.g., small groups)
  - o Use larger groups and create words/math sequences

Possible Adaptations: Health

- Use the activity to discuss other important communication skills, such as listening to ideas, providing peer feedback, etc.

Enjoy the Wellness Stations!

I Can Statement: *I can understand and engage in a variety of physical activity stations designed to help me learn to make lifelong healthy wellness choices.*

Table 10.5 Intended Learning Outcomes		
Subject	**Alberta (General Outcomes)**	**Saskatchewan (Goals)**
Physical Education	**Benefits Health:** Understand, experience and appreciate the health benefits that result from physical activity	**Active Living:** Enjoy and engage in healthy levels of movement activities to support lifelong active living in the context of self, family, and community
Health & Life Skills	**Wellness Choices:** Make responsible and informed decisions to maintain health and to promote safety for self and others	**Understanding, Skills, and Confidences:** Develop the understanding, skills, and confidences required to take action to improve health

Activity Description: To prepare for the lesson, you will create a variety of task cards describing an aspect of wellness. Each task card should have a short description of an aspect of wellness and a corresponding physical activity for students to perform. Possible task cards may include:

Wellness (Personal Health): What we eat helps to fuel our bodies. Sort the following pictures of food into healthy choices and unhealthy choices. After sorting, perform 1 jumping jack/jane for each healthy food and 1 burpee for each unhealthy food.

Wellness (Safety & Responsibility): When using scooters, there are safety guidelines to follow. Describe and apply four safety guidelines before exploring how the scooters can move throughout your designated space (within the pylons).

After you have created up to 15 task cards that include an array of wellness components and physical activities (which include different fundamental movement skills such as throwing, running, stretching), have them on hand to place one at each station. The students will be asked to participate in each station for 2-3 minutes, and move from station to station in an ordered manner.

It should be noted by the teacher that the intended learning outcomes for physical education are to perform an array of physical activities to enhance personal fitness and fundamental movement skills through various locomotor and non-locomotor movements. Each student should be provided with learning opportunities to explore their movements and enhance their movement vocabulary. For health, students will strengthen their understanding of various wellness topics (e.g., healthy vs. unhealthy food choices).

Lesson Delivery

Teacher: *"In your small groups, you will travel from station to station. Each station area includes a task card. In your groups, complete each task challenge that includes both physical education and health. I'll walk around to make sure you're all participating and meeting the challenges' expectations.*

Possible Adaptations: Physical Education
- Locomotor Skills
  - Have students use various locomotor skills to travel from station to station
- Activity
  - Increase the physical demands at each station

Possible Adaptations: Health
- Have a quiz or assessment at the end (e.g., exit pass)
- Create several sets of task cards to cover a range of health topics

Physical Education and Language Arts

According to Alberta Learning (2000), "changes in society and technology have affected, and will continue to affect, the ways in which people use language to think, to communicate and to learn. Students must be prepared to meet new literacy demands in Canada and the international community. The ability to use language effectively enhances student opportunities to experience personal satisfaction and to become responsible, contributing citizens and lifelong learners" (p. 1). Likewise, Manitoba Education and Training (2016) contended, that for all grade levels, the focus is on acquiring language and literacy skills through listening, speaking, viewing, and representing, as well as reading and writing. The following activities support the rationale behind cross-curricular connections for student learning in both physical education and language arts.

Story Steps

***I Can* Statement:** *I can listen to a story and represent my thoughts through my unique movement choices.*

Table 10.6 Intended Learning Outcomes		
Subject	**Alberta (General Outcomes)**	**Manitoba (General Outcomes)**
Physical Education	**Activity:** Acquire skills through a variety of developmentally appropriate movement activities, dance, and types of gymnastics	**Movement:** Demonstrate competency in selected movement skills, and knowledge of movement development and physical activities with respect to different types of learning experiences, environments, and cultures
Language Arts	**General Outcome 2:** Listen, speak, read, write, view, and represent to comprehend and respond personally and critically to oral and other media texts	**General Outcome 2:** Comprehend and respond personally and critically to oral, media, and literary texts

Activity Description: Students will have an opportunity to represent a piece of literature (chosen by the teacher) through physical movement. The teacher will read a short phrase from the chosen piece. Students will take a moment to think about their movement choices. As the teacher repeats the passage, the students will be asked to move around the general space in a way they choose to represent the various words.

It should be noted by the teacher that the intended learning outcomes for physical education are to develop fundamental movement skills by choosing to move according to the words spoken. Students should be provided with learning opportunities to explore their movements, enhance their movement vocabulary, develop spatial awareness, etc. For language arts, students will respond personally through physical movement to oral text being listened to.

Teacher: *"Today, you're going to use your listening skills to illustrate a story with your body. I'm going to read a passage about a seed that blossoms into a flower. Use your body to show how the seed transforms. The first line is "a small, tight, round seed lives in the dirt." Take a moment to think how your body would represent those words. When you're ready, go find your own spot, and show what those words might look like. I'll read it again."*
Possible Student Movements: *Curled up in a small ball on the floor.*

Teacher: *"I see many students making their body go low to the ground and small. Remember your movements are up to you. Let's hear the next passage. The seed gently shakes. Lightly swaying back and forth, back and forth. With the help of water and sunlight the seed begins to slowly expand. A tiny leaf begins to unfold and stretch toward the sky. Another leaf quickly follows. And another. A bud turns toward the sunlight and stretches, stretches, stretches up. Completely unfolded, wide, graceful petals blossom. Now the seed is no longer a seed but a beautiful flower."*

Following the lesson, lead a class discussion of why students made their movement choices.

Possible Adaptations: Physical Education

- Manipulative Skills
  - o Use a variety of equipment (e.g., ribbons, gymnastics sticks, parachutes)

- Locomotor Skills
    - Have students create/refine/practice a movement sequence
    - Provide movement boundaries (e.g., big, bound movements; small, low movements)

Possible Adaptations: Language Arts

- Use a story book
- Choose to project the story (words) on the wall while reading it
- Have the students write their own passages

Table 10.7 Further Learning for "Story Steps"	
Physical Education	**Language Arts**
• Classify the words used throughout the story based primarily on movement categories • Plan for a school-wide performance	• Write a poem based on the story and movements • Create a story about a lived experience • Provide students with a written copy of the story for reference

Word Search: Fractured Fairy Tale Find

I Can **Statement:** I can use a story organizer to create a fractured fairy tale with ideas from orienteering control points.

Table 10.8 Intended Learning Outcomes			
Subject	**Alberta (General Outcomes)**	**Manitoba (General Outcomes)**
Physical Education	**Activity:** Acquire skills through a variety of developmentally appropriate movement activities, dance, and types of gymnastics	**Movement:** Demonstrate competency in selected movement skills and knowledge of movement development and physical activities with respect to various types of learning experiences, environments, and cultures
Language Arts	**General Outcome 3:** Listen, speak, read, write, view and represent to manage ideas and information	**General Learning Outcome 3:** Manage ideas and information

Activity Description: Consider using this activity towards the conclusion of an orienteering unit. After being asked to collectively choose a familiar fairy tale to complete a basic story organizer chart, students will use the chart to organize their information in a fractured fairy tale (a newly created fairy tale made possible by taking pieces of other stories and joining them together in creative ways). In the school yard, the teacher will set up five orienteering control points for students to navigate between, and each group (2-3 students per group) will need a compass, map, story organizer, and writing tool. To accurately navigate the orienteering course, students will need to rely on reading a map and using a compass. After finding their way to each control point by using their mapping skills, they will be asked to perform a fundamental movement skill prior to dealing with the fairy tale. And, when they complete the orienteering course, groups will verbally retell their fractured fairy tale to another group.

It should be noted by the teacher that the intended learning outcomes for physical education are to enhance orienteering skills. Students should be provided with learning opportunities to develop communication, leadership, and cooperative skills. For language arts, students will develop greater reading and speaking skills.

Example Control Point

Setting: The setting acts as the main location where your story will take place. Choose one of the following settings and record your choice on your story organizer
   a. Deep dark forest
   b. Royal kingdom
   c. Grandma's house

Conflict:
   a. The Big Bad Wolf is blowing houses down
   b. Finding the owner of a lost shoe
   c. Delivering a basket of cookies

Control	1	2	3	4	5
Physical Activity Challenge	15 steps Bear walk	15 jumps Frog jump	15 Steps Horse gallop	15 steps Crab walk	15 Steps Bunny hops
Fairy Tale Element	Setting	Main Character(s)	Conflict	Resolution	Moral
Fairy Tale Choice					

Table 10.9 Example of a Story Organizer

Teacher: *"Last week you were introduced to orienteering. You should remember that we ventured into the school yard where we practiced using a compass. With the map serving as our guide, you are asked to find your way from control point to control point. At each control point, you will find out what to do by reading the task cards. Now, who can remember which direction the compass needs to be pointed toward?"*

Student Response: *"North!"*

Teacher: *"Again, as you should remember from our orienteering practice, at each control station there was a physical activity challenge. Who can remember one of the challenges?*

Possible Student Response: *"A bear walk for 15 steps"*

Possible Student Response: *"To jump like a frog for 12 seconds"*

Teacher: *"That's correct! Today, we are going to add another twist. On the back of your map is a story organizer that relates to each control. When you arrive at each control point, you will have two tasks. First, perform the physical activity, then you will be asked to make a choice between common fairy tale story elements. As we have been studying story writing in class, you will be familiar with the terms setting, characters, conflict, resolution, and moral of the story. You may recognize the fairy tale choices from books we have read in class. At each* *control point, write your choice on your chart. At the end of the orienteering route your group will take a moment to verbally compose your fairy tale and share with another group."*

Possible Adaptations: Physical Education

- Vary the location (e.g., local playground, school hallway, classroom)
- Vary the conditions (e.g., winter with snowshoes)
- Vary the amount of control points
- Manipulative Skills
    - o Use string orienteering
- Cooperative
    - o Have students work individually, in partners, or as a whole group
- Have students act out their constructed 'fairy tale' choosing fundamental movement skills to include throughout

Possible Adaptations: Language Arts

- Use the story organizer and verbally retell as prompts to begin a written draft
- Include as part of a larger unit on fairy tales
- Include more complex categories (e.g., protagonist, antagonist, rising actions, etc.)
- Use different writing prompts at each control point:
    - o Have students create their own control point
    - o Add phrases to be put in a poem
- Use pictures to illustrate the choices in addition to words

Physical Education and Math

According to Alberta Education (2007), the elementary school math learning environment "should value and respect the diversity of students' experiences and ways of thinking, so that students are comfortable taking intellectual risks, asking questions and posing conjectures. Students need to explore problem-solving situations in order to develop personal strategies and become mathematically literate. They must realize that it is acceptable to solve problems in a variety of ways and that a variety of solutions may be acceptable" (p. 1). The following activities support this rationale for student learning in mathematics and physical education. Likewise, the Ontario Ministry of Education (2005) in the Ontario Curriculum states that an information- and technology-based society requires individuals who are able to think critically about complex issues, analyze and adapt to new situations, solve various types of problems, and communicate effectively. The study of mathematics leads to the development of student knowledge, skills, and habits of mind essential for successful and rewarding participation in today's society. The following activities support the rationale behind cross-curricular connections for student learning in both physical education and math (see Tables 10.10 and 10.11.).

Number Balance

I Can Statement: *I can balance objects and classify numbers in different ways.*

Table 10.10 Intended Learning Outcomes		
Subject	**Alberta (General Outcomes)**	**Ontario (Overall Expectations)**
Physical Education	**Activity:** Acquire skills through a variety of developmentally appropriate movement activities; dance, games, types of gymnastics, individual activities and activities in an alternative environment; e.g., aquatics and outdoor pursuits	**Movement Competence - Skills, Concepts, and Strategies:** Develop the movement competence required to participate in physical activities through the development of movement skills and the related application of movement concepts and movement strategies
Math	**Number:** Develop number sense	**Number Sense and Numeration:** Develop an understanding of number by learning different ways of representing numbers and about the relationships among numbers

Activity Description: First, the teacher will post large posters of numbers (0-20) around the learning space. Then, the teacher will place a pile of cards representing numbers (0-20) using pictures, tally marks, equations in each of the learning environment's four corners.

In the general space of the learning environment, students will be asked to find their own spots. The teacher will call out a locomotor movement (e.g., running, bear walking, etc.), and then the students will travel to a corner to collect a card from the pile (while performing the locomotor movement while balancing a bean bag on a body part) and onward (using the same locomotor movement) to search for the corresponding digit the card relates to (placed throughout the learning environment). The teacher must ensure the students have plenty of opportunities to travel through space using a variety of locomotor skills – while balancing a bean bag on a body part. The students could be asked to assess their peers by checking if they are at the correct location (depending on the number 0-20).

It should be noted by the teacher that the intended learning outcomes for physical education are to develop various locomotor movements, and each student should be provided with learning opportunities to explore their movements and balance skills, develop spatial awareness, etc. For math, students will enhance their numeracy skills by dealing with numbers being represented in multiple ways (e.g., 2, 1 + 1, 4-2, 10-8, 30/15, etc.).

Teacher: *"All year, we've been learning that numbers can be represented in many ways. In each corner, I placed a pile of cards that show different numbers in different ways. For example, this card has a 'high 5.' What number do you think this card represents?"*

Possible Student Response: "5."

Teacher: *"Now, look at the large numbers 0-20 posted on the walls. Find and point to the number 5. That's where I would put this card. The way you will collect the cards is by balancing a bean bag on our head, while moving in a way that I will call out, like bear walk. If the* *bean bag falls off, simply put it back on. When you hear me say "number puzzle along with a locomotor movement" go pick up a card, and find its home."*

Possible Adaptations: Physical Education

- Manipulative Skills
  - o Have students use different manipulative skills (e.g., dribbling a ball while collecting a card)
- Cooperation
  - o Have students work in partners

Possible Adaptations: Math

- Change the chunk of numbers (e.g., 30-50), multiples of 5s
- Change the type of cards (e.g., equations only [3X2])
- "Mix up" the order of the large numbered posters

Workout Wednesday: 1 Minute Mania Fitness Facts

I Can **Statement:** *I can collect, organize, and display data related to my fitness.*

Table 10.11 Intended Learning Outcomes		
Subject	**Alberta (General Outcomes)**	**Ontario (Overall Expectations)**
Physical Education	**Benefits Health:** Understand, experience and appreciate the health benefits that result from physical activity	**Active Living:** Gain an understanding of the importance of regular physical activity and its relationship to developing and maintaining health-related fitness
Math	**Statistics and Probability:** Collect, display and analyze data to solve problems	**Data Management and Probability:** Learn about different ways to gather, organize, and display data

Activity Description: This cross-curricular connection will take place over a two-month period (every Wednesday). Every Wednesday (for 8 weeks), students will be asked to perform body weight fitness movements (e.g., lunges, jumping jacks, squats, push-ups, etc.) in partners (one performs while one counts). It is important for the teacher to review/discuss with the students how to perform each exercise that is requested from the lesson. One partner will perform the activity for a total of 1 minute, then the other partner will repeat. The teacher must ensure that the students (class-wide) work on the same movement at the same time (for the 1-minute duration).

It should be noted by the teacher that the intended learning outcomes for physical education are to enhance personal fitness levels while further developing a variety of fundamental movement skills. Each student should experience some personal fitness goal-setting, as well. For math, students will develop their graphing skills and overall understanding of how graphs can illustrate their personal data through time.

Teacher: *"It's Workout Wednesday! Today is our first day of a long-term fitness project. For one minute at a time, one partner will work, and the other will count. After the minute is up,* *record your numbers in your chart. Over time, the chart will be used to show improvements in your activity levels. Now, let's start Workout Wednesday!"*

As the teacher, use a timer and call out "Go & Stop" after each minute. Have the students record their results in a pre-made chart format. Students will then use their data to create a line graph displaying their progress over time. The line graphs will be used to show the date, time, and performance numbers (see Table 10.12 and Figure 10.1).

Week	Jumping Jacks/Janes	Wall Touches	Squats	Step-Ups
Table 10.12 Example Student Data Chart				
1	62	17	18	44
2	69	19	23	49

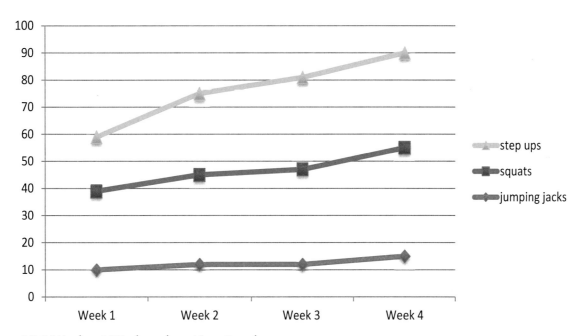

Figure 10.1 Workout Wednesdays Line Graph

This weekly lesson can be used as a spring board to discuss the importance of daily physical activity as a way to improve student health.

Possible Adaptations: Physical Education
- Manipulative Skills
  - Use various objects to enhance the difficulty of activity (benches to step up and down)
- Benefits Health
  - Use a Physical Activity Log (PAL) to write down personal reflections on improvements through time
  - Practice goal-setting
- Fitness
  - Use different body weight movements

Possible Adaptations: Math
- Combine the data to create a class graph
- Use the data to create and discuss different types of graphs
- Have students respond to assessment questions based on graph results
- Consider having students keep a 'pulse log' (heart rates for different aerobic activities) throughout each unit and graph these to show how activities have different fitness requirements

Checklist for Designing Quality Cross-Curricular Connections

According to Drake and Reid (2010), when students are provided with cross-curricular learning experiences, the following have been found to occur:
- students demonstrate academic performance equal to, or better than, students in discipline-based programs
- benefits include greater student engagement, increased teacher collaboration, professional growth, and more opportunities to differentiate learning

Table 10.13 Checklist for Designing Quality Cross-Curricular Connection	
Criteria	**Yes/No**
• Physical Education intended learning outcomes are being met	
• Physical Education learning experiences are developmentally appropriate	
• Other subject area's intended learning outcomes are being met	
• Students are understanding the connections between the subject areas	
• Assessment is used to ensure intended learning outcomes are understood in both subject areas	
• Student work is sufficient in both subject areas	

Concluding Thoughts

Early childhood educators and educational researchers know that young children perceive the world to be a connective whole rather than isolated parts (Alberta Education, 2007). Although the Program of Studies describes learning in subject areas that have their own distinctive knowledge and understandings, skills, values and attitudes, these subject areas include outcomes which are common to other subjects (Alberta Education, 2007). In addition, along with the need to help students develop physical literacy (PHE Canada, 2016), teachers need to address other initiatives such as environmental education, character education and the new literacies (e.g., media, technological). With so many curricular expectations to cover and assess, it should not be a surprise that teachers sometimes feel overwhelmed (Drake & Reid, 2010). In knowing this regarding student learning and teacher needs, developing integrative activities across different subjects with physical education is an effective way to foster student learning, while maintaining high levels of motivation, creativity and discovery, and to help teachers develop more effective planning practices, preferably lessening occurrences of becoming overwhelmed by all the curricular expectations.

Checking for Understanding

I Can...

- Explain the rationale behind cross-curricular learning
- Explain the benefits of connecting learning outcomes from other subject areas to physical education
- Describe the importance of 'true' cross-curricular lessons that meet the intended learning outcomes of each subject area
- Share a variety of approaches for connecting physical education with other subject areas
- Demonstrate confidence toward making cross-curricular connections between physical education and other subject areas while maintaining a focus on student learning

Chapter 11
Being an Advocate for Physical Education

Introduction: Why Do We Need to be Advocates?

Article 1 – The practice of physical education, physical activity and sport is a fundamental right for all

1.1 Every human being has a fundamental right to physical education, physical activity, and sport without discrimination on the basis of ethnicity, gender, sexual orientation, language, religion, political or other opinion, national or social origin, property or any other basis.

1.2 The freedom to develop physical, psychological and social well-being and capabilities through these activities must be supported by all governmental, sport and educational institutions.

1.3 Inclusive, adapted and safe opportunities to participate in physical education, physical activity and sport must be available to all human beings, notably children of preschool age, women and girls, the aged, persons with disabilities and indigenous people.

(International Charter of Physical Education, Physical Activity and Sport, UNESCO, 2016)

The Oxford Canadian Dictionary (online) defines advocacy as, "Public support for or recommendation of a particular cause or policy." An advocate is defined as, "A person who publicly supports or recommends a particular cause or policy." Physical education has long been a marginalized subject in schools, often shunted aside in favour of more time for literacy and numeracy (Trost & van der Mars, 2010; Fishburne, 1983). Consistent with our goals for this textbook, however, is a realization of the value of physical education; its place within elementary school education; how it is part of the education of the whole child; and how it is critical to a student's overall development and lifelong journey of physical literacy. It is now time to examine how we can share our passion and expertise in physical education to convince others of the value of physical education - in our schools and beyond! By the end of the chapter our hope is that you will:

- Understand the need for advocacy
- Be able to apply an ecological model to your own reality
- Be prepared to advocate for physical education in your own context

Background

Who needs 'convincing'?

There are a number of reasons that others may need to be 'convinced' of the value and efficacy of elementary school physical education. Firstly, as we have studied in Chapter 1, there are those who did not have a positive K-6 (or 7-12!) physical education experience. Without even realizing it, those people may marginalize physical education due to its lack of value in their own lives. When these people become teachers, their poor perception and experience of physical education can become even more problematic as it can negatively impact the experience of their own students. Secondly, others are feeling intense pressure for students to 'succeed' in math and language arts, and may believe that the only way to answer this pressure is with less time and space for physical education. Thirdly, some people may just not realize the many benefits and advantages that a quality physical education program can bring to a school community. Finally, there are those who may not feel competent to teach physical education either because of minimal training and/or experience or a sense that they are not "athletic enough" (which we know is not a requirement!). This last category of people might just need help with certain aspects of their performance confidence in regards to physical education. All of these people can become allies and advocates for quality physical education!

In other words, this means that we have circles of people around us: students; colleagues; parents; administrators; trustees; etc. that we might need to influence in a positive manner. Ecological theory (Bronfenbrenner, 1977; Kelly, 1990; Sallis & Owen, 1997) recognizes the interplay and complexity within and between these circles: individual; social; organizational; community; and policy.

Through our interactions between and among these circles of influence, we can advocate for quality daily physical education on five different levels. The rest of this chapter is organized according to this model. See Figure 11.1.

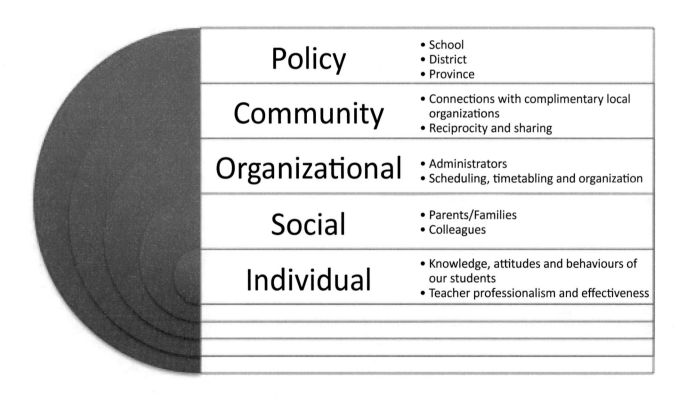

Figure 11.1 An Ecological Model applied to Advocacy (Adapted from Bronfenbrenner, 1977)

Moral Purpose

A compelling and inclusive moral purpose steers a system, binds it together, and draws the best people to work in it. Literacy and numeracy are sometimes such a purpose and should always be an educational priority. But they are not always the right reform priority, especially when schools and nations are already high performers in those areas, or when they sideline other emphases that need more attention.

Hargreaves & Shirley, 2009, p. 76

Reflection Corner...
Why do you think physical education is important and belongs in elementary schools?

Your answer to this question is your moral purpose for physical education – it is the "WHY" of why we do what we do. In fact, a major component of this textbook has been about helping you to answer that very question! If we indeed believe that physical education is important and should be a valued part of elementary school education, then we have a moral purpose, and indeed a moral obligation, to pursue a goal of quality daily physical education – and not only for our own students!

Of course, we also learned in Chapter 4 that physical education is a required element of every K-6 education program across the country. Therefore, we are legally mandated by our respective Ministries of Education to teach physical education to all children. It is not a choice. It is a requirement. Imagine if a teacher made a 'choice' to not teach mathematics, and just decided that it was not a valuable part of their personal view of education? How long would this teacher keep a teaching position? Who would hold this teacher accountable? We should expect – and maybe even demand – the same for physical education.

Your Role

As you know, not everyone is on board with physical education. As well, many elementary schools do not have specialist teachers in physical education. But, your school has you.

And, you can make a difference!

You are a well-trained, passionate, advocate for physical education. However, this does not mean that you try and take on everything for everyone. It means, quite simply, that you first lead by example (Bradford, 2014), and then look for ways to support others in the ecological circles surrounding you, and continually 'stand up' for physical education. In this case, advocacy does not mean marching in the streets with a placard that reads, "MORE PHYSED!" What it does mean, however, is that you take advantage of opportunities to promote and support what you believe to be right and true about physical education in elementary schools. It means you help people 'remember' that physical education is required for all students. Presented here is a practical look at how to make a difference – one ecological level at a time.

Five Layers of Advocacy

1. Individual Advocacy

Be the change you wish to see in the world.
Ghandi

Your Own Class

The first place to start your advocacy journey is with your own class. You have students of your own, a class and a mission: to provide your students with the best quality physical education program they have ever experienced! Remember that students (especially in the upper elementary grades) may have had less than stellar experiences and therefore could perceive physical education as unimportant. They may even ascribe to the view that, "… physical education is not a real subject" (Bradford, Hickson, & Evaniew, 2015a). Or, they may have enjoyed physical education because it was a chance to run around, do what they wanted, and blow off steam. Regardless of what your students may have experienced before – they are in your class now (see Vignette on page 226). Due to your education and knowledge, you will ensure quality daily physical education happens by starting with some of the basics in Table 11.1.

Table 11.1 Quality Daily Physical Education
Scheduling daily physical education, even if you don't have daily gymnasium access
Following the Provincial Program of Studies for physical education
NEVER missing physical education to provide more time for other subject areas
Teaching across the dimensions: alternative environments; dance; games; gymnastics; and individual activities, while promoting lifelong physical literacy
Creating and implementing quality year, unit, and lesson plans that include all learners, promote safety, and are developmentally appropriate
ALWAYS referring to physical education – not "gym" (I teach physical education – 'Jim' lives down the street!)
Assessing and reporting on the learning outcomes found in the Program of Studies

Be a Professional Physical Educator

Teachers are professionals. This concept also applies to your teaching of physical education (and why wouldn't it?). There are a number of actions you can take to be a professional physical educator.

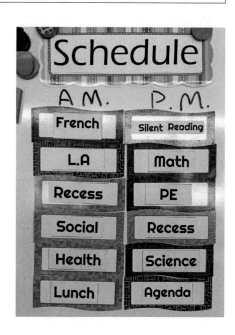

- **Attend to Current Research:** You have a responsibility to stay up-to-date with what the research says about developments in pedagogy, child development, physical activity, wellness, fundamental movement skill development, and more. You can do this through reading quality journals, checking out online articles, being involved in #physed groups (essentially discussion groups) on social media, and attending research-based or professional talks.

- **Be a Reflective Teacher (see Chapter 2):** Examine your planning, teaching, and assessment practices on a regular basis. Consider recording yourself periodically. Provide students with a way to offer feedback on your teaching. If possible, have an experienced physical educator mentor you as you develop as a professional.

- **Teach Effectively (see Chapter 5):** Quality physical education is not about being a former athlete and/or "good" at sports. It is about understanding curriculum and pedagogy as applied to the unique and complex field of human movement. How a teacher organizes the program, plans for assessment, engages learners, and dresses for teaching in an active learning environment are just a few components that have become part of effective teaching in physical education.

- **Join Your Provincial/National Physical Education Association:** These organizations offer a wide range of professional development and learning opportunities. In its simplest form, joining a provincial/national physical education association can play an integral part in your networking advantages. Like-minded educators getting together can only help develop further knowledge and skills for teaching quality physical education.

- **Engage in Regular, Intentional Professional Development**: Not sure how to teach dance? Attend a workshop or learn online! Need help with formative assessment in physical education? Take advantage of sessions at your local teachers' convention. Professional development opportunities are always available. You just need to know how to discover where and when they are scheduled (e.g., contact your school jurisdiction's physical education consultant, join a #physed professional learning community on social media, etc.).

- **Be a Role Model:** When becoming an advocate for physical education, it is essential that you "do as you say!" If students are learning in physical education that being physically active is important for healthy living, they should be exposed to teachers who are engaged in a health journey.

  - **Fitness and Physical Activity.** We need to begin here by saying that physical education teachers do NOT need to be super athletes or fitlets to be exceptional at what they do. Your goal is to model a healthy, active lifestyle, not be on the front cover of a Muscle and Fitness periodical. This can be as simple as parking a few blocks away and walking to work, doing yoga with other teachers at lunch, sharing your love of orienteering, or discussing active recreation opportunities with your class. Remember, health is a journey, not a destination and it is important to reinforce that message in your own walk.

  - **Food and Drink Consumption.** Consider what message students may perceive when they observe teachers drinking pop and eating bags of chips during the school day (Bradford, Hickson, & Evaniew, 2015b; Hickson & Bradford, 2010). Be aware of your own healthy (and unhealthy) food and drink choices as an integral part of student learning; they are watching you!

  - **Appropriate Clothing.** What you choose to wear while teaching is a powerful communicator (Damhorst, Miller-Spillman, & Michelman, 2005; Roach, 1997). The clothing being worn by a teacher in physical education must fit that of a teacher who is prepared to engage in physical activity or students may perceive the teacher as uncaring toward the subject area, not prepared to demonstrate the skills, and/or disinterested in engaging in physical activities (Hickson & Bradford, 2010).

Student Voice: Grade 4 student

I think physical education teachers are supposed to be role models because if you're going to be a physical education teacher, you're supposed to show students how to do it, and, if you're not showing us what to do, what are we going to learn, what are we going to accomplish? (Bradford, 2015)

Teacher Clothing for Physical Education

In a recent study, Bradford (2015) found that running shoes are the most important part of teacher clothing that should be worn while teaching physical education. Other items of clothing that should be worn include a golf shirt and khaki or sweat-type pants, or shorts. Students in the study were shown a mannequin (teacher) dressed in the two ways depicted below. In reference to Figure 11.2, a Grade 6 student contended that the teacher is wearing "all appropriate clothes" for teaching physical education (p. 123), while a Grade 5 student stated "the teacher can move around and help you more" (p. 102).

On the contrary, when referring to the mannequin in Figure 11.3, wearing a blouse, skirt, with dress shoes, a Grade 6 student stated, "This teacher is not prepared and does not show an interest in what she is teaching." (p. 123). Likewise, a Grade 5 student contended, "I feel that she does not want to teach physical education," (p. 123), while a Grade 6 student believed that, "This shows that the teacher does not care." (p. 158).

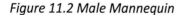

Figure 11.2 Male Mannequin   *Figure 11.3. Female Mannequin*

2. Social Advocacy

As generalists are in a unique and privileged position to teach the 'whole' child using an interdisciplinary approach to the curriculum (e.g., bridging the gap between math,science, language arts, social studies), each one of them should aim to assist every child in his/her development of the knowledge, skills, and attitudes necessary to lead an active, healthy lifestyle because they are simplyin the best position to do so.

Lu & DeLisio, 2009, p. 184

Colleagues

As you broaden your views in your advocacy, begin with other teachers in your school. It might be in the same grade or just a teacher-friend across the hall. As you have already done a superb job of advocating for PE in your own class, there are bound to be questions. For example, your schedule outside the classroom door (with Daily Physical Education!) might draw the question, "Do you REALLY do physical education every day?" Use questions such as this to open up a conversation about the value and purpose of physical education.

What can often be overlooked are the advantages that a generalist-trained teacher of physical education possesses over the specialist (Lu & DeLisio, 2009). Do your colleagues know that they:

- Are better able to have a holistic view of each student (see them all day in every subject)?
- Are better able to plan interdisciplinary teaching based on knowledge of all curricula?
- Have more opportunities to observe students in unique settings?
- Can address cooperation and conflict issues through curriculum in physical education?

In addition to sharing your ideas, passion, and practices for quality physical education, consider other areas that include physical activity and healthy behaviours (See Chapter 8 & 9). These classroom and staff activities can be a way for colleagues to feel the benefits of quality movement for themselves – and their students. This process may encourage and support the delivery of physical education. Begin with small, manageable steps – maybe begin with activity breaks during classes first before convincing others of daily physical education. Providing all teachers in the school with ideas/strategies to infuse physical activity breaks during regular class time can help support the benefits of regular physical activity. Consider sharing several activities at each staff meeting as a way to build confidence and competence. As well, one of the best ways to convince teachers that their students need to move regularly is to have them experience the joy of movement for themselves (Kretchmar, 2008). Encourage a walking group, yoga class, Zumba session, learn-to-run club, etc.

Share your learning (professionalism) with your colleagues. Consider how you can communicate ideas in the staff room, shared spaces like a copier or work room or at grade-level meetings. Consider posting a practice-based research article with key points conveniently highlighted above the coffee machine. Email out a blog post and suggest a time to meet to discuss applications to your school's context. In this way, colleagues can become more knowledgeable and equipped to develop quality physical education programming benefitting all students in your school.

Parents and Families

Often neglected as advocacy partners, parents and families can be powerful allies for physical education. Consider the strategies identified in Table 11.2.

Table 11.2 Keeping Parents and Families Informed
Communicate (share) with parents and families why you have daily physical education, and what is being learned in classes • Newsletters, class website, etc.
Be firm and consistent as you explain your rationale • Back up your position with research, and explain why
Include physical education as part of student-led or parent-teacher interviews, homework activities (Bradford & Evaniew, 2014), family projects, etc. • Connect what students are learning to what they can do at home with their families and in the local community
Remember the importance of the school's parent council and take the time to educate and encourage them towards quality programming and support • Attend parent council meetings, and share the importance of physically active lifestyles and quality daily physical education
Develop and update physical education bulletin boards throughout the school • Current physical education information/learning on the bulletin boards may be read by parents and families walking through the hallways • Consider a healthy, active living page on your school's website that includes physical education information, key research, community links, and other ideas

Remember, parents want their children to succeed – not just in school, but in life. Highlighting the relational, affective nature of physical education as well as its intrinsic, joyful purpose can be very effective. And, as we learned in Chapter 1, students will also have an improved academic experience!

3. Organizational Advocacy

Administration

With the considerable amount of research that points to the importance of teaching quality physical education, it continues to be disheartening to observe that such opportunities for learning are often marginalized in schools (Lounsbery, McKenzie, Trost, & Smith, 2011; Gaudreault & Woods, 2012). According to Lounsbery, et al. (2011), the support of school leadership personnel is most important to physical education programming and, wherever possible, school administrators should be encouraged to champion their schools' physical education programs at all times. Hence, instead of blindly accepting a potentially bleak outcome for physical education programming, there are potential ways to offset this pattern and create a different outcome for learning in physical education (Hickson, Berg & Bradford, 2015).

Hickson, et al. (2015) contended that *"...schools and teachers must be the front-line advocates for students, and school leadership personnel can be the catalysts for change. Although there are likely challenging obstacles that school leaders need to overcome, these challenges are not insurmountable..." (p. 10).*

Figure 11.4. The Facilitation of Change (Hickson, et al., 2015)

Various ways you can get your administration team on board (see Figure 11.4) include:

- Inviting them into your class to see quality physical education in action
- Asking to share some key research information at a staff meeting
- Demonstrating your quality assessment practice in physical education
- Getting to know them and their background with physical education and physical activity
- Reminding them of the provincial guidelines and documents

Scheduling

Plan for the gymnasium to be used all day every day – no gaps! In order to promote the importance of physical education across all grade levels, timetabling should be attended to so that all classes are allotted a fair amount of time each day, which vary throughout the day (similar to a *Learning Commons*). For example, Grade One students should be afforded physical education time each day at various times throughout the week. It seems unfair for one class to always benefit from having physical education scheduled in the morning. According to Tomporowski (2003), following just one session of physical activity, children's attention and memory can increase, and inappropriate behaviour has been found to reduce. Therefore, when the time comes for planning timetables, speak up about the importance of daily physical education and to the fact that each class would benefit from having physical education at different times throughout the week. Since elementary school gymnasiums tend to be small and two-gymnasium schools are rare, you will have conflicts. Not only might there be too many classes for the time allotments, you also lose space for holiday concerts, plays, etc. Set an example and plan to use local facilities to meet your plans to deliver daily physical education experiences.

- **On Campus and Free**
  - o Playgrounds
  - o Hallways
  - o Portables
  - o School Fields
  - o Classrooms

- **Off Campus (walking distance) and Free**
  - o Community halls
  - o Skating rinks (can be used for curling, broomball, skating, etc. and as a grass surface in Spring/Fall)
  - o Local parks (orienteering, cross-curricular activities, team-building)
  - o Spray parks

- **Off Campus (bused) and Fee for Service (most of these have discount rates for schools)**
  - o Gymnastics centres
  - o Dance studios
  - o Fitness centres
  - o Recreation centres
  - o Swimming pools

Equipment and Budget

In addition to attending to timetabling issues, maintaining an equipment room is another initiative that can be focused on by the school's physical education advocate. Equipment must be safe and maintained (e.g., poles, nets). As well, it is quite difficult to teach a quality physical education program without proper class sets of equipment (e.g., skipping ropes, balls, etc.). In the classroom, we do not ask several students to share one book, pen, or tablet computer, likewise we should not expect students to learn physical education outcomes by always having to share equipment that minimizes their participation rates. Scheduling regular equipment room organization and planning time will make teaching physical education much easier. With this practice, throughout the school year, there will be minimal issues concerning equipment while all teachers enter the gymnasium and other learning environments to teach their physical education lessons.

Advocate for a proper physical education budget. Use other areas (e.g., science) as examples and inquire about equity. Approach your parent council for extra funds for special purchases as needed. For example, when 'big ticket' items are needed, you do not want to be faced with limited funds. Therefore, develop a planned budget (possibly with parent council financial support) for upcoming items (e.g., volleyball nets, gymnastics equipment). When developing your physical education budget, make a five-year plan, considering local and provincial grants that can benefit your teaching and students' learning.

Extra-Curricular Activity Opportunities (see Chapter 9)

Physical activity opportunities outside of physical education are a fabulous way for students to develop physical literacy and build upon the skills learned. All students should be encouraged to participate in an array of physical activities during their time at school. Activities organized by the school can happen before or after school, at recess and lunchtime, and could include:
- Organized sports
- Dance opportunities
- Fitness activities
- Recess activities supported through class or grade specific, colour identified, equipment

Providing students with opportunities to be physically active in a supervised environment (e.g., recess volleyball-type games) can help develop their levels of self-confidence, team skills, and much more. Remember, when considering connections to lifelong physical activity, it is essential to offer an array of activities across the five dimensions (see Chapter 4) so that students have a better opportunity of finding their niche.

4. Community Advocacy

School District/Province

Inquiring about and attending school district professional development (e.g., teachers' conventions) can provide opportunities to engage in workshops aimed to enhance your physical education teaching. Attending workshops can be a terrific strategy to learn about and collect quality resources to support your teaching, and the teaching across all grade levels via your willingness to share the materials. Moreover, connecting directly with individuals and organizations that focus their work along the lines of effective teaching of physical education (e.g., school consultants, Ever Active Schools, Saskatchewan Physical Educators Association) will be a terrific step toward community advocacy. These connections will help you develop greater skills in your teaching while also proving to be an effective networking strategy; they will most likely connect you with other individuals with similar interests along with local and provincial resources and organizations.

Comprehensive School Health/Healthy School Communities

As explained in Chapter 8, embedding your physical education practice and program within a broader, healthy school community framework is very important. If you look again at Figure 8.1 (Chapter 8), consider explicitly how quality physical education (and you) can be an important contributor to a healthy school community.

- **Social and Physical Environment:** a school culture that is supportive of physical education provides opportunities for students, staff and families to be active

- **Teaching and Learning:** physical education is part of teaching the whole child

- **Healthy School Policy:** a policy of equitable gymnasium access supports healthy and active students

- **Partnerships and Services:** cooperating with the local community league provides access to activity space such as community halls and rinks

Connections to Lifelong Physical Activity and Opportunities in the Community

One way to connect to your community would be to organize a Physical and Health Education Fair. Scheduled outside of regular physical education teaching time, a PHE Fair is a terrific way to educate students, parents, and other family members about an array of topics concerning the importance of active living and healthy lifestyles. Invite local sport and activity clubs, the neighbourhood grocery store, local health support people, and other community resources to share what is available throughout the community.

5. Policy Advocacy

School Policy: Linking Physical Education to Healthy School Community Policy

Once you have reached this level of advocacy, it is time to look into what your school has for policies. Inquire as to whether your school's policy includes access to quality physical education. Consider forming a healthy school policy committee formed of multiple stakeholders (e.g., students, staff, parents, community members, public health) and begin to discuss what processes and polices will be effective. Look into what resources are available in your province to assist with this process. For example, both Ever Active Schools (2016) in Alberta and OPHEA (2016) in Ontario have tools, events, and assistance for local school communities. As well, the Joint Consortium for School Health (JCSH, 2016) has myriad of information and tools to help schools along their journey to be healthy.

District Policy

Policy also exists at the school jurisdictional level. More and more school jurisdictions are recognizing the importance of quality physical education, nutrition, and mental health, and care about the effectiveness of a healthy school community. For example, the Battle River School District (BRSD) (Gleddie, 2012a), as they developed district policy on healthy schools, added a foundation of health to their Pyramid of Success. The Pyramid is a graphic used to represent the priorities and values of the BRSD. Now everyone can see the role of health within the district's priorities, and school health has become embedded in the BRSD (Gleddie, 2012b). See Figure 11.5.

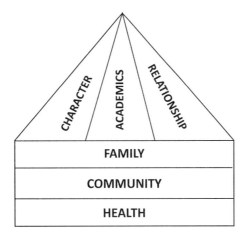

Figure 11.5. BRSD Pyramid of Success

Provincial Policy

For the most part, policy at the Provincial level means curriculum. It could also, however, involve recommendations of time and frequency for physical education, or relatively recent policies like DPA (see Chapter 9). Opportunities to influence and change provincial policy can include:

- Volunteering to serve on the executive of your provincial health and physical education association
- Participating in curriculum development activities
- Signing up for pilot or research projects that will inform policy
- Being a part of grants and research studies examining policy implementation

Case Study

You have 5 years of experience teaching Grade 2 and have always implemented daily physical education, an outcome-based program, and engaged in collaborative planning. You recently moved to a new school and during your first staff meeting, a week before school starts, the principal shared the school physical education schedule. You are dismayed to see that your Grade 2 class has only 3 scheduled times in the gymnasium and two of these times are combined with two other Grade 2 classes! As part of the staff meeting, you have time to meet with your grade level colleagues. Based on your discrete questioning, it doesn't seem that either of the other Grade 2 teachers have any issues with the physical education schedule and sharing the gymnasium. Your colleagues also share with you their previous year plans, which do not include gymnastics or alternative environments. They do, however, seem very receptive to change and open to suggestions, as neither would consider themselves a physical education leader. Given what you know about planning and being a physical education leader:

- **How would you begin to effect change to move towards quality daily physical education?**

Vignette

One of the best student papers I ever received was on the topic of media stereotypes and myths surrounding physical education. I had asked pre-service teachers to reflect on how negative media portrayals of physical education might impact their own future students' perceptions of the course and physical education teachers themselves. Sharif (pseudonym) not only had an excellent summary and analysis of these stereotypes, he had a very unique and wonderful way of responding. In his conclusion, he wrote (rough paraphrase from my memory):

> *In the end, it won't matter what stereotypes or myths my students have seen and/ or believe about physical education. Once they walk into my gym and experience my physical education, they will know that is NOT me. Humiliation?* **Not in my gym..** *Athlete-centric?* **Not in my gym.** *Gender biased?* **Not in my gym.** *Sports only?* **Not in my gym.** *Picked last?* **Not in my gym.**

Gleddie, 2013

> *" Classroom teachers need a coordinated strategy for addressing all the components of a quality physical education program, both during and after class time."*
>
> DeCorby, Halas, Dixon, Wintrup, & Janzen, 2005

Concluding Thoughts

Although some teachers will have had incredibly successful learning experiences in elementary school physical education, there will be other teachers who did not. Sometimes, without even realizing it, these teachers may marginalize physical education for their own classes. Recognizing that not everyone is supportive of physical education, this chapter aimed to show how you can be a leader and help your school develop a culture that promotes quality physical education programming. Leadership means, quite simply, that you first lead by example (Bradford, 2014), and then look for ways to support others in the ecological circles surrounding you by advocating for physical education. Advocacy refers to taking advantage of opportunities to promote and stand up for what you believe to be right and true about physical education in elementary schools. Becoming an advocate for physical education is important, similar to how we also need to be advocates for numeracy and literacy. By attending to the five layers of advocacy included in this chapter, we can ensure that we are supporting physical education programming in our schools, physical activity opportunities in our communities, and developing the basis for the physical literacy journeys of our students.

Checking for Understanding

I can:

- Use the ecological model to advocate for physical education at my school
- Explain the importance of personal leadership
- Understand that although quality physical education in my school might start with me... it certainly does not end there
- Understand how to advocate for physical education at an organizational level
- Delineate the various ways to connect with community – to the benefit of your physical education program
- Consider big and little picture policy and how physical education can enhance and support healthy schools

Chapter 12

An Open Letter from the Authors and Contributors

Introduction

Over the course of your class, through the readings, discussions, and applications of this text and much more, you have been learning about quality physical education and how to teach effectively and successfully. In the previous chapters, you will have seen the following four themes explored in a variety of ways.

The Importance of Safe Physical and Social-Emotional Environments. It is essential that your physical education program create and support a safe learning environment for all students: physically, socially and emotionally.

Developmental Appropriateness. The best opportunity for effective learning in physical education comes through an approach that is developmentally appropriate from psychomotor, growth, affective and cognitive perspectives.

Inclusive Practices. Teaching for all ensures that every student is recognized and considered during the planning, delivery, and assessment phases of physical education lessons.

Physical Literacy. Quality physical education enables students to take steps on the individual, lifelong journey that is physical literacy; supporting a lifetime of confidence and competence across a wide variety of activities and environments.

With a focus on these four themes when planning for quality physical education programming, it is important for teachers to fully understand why physical education is relevant and valuable for students. The following section shares some of this information.

Based on the Evidence, Physical Education is Relevant and Valuable because:

Physical education is an important part of the elementary school experience:
- More physical education time is related to reduced obesity rates in grade 5 students (Cawley, Friswold & Meyerhoefer, 2013)
- High school students who take more physical education were found to be more physically active after high school (Mears, 2005)
- Movement that is joyful and meaningful allows for creativity, development, discovery and expression (Kretchmar, 2008)

Physical education is essential for the development of fundamental movement skills:
- Motor skills were found to improve with increased physical education and physical activity time (Ericsson, 2008)
- When daily physical education was not occurring, students were more likely to have motor deficits (Ericsson & Karlsson, 2014)

Physical education informs the necessary skills and attitudes for all individuals to be successful in their activities of daily living:

- Physical activity is associated with a stronger self-image, quality of life and quality of peer and family relationships for children and youth (Iannotti et al., 2009)
- Students who did NOT have daily physical education were more likely to have motor deficits (Ericsson & Karlsson, 2014)

Physical education is a great way to energize and provide an emotional and physical outlet for children:

- Physical activity has the potential to enhance mood and improve self-esteem and self-perception (Fox et al., & 2000)
- "When movement is joyful and meaningful, it may even inspire us to do things that were never thought possible." (Kretchmar, 2008, p. 162)

Physical education is hands-on, exploratory, and practical in nature, which supports a variety of learning styles and student success:

- Kinaesthetic learners have opportunities for hands-on learning
- It allows students to show different forms of expression and provides opportunities to express themselves in a variety of ways

Physical education provides a unique and distinct contribution to a child's education:

- Distinct from many other subject areas, physical education addresses the interplay of mind, body, and spirit
- Physical education enables individuals to develop the knowledge, skills and attitudes necessary to lead an active, healthy lifestyle (Alberta Education, 2016)

Physical education is a place for planned and assessed intentional learning opportunities:

- A planned physical education experience will ensure opportunities for student learning
- Assessment practices should be conducted in a manner that promotes, encourages, and supports ongoing learning and contributes to the overall development of students (Alberta Education, 2000)

Physical education is a key part of a healthy school community (Comprehensive School Health - CSH):

- Physical education provides a clear connection between health and education
- CSH provides an opportunity for students to learn about how to lead active, healthy lifestyles in school and beyond; physical education can reinforce and support what happens outside the classroom walls

Physical education has been found to enhance student's academic performance:

- Academic grades for students enrolled in physical education, despite having almost an hour less of 'core academic instruction', were similar to those of students who did not have physical education (Coe, Pivarnik, Womack, Reeves & Malina, 2006)

- Girls who had physical education for 70 or more minutes per week attained significantly higher reading and mathematics scores than did girls with 35 or fewer minutes per week (Carlson, et al., 2008)

Physical education can help students experience the benefits of cross-curricular connections:
- Cross-curricular connections help students, through meaningful connections among subjects, build on their diverse prior knowledge and experiences (Alberta Education, 2007)
- Connecting subject areas enables students to develop a unified curriculum view to broaden the context of their learning beyond single subjects (Alberta Education, 2007)

Considerations for Your Physical Education Journey

"Start Small" - It is impossible to know, be and do everything – especially when you are a new teacher! Consider your strengths and weaknesses; the context you work in; your students and colleagues and begin to set specific, measurable, attainable, realistic, time-based (SMART) goals for yourself and your program. Evaluate regularly, then re-set those goals and keep moving forward!

"Start with YOU!" - Recognize the importance of physical education as an academic subject that contributes to the holistic development of children as citizens: now and for the future. Embrace quality health and physical education, and find people, resources, and professional development opportunities to fill gaps in your own practice. Don't settle for 'throwing out a ball' and watching students play – ensure learning!

"Find Partners" - 'You can go faster alone, but you go further together.' Connect with others who share your love and commitment to physical education. Share ideas, lessons and resources and above all, support each other on your professional journeys in physical education. These colleagues can be in your school, district, or around the world through social media platforms!

"You are a Role Model" - When teaching physical education, students will always be watching you. It is important to understand that you are, by nature, a role model to your students. Always pay attention to what you are wearing while teaching, and how you are communicating the importance of physical education to your students. Your students will soon realize, from your actions and attitudes, how important physical education really is.

"Engage in Professional Development" - You will be the best teacher you can be when you engage in professional development opportunities. It will help you stay current with your teaching practices. Professional development opportunities are always available. You just need to know how to discover where and when they are scheduled (e.g., contact your school jurisdiction's physical education consultant, join a #physed professional learning community on social media, etc.). Be open to multiple perspectives during professional development sessions, and use what works for your students.

"Teach Effectively" - Teaching effectively in physical education is about understanding curriculum and pedagogy as applied to the unique and complex field of human movement. Stay alert to effective teaching practices, and ensure your intended learning outcomes are focused on during your physical education lessons. Remember, how a teacher organizes the program, plans for assessment, engages learners through quality lessons, and dresses for teaching in an active learning environment, are just a few components that are associated with effective teaching in physical education.

"Time to Move" - As you continue your journey into the realm of teaching physical education, it is important to provide ample time for children and youth to be active not only for their physical health, but their overall well-being and health. Think about ways you can incorporate meaningful movement into the rest of the day. Support recess time and alternatives to sit-down desks. This may require advocacy on your part and perhaps even some creativity within the school day. It is worth it!

"Step Outside the Box" - There are endless resources, organizations, colleagues, friends, etc. available to support you. It's okay to not know everything; try to step outside your comfort zone to learn something new to teach in physical education, or ask someone to come in to help you out so you can provide diverse and meaningful experiences for your students.

"Create THAT Environment" - If the environment is open, engaging, supportive, positive, focused on strengths, diverse with variety, provides choice, developmentally appropriate...; then your students will be more than willing to participate, learn, and explore with you on new adventures through movement.

"Reflect and Listen" - Be self-reflective and talk to your students! Actively reflect on your teaching, question traditional practices, and ask your students for their feedback.

Our Concluding Thoughts for You...

Shannon Kell: Focus on the relationships you will build with students; the rest will come with time and practice.

Joanna Sheppard: Do not sell yourself short! You are not just a PE teacher. You are not just a "jock". You are a trained teacher, you are an educator, and you are a role model of physical activity in every sense of the word to your students, colleagues, friends and family!

Hayley Morrison: Take the time to get to know all of your students (strengths, interests, needs, wants, engagements outside school, etc.) so you can plan for an engaging and diverse experience for students in physical education.

Ashleigh Evaniew: It is important for you to recognize that physical education is essential for student growth and development. Through quality physical education, your students will increase their fundamental movement skills, self-efficacy, and overall passion for living healthy, active lifestyles.

Lauren Sulz: Create a "Physical Education Family" – establish a community of physical education teachers who you can share resources, have dialogue with regarding your practices, and support one another through your physical education journey.

Steve Berg: Have fun and enjoy the process! Sometimes, educators 'go through the motions' day in and day out. Enjoy the fact that you are making a positive difference in the lives of children. Smile and laugh with your students, and take some of their enthusiasm into your lessons.

Brent Bradford: When planning, teaching, and assessing for quality physical education, always consider: role modeling; maximum participation; inclusiveness; developmental appropriateness; and safety! Remember you are a role model!

Clive Hickson: Care about what and how you teach physical education, and take pride in knowing that you can provide a program that can positively impact children for their whole lives.

Doug Gleddie: Remember that to move is to be human and to be human is to be joyful. As you engage and relate with your students, help them embrace or re-connect with joyful movement through the wonder that is physical education!

We wish you much success in your journey of teaching physical education!

Reference List

AbilityPath.org. (2016). *Finding balance, obesity and children with special needs.* Retrieved from: http://www.abilitypath.org/health-daily-care/health/growth-and-nutrition

Active Healthy Kids Canada (2014). *Report card on the physical activity of children and youth: Is Canada in the running?* Retrieved from: http://www.activehealthykids.ca/ReportCard/2014ReportCard.aspx

Alberta Centre for Injury Control & Research. (2013). *Safety guidelines for physical activity in Alberta schools 2013.* Edmonton, AB: ACICR

Alberta Education. Alberta, Canada. Programs of Study. Retrieved from: https://education.alberta.ca/programs-of-study/programs-of-study

  1985. *Art Program of Studies.*

  2000. *English Language Arts Program of Studies.*

  2002. *Health and Life Skills Program of Studies.*

  2007. *Primary programs framework - Curriculum integration: Making connections.*

  2007; Updated 2014. *Mathematics Program of Studies.*

Alberta Education. (2005). Programming for students with Learning disabilities: Individualized program plans. Retrieved from: http://www.learnalberta.ca/content/kes/pdf/or_ws_tea_ld_b_01_ipp.pdf

Alberta Education. (2006). *Daily Physical Activity: A Handbook for Grades 1-9 Schools.* Edmonton, AB: Alberta Education.

Alberta Education. (2013). *Inclusive education library: Revised sample IPP templates.* Retrieved from: http://www.learnalberta.ca/content/ieptLibrary/lib07.html

Alberta Education (2015). *Guide to Education.* Retrieved from: https://education.alberta.ca/admin/resources/guidetoed

Alberta Education. (2016). *The daily physical activity initiative.* Retrieved from: https://education.alberta.ca/daily-physical-activity-dpa-initiative/program-supports

Alberta Education. (2016). *Guidelines for best practices: Creating learning environments that respect diverse sexual orientations, gender identities, and gender expressions.* Retrieved from: https://education.alberta.ca/media/1626737/91383-attachment-1-guidelines-final.pdf

Alberta Education. (2016). *What is inclusion? Retrieved from:* https://education.alberta.ca/inclusion/what-is-inclusion/?journeyId=1090&resetFilter=1

Alberta Learning. (2000). *Physical education program of studies.* Alberta Learning, Alberta, Canada.

Alberta Learning. (2000). *Physical Education Kindergarten to Grade 12.* Edmonton, Alberta: Alberta Education, 1.

Alberta Teachers' Association (2015). *History of Public Education, before 1905.* Retrieved from: http://www.teachers.ab.ca/Teaching%20in%20Alberta/History%20of%20Public%20Education/Pages/Before%201905.aspx

Almond, L., & Whitehead, M. (2012) Physical literacy: Clarifying the nature of the concept. *Practice Matters, Spring,* 68-71.

Armour, K.M., & Jones, R.L. (1998). *Physical education teachers' lives and careers: PE, sport and educational status.* London: Falmer.

Armstrong, Henson, and Savage (2015). *Teaching Today: An Introduction to Education.* Upper Saddle River, NJ: Person Education

Azzarito, L., & Solomon, M. A. (2005). A reconceptualization of physical education: The intersection of gender/race/social class. Sport, Education and Society, 10(1), 25-47.

Bandura. A. (1977). *Self-efficacy: Toward a unifying theory of behavioral change.* Psychological Review, 84, 191-215.

Barber, K. (Ed.). (1998). *The Canadian Oxford dictionary.* Oxford: Oxford University Press.

Barrett, J. M., & Winters, K-L. (2013). Dancing toward physical literacy from stage right and stage left: Pedagogical approaches from both physical education and arts educators. *Physical and Health Education Journal. Spring Special Issue,* 79(1), 12-17.

Barthel, S. and Gleddie, D.L. (2005). *Run, Jump and Throw: Implementing Daily Physical Activity in Alberta Schools.* Wellspring, 16(6).

Bassett-Gunter, R., Yessis, J., Manske, S., & Gleddie, D. (2015). Healthy school communities in Canada. *Health Education Journal, 1-14. DOI: 10.1177/0017896915570397.*

Beauchamp, C., & Thomas, L. (2009). Understanding teacher identity: An overview of issues in the literature and implications for teacher education. *Cambridge Journal of Education, 39(2),* 175-189. DOI:10.1080/03057640902902252

Beatty, J.E., Leigh, J.S., & Dean, K.L. (2009). Finding our roots: An exercise for creating a personal teaching philosophy statement. *Journal of Management Education, 33, 115-130.* DOI: 10.1177/1052562907310642

Belka, D.E. (1994). *Teaching Children Games.* Champaign, IL: Human Kinetics.

Bellon, J.J., Bellon, E.C., & Blank, M.A. (1992). *Teaching from a research knowledge base: A development and renewal process.* New York: Macmillan Publishing Company.

Berg, S., Hickson, C., & Fishburne, G.J. (2010). *Teaching children about health and wellness.* Edmonton, AB: Ripon Publishing.

Berg, S., Hickson, C., Bradford, B., & Fishburne, G.J. (2016). *Teaching for health and wellness in children and youth.* Edmonton, AB: Ripon Publishing.

Block, M. (2007). *A Teacher's Guide to Including Students with Disabilities in General Physical Education.* Baltimore, MD: Brookes Publishing.

Bonell, C., Humphrey, N., Fletcher, A., Moore, L., Anderson, R., & Campbell, R. (2014). *Why schools should promote students' health and wellbeing.* BMJ, 348(7958), g3078.

Borich, G.D. (1996). *Effective Teaching Methods (3rd ed.).* New Jersey: Prentice-Hall.

Borys, A.H. & Fishburne G.J. (1986). *Student teachers' conceptions of successful and unsuccessful teaching: Implications for student learning and teacher preparation.* Proceedings of the 1986 International Conference on Research in Teacher Education and Teaching in Physical Education (124-129). Vancouver: University of British Columbia.

Bradford, B. (2014). Leading by example: An effective motivational strategy! *Active & Healthy Magazine. Australian Council for Health, Physical Education and Recreation (ACHPER). 21(1): p. 19-22.*

Bradford, B.D. (2015). *Symbolism of clothing: The relationship between teacher clothing and children's perceptions in elementary school physical education.* Dissertation. University of Alberta. Retrieved from https://era.library.ualberta.ca/downloads/dj52w739f

Bradford, B. & Evaniew, A. (2014). Physical education homework: Learning outside the school walls! *The Canadian Teacher Magazine. (Issue: September/October 2014). p. 16-18. Retrieved from:* http://canadianteachermagazine.com/issues/2014/CTM_SeptOct14/index.html

Bradford, B., Hickson, C., & Evaniew, A. (2015a). *Professional development: Take time to improve yourself and others this year!* P.E. Links 4U Physical Education Website. 17(7). Retrieved from: http://www.pelinks4u.org/articles/hickson8_2015.html

Bradford, B., Hickson, C., & Evaniew, A. (2015b). Role modeling: The forgotten part of elementary school physical education. *Journal of Higher Education Theory and Practice.* 14(5), 18-23.

Bradford, B., & Hickson, C. (2014). *Teaching styles in elementary school physical education: The effect on children's learning.* International Journal of Pedagogy and Curriculum, 20(3).

Bradford, B., Hickson, C. & Berg, S. (2015). *Classrooms can be your gymnasium too. Presentation Proceedings.* SHAPE America National Convention and Expo. Seattle, Washington, USA. Retrieved from: https://shapeamerica.confex.com/shapeamerica/2015/webprogram/Session59642.html

Bradley, B.J., & Greene, A.C. (2013). Do health and education agencies in the United States share responsibility for academic achievement and health? A review of 25 years of evidence about the relationship of adolescents'' academic achievement and health behaviors. *Journal of Adolescent Health, 52(5), 523-532.*

British Columbia. (2016). *BC's New Curriculum.* Retrieved from: https://curriculum.gov.bc.ca/curriculum

British Columbia. (2016). *Health and physical activity.* Retrieved from: http://www2.gov.bc.ca/gov/content/education-training/k-12/teach/teaching-tools/health-and-physical-activity

British Columbia Ministry of Education. (2006). Physical education K-7: Grade 1. Retrieved from: https://www.bced.gov.bc.ca/irp/course.php?lang=en&subject=PhysicalEducation&course=Physical_Education_K_to_7&year=2006

British Columbia Ministry of Education. (2016). *Special education services: A manual of policies, procedures and guidelines*. Victoria, BC: BC Ministry of Education.

British Columbia. (2016). Health and physical activity. Retrieved from: http://www2.gov.bc.ca/gov/content/education-training/k-12/teach/teaching-tools/health-and-physical-activity

Britzman, D.P. (2003). *Practice makes practice: A critical study of learning to teach.* New York, N.Y.: State University of New York Press.

Bronfenbrenner, U. (1977). *Toward an experimental ecology of human development.* American Psychologist, 32, 513-531.

Brownlee, K., Rawana, E.P., & MacArthur, J. (2012). Implementation of a strengths-based approach to teaching in an elementary school. *Journal of Teaching and Learning, 8*(1), 1–12.

Bower, J. M., Carroll, A., & Ashman, A. (2014). The development and validation of the Contextualized Assessment Tool for Risk and Protection Management (CAT-   RPM). *Journal of Psychoeducational Assessment, 32*(2), 107–122.

Bunker, D., & Thorpe, R. (1982). A model for the teaching of games in secondary schools. *Bulletin of physical education, 18*(1), 5-8.

Cale, L., & Harris, J. (2013). Every child (of every size) matters' in physical education! Physical education's role in childhood obesity. *Sport, Education and Society, 18*(4), 433-452.

Canadian Active After School. (2016). Jiffy mixer dance. Retrieved from: http://activeafterschool.ca/activities/jiffy-mixer-dance

Canadian Centre for Ethics in Sport. (2016). Concussion prevention. Retrieved from: http://cces.ca/concussion-prevention

Canadian Council on Learning (2007). Health literacy in Canada: *Initial results from the international adult literacy and skills survey.* Retrieved from: http://www.ccl.cca.ca/ccl/Reports/HealthLiteracy/HealthLiteracy2007.html

Canadian Fitness and Lifestyle Research Institute (CFLRI). (2011). *Physical activity monitor 2010-2011*. Ottawa: ON.

Canadian Mental Health Association (2016). *Fast facts about mental illness.* Retrieved from: http://www.cmha.ca/media/fast-facts-about-mental-illness/#.V2bQrGgrKUk

Canadian Sport for Life (2015). Canada's physical literacy consensus statement. Downloaded from: http://www.physicalliteracy.ca/resources/canada%E2%80%99s-physical-literacy-consensus-statement

Canadian Sport for Life (2015). Long term athlete development model. Retrieved from:http://canadiansportforlife.ca/learn-about-canadian-sport-life/ltad-stages

Carlson, S.A., Fulton, J.E., Lee, S.M., Maynard, M., Brown, D.R., Kohl, III, H.W, & Dietz, W.H. (2008). *Physical education and academic achievement in elementary school: Data from the early childhood longitudinal study.* American Journal of Public Health, 98(4), 721-727

Cawley, J., Frisvold, D., & Meyerhoefer, C. (2013). *The impact of physical education on obesity among elementary school children.* Journal of Health Economics, 32(4), 743–755.

Cervantes, C. M., Lieberman, L. J., Magnesio, B., & Wood, J. (2013). Peer tutoring: meeting the demands of inclusion in physical education today. *Journal of Physical Education, Recreation & Dance, 84*(3), 43–48.

Chaput, J.P., Carson, V., Gray, C.E., & Tremblay, M.S. (2014). Importance of all movement behaviors in a 24 hour period for overall health. *International Journal of Environmental Research and Public Health. 11*(12), 12575-12581. DOI:10.3390/ijerph111212575

Clandinin, D.J., & Connelly, F.M. (2000). *Narrative inquiry: Experience and story in qualitative research.* San Francisco: Jossey-Bass.

Clandinin, D.J., & Rosiek, J. (2007) Mapping a landscape of narrative inquiry: Borderland spaces and tensions, pp. 35- 75 in Clandinin, J. (Ed.), *Handbook of Narrative Inquiry: Mapping Methodology,* Thousand Islands, London, New Dehli: Sage.

Clandinin, D. J., (1985). Personal, practical knowledge: A study of teachers' classroom images. *Curriculum Inquiry, 15*(4), 361-385.

Coe, D.P., Pivarnik, J.M., Womack, C.J., Reeves, M.J., & Malina, R.M. *(2006).* Effect of physical education and activity levels on academic achievement in children. *Medicine and Science in Sport and Exercise, 38*(8), 1515-1519.

Coelho, J. (2010). Gymnastics and Movement Instruction: fighting the decline in motor fitness. *Journal of Physical Education, Recreation & Dance, 81*(1),14-18.

Corlett, J., & Mandigo, J. (2013). A day in the life: Teaching physical literacy. *PHE Journal, 78*(4), 18-24.

Damhorst, M.L., Miller-Spillman, K.A., & Michelman, S.O. (2005). *The meanings of dress (2nd Ed.)*. New York, NY: Fairchild Publications, Inc.

Dean, M.B., Adams, T.M., & Comeau, M.J. (2005). The effect of a female physical educator's physical appearance on physical fitness knowledge and attitudes of junior high students. *The Physical Educator, 62*(1), 14-25.

DeCorby, K., Halas, J., Dixon, S., Wintrup, L., & Janzen, H. (2005). Classroom teachers and the challenges of delivering quality physical education. *Journal of Educational Research, 98*(4), 208-220.

De Koning L, Vasanti S, Malik MD, et al. (2012). Sweetened beverage consumption, Incident coronary heart disease and biomarkers of risk in men. *Circulation* 125, 1735-1741.

Dewey, J. (1938). *Experience and education*. New York: Collier Books

Dodds, P. & Placek, J. H. (1991). Silverman's RT-PE review: Too simple a summary of a complex field. *Research Quarterly for Exercise and Sport, 62,* (4), 365-368.

Donald, D. (2013). Teachers, aboriginal perspectives and the logic of the fort: We need a new story to guide us. Retrieved from: http://www.teachers.ab.ca/Publications/ATA%20Magazine/Volume-93/Number-4/Pages/Teachers-aboriginal-perspectives.aspx

Donnelly J.E., & Lambourne K. (2011). Classroom-based physical activity, cognition, and academic achievement. *Preventive Medicine.* 52 Suppl 1: S36-S42. 36, DOI:10.1016/j.ypmed.2011.01.021

Donham-Foutch, S. (2007). Teaching skills and health-related fitness through a pre-service gymnastics program. *Journal of Physical Education, Recreation & Dance, 78*(5), 1-58.

Drake, S.M., & Reid, J. (2010). Integrated curriculum: Increasing relevance while maintaining accountability. T*he Literacy and Numeracy Secretariat.* (September 2010).

Dunn, A. L., Trivedi, M. H., & O'Neal, H. A. (2001). Physical activity dose–response effects on outcomes of depression and anxiety. *Medicine & Science in Sports & Exercise.*

Ericsson, I. (2008). Motor skills, attention and academic achievements: An intervention study in school years 1-3. *British Educational Research Journal, 34*(3), 301–313.

Ericsson, I., & Karlsson, M. K. (2014). Motor skills and school performance in children with daily physical education in school – a 9-year intervention study. *Scandinavian Journal of Medicine & Science in Sports, 24*(2), 273–278.

Espiritu, J. K. (1987). Quality physical education programs: Cognitive emphases. *Journal of Physical Education, Recreation and Dance, 58*(6), 38–40.

Ever Active Schools. (2016). Retrieved from: http://www.everactive.org

Fishburne, G.J. (1983). Is reading more important than physical education? *Elements: A Journal for Elementary Education.* 15(1), 3-5.

Fishburne G. J. & Borys, A. H. (1987). A comparison between elementary school teachers' and student-teachers' conceptions of successful teaching. Proceedings of the 30th ICHPER World Congress and the 34th CAHPER Conference in conjunction with the British Columbia Physical Education Teachers' Conference (pp. 82-85). Vancouver: University of British Columbia.

Fishburne, G.J. (2005). *Developmentally appropriate physical education for children and youth.* University of Alberta: Ripon Publishing.

Fishburne, G. J. (2005). Unit Plans, Lesson Plans, and Yearly Programs for Developmentally Appropriate Physical Education for Children and Youth. Sherwood Park, AL: Ripon Publishing

Fishburne, G. J. & Hickson, C. (2005). *What is the Relationship between Physical Education and Physical Activity?* National Major Position paper for Canadian Association for Health, Physical Education, Recreation and Dance. Ottawa: CAHPERD.

Fitts, P.M., & Posner, M.L. (1967). *Human performance.* Belmont, CA: Brooks-Cole.

Fitzgerald, H., & Stride, A. (2012). Stories about physical education from young people with disabilities. *International Journal of Disability, Development and Education, 59(*3), 283-293.

Forsberg, N., & Chorney, D. (2014). *Physical education looking back, looking forward. In D. B. Robinson & L. Randall (Ed.)* Teaching Physical Education Today: Canadian Perspectives (pp. 2-19). Toronto, ON: Thompson Educational Publishing.

Fox, K. R., Boutcher, S. H., Faulkner, G. E., & Biddle, S. J. (2000). The case for exercise in the promotion of mental health and psychological well-being. *Physical activity and psychological well-being*, 1-9.

Fung, C., Kuhl, S., Lu, M., Purcell, M., Schwartz, M., Storey, K., & Veugelers, P.J. (2012). From "best practice" to "next practice": the effectiveness of school-based health promotion in improving healthy eating and physical activity and preventing childhood obesity. *International Journal of Behavioral Nutrition and Physical Activity*, 9(27), 1-9.

Garrett, R. (2006). Critical storytelling as a teaching strategy in physical education teacher education. *European Physical Education Review,* 12(3), 339-360.

Gaudreault, K.L. & Woods, A.M. (2012). The effects of achieved National Board for Professional Teaching Standards Certification on the marginality of physical education teachers. *Teacher Educator.* 47(4), 283-301. DOI: 10.1080/08878730.2012.707760

Gleddie, D.L. (2006) Daily physical activity: Overcoming two challenges. *Wellspring,* 17(3).

Gleddie, D.L. (2010). *Health Promoting Schools: Administrator's Guide.* Physical and Health Education Canada, Ottawa.

Gleddie, D.L. (2012). A journey into school health promotion: District implementation of the health promoting schools approach. *Health Promotion International*, 27(1), 82-89. DOI: 10.1093/heapro/dar053

Gleddie, D.L. (2013). Not in my gym. Retrieved from http://purposefulmovement.net/2013/05/14/not-in-my-gym/

Gleddie, D.L. (2015). Fit for #physed? Retrieved from: https://purposefulmovement.net/2015/02/20/fit-for-physed

Gleddie, D.L., & Schaefer, L. (2014). Autobiographical narrative inquiry into movement and physical education: The beginning of a journey. *PHEnex Journal*, 6(3), 1-14.

Gibbons, S., & Naylor, P.J. (2007). Whole school obesity prevention models: Considerations for secondary schools. *Physical and Health Education Journal,* 72(4), 8-13.

Government of Canada. (2016). Children and physical activity. Retrieved from: http://healthycanadians.gc.ca/healthy-living-vie-saine/being-active-etre-actif/tips-conseils-eng.php

Grasha, A, F. (1996). *Teaching with style: a practical guide to enhancing learning by understanding teaching and learning styles.* Pittsburgh: Alliance Publishers.

Goodwin, D.L., & Watkinson, E. J. (2000). Inclusive physical education from the perspective of students with disabilities. *Adapted Physical Activity Quarterly,* 17, 144–160.

Goodwin, D.L. (2001). The meaning of help in PE: Perceptions of students with physical disabilities. *Adapted Physical Activity Quarterly*, 18(3), 289–303.

Greene, M. (1993). Diversity and inclusion: Toward a curriculum for human beings. *Teachers College Record*, 95(2), 211-221.

Greene, M. (1995). *Releasing the imagination: Essays on education, the arts and social change.* San-Francisco, CA: Jossey-Bass.

Hargreaves, A., & Shirley, D. (2009). *The fourth way: The inspiring future for educational change.* Thousand Oaks, CA: Corwin.

Halas, J. M. (2011). Aboriginal youth and their experiences in physical education: "This is what you've taught me". *Revue phénEPS/PHEnex Journal*, 3(2), 1–23.

Halas, J., McRae, H., & Petherick, L. (2012). Advice for Physical Education Teachers from Aboriginal Youth: Become an Ally. *Physical & Health Education Journal*, 78(3), 6–11.

Halas, J., McCrae, H., & Carpenter, A. (2013). The quality and cultural relevance of physical education for Aboriginal youth: Challenges and opportunities. In J. Forsythe & A. R. Giles(Eds.), Aboriginal peoples and sport in Canada: Historical foundations and contemporary issues (pp. 182-205). Vancouver, Canada: UBC Press

Hall, N., Bradford, B., & Hickson, C. (2015). Orienteering: A fun way to get physically active in an outdoor environment. *Runner - Journal of the Health and Physical Education Council of the Alberta Teachers' Association* (HPEC), 47(1), 9-12.

Hart, M.A. (1999). Seeking mino-pimatasiwin (the good life): An aboriginal approach to social work practice. *Native Social Work Journal*, 2(1), 91-112.

Hastie, P. & Martin, E. (2006). *Teaching elementary physical education: Strategies for the classroom teacher*. Pearson: New York, NY.

Hay, P.J. & Macdonald, D. (2010). The gendering of abilities in senior Physical Education. *Physical Education & Sport Pedagogy, 15* (3), 271-285.

Haywood, K.M., & Getchell, N. (2014). *Life Span Motor Development (6th Edition).* Champaign, IL: Human Kinetics

Health Canada. (2012). Do Canadian children meet their nutrient requirements through food intake alone? Retrieved from: http://www.hc-sc.gc.ca/fn-an/surveill/nutrition/commun/art-nutr-child-enf-eng.php#a1

Health Canada. (2013). *Canadian alcohol and drug use monitoring survey:* Summary of results for 2012. Ottawa, ON:Author.

Heart and Stroke Foundation. (2016). *Schools and nutrition*. Retrieved from: http://www.heartandstroke.com/site/c.ikIQLcMWJtE/b.3799205/k.DBDC/Position_Statements__Schools_and_Nutrition_Position_Statement.htm

Hickson, C. (2005). *Teacher development: Effective P.E. teaching*. Unpublished dissertation, University of Alberta.

Hickson, C., & Saby, C. (2008). *Making Games Activities Developmentally Appropriate for Elementary School Children*. Presentation at Health and Physical Education Council. AB, Grande Prairie.

Hickson, C. (2009). Spreading the Word, Sharing the Value! P.E. Links 4U. Retrieved from: http://www.pelinks4u.org/articles/hicks0509.htm

Hickson, C. (2010). Physical Activity Programming: The new kid on the block! Friend, foe, or just what we needed? P.E. Links 4U. Retrieved from: http://www.pelinks4u.org/articles/hickson0310.htm

Hickson, C. & Bradford, B. (2010). Healthy, active messages: What are we telling our students? P.E.Links4U Physical Education Website. Retrieved from http://www.pelinks4u.org/articles/hick_brad_1210.htm

Hickson, C., Robinson, D., Berg, S. & Hall, N. (2012). Active in the north: School and community physical activity programming in Canada. *International Journal of Physical Education 2(12)*, 16-30.

Hickson, C.N., & Fishburne, G.J. (2001) Learning through effective teaching: Research studies in physical education. In B. Cope, & M. Kalantzis (Eds.), *Learning for the Future*. Proceedings of the Learning Conference 2001. Spetses: Greece.

Hickson, C. & Fishburne, G.J. (2002, April). *Effective teaching in elementary schools: Subject area differences*. Presentation at the Annual Convention of the American Alliance for Health, Physical Education, Recreation & Dance, San Diego, CA.

Hickson, C., Berg, S., & Bradford, B. (2015). School leadership personnel: A critical piece of the puzzle for health and physical education programming? *Physical and Health Education Journal.* 81(1), 8-13.

Hillman C.H., Pontifex, M.B., Raine, L.B., Castelli, D.M., Hall, E.E., & Kramer, A.F. (2009). The effect of acute treadmill walking on cognitive control and academic achievement in preadolescent children. Neuroscience. 159(3), 1044-1054.

Hyde, A.L., Maher, J.P., & Elavsky, S. (2013). Enhancing our understanding of physical activity and wellbeing with a lifespan perspective. I*nternational Journal of Wellbeing*, 3(1), 98-115.

Hogan, A., McLellan, L., & Bauman, A. (2000). *Health promotion needs of young people with disabilities – A population study*. Disabil Rehabil, 22(8), 352-7.

Holt, B., & Hannon, J. (2006). *Teaching-learning in the affective domain. Strategies*, 20(1), 11–13.

Iannotti, R.J., Kogan, M.D., Janssen, I., & Boyce, W.F. (2009). Patterns of adolescent physical activity, screen-based media use, and positive and negative health indicators in the US and Canada. *Journal of Adolescent Health,* 44(5), 493-499.

Irish, C., & O'Callaghan, W. (2013). Who Is responsible for education in a community? Implications of living in the education silo. *National Civic Review*, (102)2, 17-19.

Iserbyt, P., & Byra, M. (2013). Design and use of task cards in the reciprocal style of teaching. *Journal of Physical Education, Recreation & Dance*, 84(2), 20–26

Jenkinson, K.A., & Benson, A.C. (2010). Barriers to providing physical education and physical activity in Victorian state secondary schools. *Australian Journal of Teacher Education*, 35(8).

Joint Consortium for School Health. (2010). What is comprehensive school health? Retrieved from www.jcsh-cces.ca

Joint Consortium for School Health. (2016). Retrieved from: http://www.jcsh-cces.ca

Karhioo, E. (2009). Reframing physical activity programs for aboriginal communities. *WellSpring*, 20(6), n.p.

Kell, S. D. (2015). Program of studies and curriculum instruction in teaching physical education [Course syllabus]. Department of Health and Physical Education, Mount Royal University, Calgary, AB.

Kelly, J.G. (1990). Changing contexts and the field of community psychology. *American Journal of Community Psychology,* 18, 769-792.

Keshavarz, N., Nutbeam, D., Rowling, L., & Khavarpour, F. (2010). Schools as social complex adaptive systems: a new way to understand the challenges of introducing the health promoting schools concept. *Social science & medicine*, 70(10), 1467-1474.

Kilborn, M., Lorusso, J., & Francis, N. (2015). An analysis of Canadian physical education curricula. *European Physical Education Review*, 1-24: DOI: 10.1177/1356336X15586909

Kirk, D. (2010). *Physical education futures*. New York, NY: Routledge.

Kretchmar, R.S. (1990). Values, passion, and the expected lifespan of physical education. *Quest*, 42, 95-112.

Kretchmar, R.S. (2008). The increasing utility of elementary school physical education: A mixed blessing and a unique challenge. *The Elementary School Journal*, 108(3), 161-170.

Kriemler, S., Meyer, U., Martin, E., van Sluijs, E.M., Andersen, L.B., & Martin, B.W. (2011). Effect of school-based interventions on physical activity and fitness in children and adolescents: a review of reviews and systematic update. *British Journal of Sports Medicine*, 45(11), 923-930.

LaBillois, J.M., & Lagacé-Séguin, D.G. (2009). Does a good fit matter? Exploring teaching styles, emotion regulation, and child anxiety in the classroom. *Early Childhood Development and Care,* 179(3):303-315.

Lešnik, B., Glinšek, V., & Žvan, M. (2015). Correlation between gymnastics elements knowledge and performance success in younger categories of alpine skiing. *Science of Gymnastics Journal,* 7(2), 67-79.

Lieberman, L.J., Houston-Wilson, C., & Kozub, F.M. (2002). Perceived barriers to including students with visual impairments in general physical education. *Adapted Physical Activity Quarterly*, 19, 364–377.

Lloyd, R. & Smith, S. (2013). Physical literacy. In. In. D. Robinson, & L. Randall (Eds.), Teaching physical education today: *Canadian perspectives*. Toronto: Thompson Education.

Long, M.W., Sobol, A.M., Cradock, A.L., Subramanian, S.V., Blendon, M.J., & Gortmaker, S.L. (2013). School-day and overall physical activity among youth. *American Journal of Preventive Medicine*, 45(2), 150–157.

Lounsbery, M.A.F., McKenzie, T.L., Trost, S., & Smith, N.J. (2011). Facilitators and barriers to adopting evidence-based physical education in elementary school. *Journal of Physical Activity and Health*, 8(Suppl 1), S17-S28.

Louv, R. (2008). *Last child in the woods: Saving our children from nature-deficit disorder*. Algonquin: Chapel Hill, North Carolina.

Lu, C., & De Lisio, A. (2009). Specifics for generalists: Teaching elementary physical education. *International Electronic Journal of Elementary Education,* 1(3), 170–187.

Lugones, M. (1997). Playfulness, "world"–travelling and loving perception. *Hypatia*, 2(2), 3-18.

Mandigo, J., Francis, N., Lodewyk, K, & Lopez, R. (2009) Position paper: Physical literacy for educators. *Physical and Health Education Canada*. 1-13.

Mandigo, J.L. (2010). Presenting the evidence: Quality physical education for Canadian children and youth position statement by Physical and Health Education Canada. Position statement by: Physical and Health Education Canada. *PHEnex*. 2(1).

Manitoba Education and Training (2016). Retrieved from: http://www.edu.gov.mb.ca/index.html

Manitoba Education and Training. (2000). Kindergarten to Senior 4 Physical Education/Health Education: Manitoba Curriculum Framework of Outcomes for Active Healthy Lifestyles. Winnipeg, Manitoba: Manitoba Education and Training, 3.

Manuel, D.G., Rosella, L.C.A., Tuna, M., & Bennett, C. (2010). How many Canadians will be diagnosed with diabetes between 2007 and 2017? Assessing population risk. *ICES Investigative Report.* Toronto: Institute for Clinical Evaluative Sciences.

Marzano, R.J. (2003). *Classroom Management that works: Research-based strategies for every teacher*. ASCD, Virginia, US.

Mawer, M. (1995). *The effective teaching of physical education*. New York, NY: Longman.

Mawer, M. 1999. Teaching Styles and Teaching Approaches in Physical Education: Research Developments. In C. A. Hardy & M. Mawer (Eds.), *Learning and teaching in physical education.* (pp. 83-104). Philadelphia, PA: Falmer Press.

McCashen, W. (2004). *Communities of hope: A strengths-based resource for building community.* Bendigo, VIC: St. Luke's Innovative Resources.

McCaughtry, N., & Centeio, E.E. (2014). Physical Education Curriculum in the Age of Cultural Relevance and Popular Physical Activity Culture (pp. 1-18). In S. Bernard Flory, A. Tischler, and S. Sander, Sociocultural Issues in Physical Education: Case Studies for Teachers (Eds.), London, UK: Rowman & Littlefield.

McLean, C. (2012). Play it forward: The influence of Action Schools! BC on high School students' physical activity levels (Unpublished Masters Thesis). University of Victoria, Victoria, BC.

McMahon, J.A., & Penney, D. (2013). *Using narrative as a tool to locate and challenge pre- service teacher bodies in health and physical education. Australian Journal of Teacher Education,* 38(1), 115–133.

Mears, D. (2005). Do Missouri high school physical education programs have an impact on life-time physical activity? *Missouri Journal of Health, Physical Education, Recreation and Dance,* 15(1), 51–61.

Medley, D.M. (1987). Evolution of research on teaching. In M. J. Dunkin (Ed.). *The International encyclopediu of teaching and teacher education.* (pp. 105-113). New York: Pergamon.

Metzler, M.W. (2011). *Instructional models for physical education, (3rd ed.).* Scottsdale, AZ: Holcomb Hathaway.

Morgan, P.J. & Hansen, V. (2008). Classroom teachers' perceptions of the impact of barriers to teaching physical education on the quality of physical education programs. *Research Quarterly for Exercise and Sport*, 79(4), 506-516.

Mosston, M., & Ashworth, S. (1986). *Teaching physical education. (3rd ed.).* Columbus: Merrill Publishing Company.

Mosston, M., & Ashworth, S. (1994). *Teaching physical education.* (4th ed.). New York: NY: Macmillan College Publishing Company.

Mullender-Wijnsma, M.J., Hartman, E., de Greeff, J.W., Doolaard, S., Bosker, R.J., Visscher, C. (2016). Physically active math and language lessons improve academic achievement: a cluster randomized controlled trial. *Pediatrics.* 137(3), 1-9.

Murray, N.G., Low, B.J., Hollis, C., Cross, & Davis. (2007). Coordinated health school programs and academic achievement: A systematic review of the literature. *Journal of School Health,* 77(9), p.589-600.

Mutrie, N. (2000). The relationship between physical activity and clinically defined depression. Physical activity and psychological well-being, 46-62.

Naylor, P.J., Macdonald, H.M., Warburton, D.E.R., Reed, K.E., & McKay, H.A. (2008). An active school model to promote physical activity in elementary schools: Action Schools! BC. *British Journal of Sports Medicine,* 42(5), 338-343.

Nickel, J. (2013). Self-assessment of professional growth through reflective portfolios. Phronesis, 2(1). 67-79.

Nickel, J. (2015). *Professional identity in graduating teacher candidates.* Unpublished manuscript.

Noddings, N. (2005). Caring in education. The encyclopedia of informal education. Retrieved from: www.infed.org/ biblio/noddings_caring_in_education.htm

Ontario Ministry of Education. (2005). Mathematics. Retrieved from: http://www.edu.gov.on.ca/eng/curriculum/ elementary/math18curr.pdf

Ontario Ministry of Education. (2010). The Ontario curriculum grades 1-8: Physical and health education. Retrieved from: http://www.edu.gov.on.ca/eng/curriculum/elementary/health.html

Ontario Ministry of Education (2015). Achieving excellence: A renewed vision for education in Ontario. Retrieved from: http://www.edu.gov.on.ca/eng/about/excellent.html

OPHEA. (2010). Building Health & Physical literacy for Schools & Communities across Ontario. *Physical & Health Education Journal*. 76(2), 28-31.

OPHEA. (2014). Play Sport. Teaching games for understanding (TGfU) Approach. Toronto, ON. Retrieved from: http://www.playsport.net/about-playsport/teaching-games-understanding-tgfu

OPHEA. (2014). Playsport Teaching kids games by playing games. Retrieved from: http://www.playsport.net/Ophea/PlaySport/overview.cfm

OPHEA. (2016). Retrieved from https://www.ophea.net/

O'Reilly, E., Tomkins, J., & Gallant, M. (2001). They ought to enjoy physical activity, you know?": Struggling with fun in physical education. *Sport, Education and Society*, 6(2), 211 – 221.

O'Sullivan, M. (2006). Professional lives of Irish physical education teachers: stories of resilience, respect and resignation. *Physical Education and Sport Pedagogy,* 11(3), 265-284.

Pangrazi, R.P., & Gibbons, S.L. (2009). *Dynamic physical education for elementary school children.* (2nd Ed.). Toronto, ON: Pearson, Allyn & Bacon.

Pangrazi, R.P., & Beighle, A. (2013). *Dynamic physical education for elementary school children.* (17th ed.). New York, NY: Pearson.

Pardo, B.M., Bengoechea, E.G., Lanaspa, E.G., Bush, P.L., Casterad, J.Z., Clemente, J.A.J., & Gonzalez, L.G. (2013). Promising school-based strategies and intervention guidelines to increase physical activity of adolescents. *Health Education Research*, 29(3), 1-9.

Parfitt, G., Pavey, T., & Rowlands, A. V. (2009). Children's physical activity and psychological health: the relevance of intensity. *Acta Paediatrica*, 98(6), 1037-1043.

Parkay, F.W., Stanford, B.H., Vailancourt, J.P. Stephens, H.C., & Harris, J.R. (2010). *Becoming a teacher*. Toronto, ON: Pearson

ParticipACTION. (2013). Why Kids are not playing anymore. Toronto: ON. Retrieved from: http://www.participaction.com/get-moving/bring-back-play

ParticipACTION. (2015). *The biggest risk is keeping kids indoors.* Toronto, ON. Retrieved from: http://www.participaction.com/sites/default/files/downloads/Participaction-2015 ReportCard-FullReport_4.pdf

ParticipACTION (2016). The ParticipACTION report card on physical activity for children and youth. Retrieved from http://www.participaction.com/en-ca/thought-leadership/report-card/archive

Passarelli, A., Hall, E., & Anderson, M. (2010). A strengths-based approach to outdoor and adventure education: Possibilities for personal growth. *Journal of Experiential Education*, 33(2), 120–135.

Pavlovic, B., Popovic, B., & Zrnzevic, N. (2015). Traditional folk dances of south-west Serbia in teaching musical culture and physical education. *Activities in Physical Education and Sport.* 5(1), 24-29.

Pearson, P. & Webb, P. (2008). Developing effective questioning in teaching games for understanding (TGfU). (Paper Presentation). *1st Asia Pacific Sport in Education Conference.* Adelaide. Retrieved from: http://ro.uow.edu.au/cgi/viewcontent.cgi?article=1054&context=edupapers

PHE Canada (2010). *Fundamental movement skills: Active start and FUNdamentals stages – for children with developmental and/or behavioural disabilities.* Ottawa, ON: PHE Canada.

PHE Canada. (2011). *Fundamental Movement Skills: The Building Blocks for the Development of Physical Literacy.* Ottawa, ON.

PHE Canada. (2015). *Physical and Health Education Canada.* Retrieved from: www.phecanada.ca

PHE Canada. (2016). *Physical and Health Education Canada.* Retrieved from: www.phecanada.ca

PHE Canada (2016). *Time to move!* Retrieved from: http://www.phecanada.ca/sites/default/files/advocacy_tools/TimetoMoveEnglish_crop.pdf

Phillips, S., & Silverman, S. (2012). Development of an instrument to assess fourth and fifth grade students' attitudes toward physical education. *Measurement in Physical Education and Exercise Science.* 16, 316–327.

Placek, J. (1983). Conceptions of success in teaching: Busy, happy and good. *Teaching in Physical Education*, 46-56.

Prince Edward Island Department of Education and Early Childhood Development. (2011). Prince Edward Island Physical Education Curriculum Grades K-6. Summerside, Prince Edward Island: Prince Edward Island Department of Education and Early Childhood Development, 3.

Public Health Agency of Canada (2015). *Health behaviour in school-aged children (HBSC) in Canada.* Retrieved from: http://healthycanadians.gc.ca/publications/science-research-sciences-recherches/health-behaviour-children-canada-2015-comportements-sante-jeunes/alt/health-behaviour-children-canada-2015-comportements-sant%C3%A9-jeunes-eng.pdf

Public Health Agency of Canada (2016). *Health literacy.* Retrieved from: http://www.phac-aspc.gc.ca/cd-mc/hl-ls/index-eng.php#tabs-2

Rauschenbach, J. (1996). Tying it all together: Integrating physical education and other subject areas. *Journal of Physical Education, Recreation & Dance (JOPERD).* 67(2), 49-51.

Reed, K.E., Warburton, D.E.R., Macdonald, H.M., Naylor, P.J., & McKay, H.A. (2008). Action Schools! BC: a school-based physical activity intervention designed to decrease cardiovascular disease risk factors in children. *Preventive Medicine*, 46(6), 525-531.

Richard, M. (2013). Dance as a language of learning and a source of embodied knowledge. *Physical and Health Education. Spring Special Issue,* 79(1), 6-10.

Richie, J.S. & Wilson, D.E. (2000). *Teacher narrative as critical inquiry: Rewriting the script.* NewYork, N.Y.: Teachers College Press.

Rink, J.E. (1993). *Teaching physical education for learning.* St. Louis: Mosby Year Book.

Rink, J. (1999). *What do students learn in physical education and how do they learn?* The José Maria Cagigal Lecture presented at the 1999 International AIESEP Congress, Besançon.

Rink, J.E. (2010). *Teaching physical education for learning.* (6th ed.). Boston: McGraw-Hill.

Roach, K.D. (1997). Effects of graduate teaching assistant attire on student learning, misbehaviors, and ratings of instruction. *Communication Quarterly.* 45(3), 125-141.

Robinson, D.B., & Gleddie, D.L. (2011). Gym class with Ed Fizz: Exploring questionable and taken for granted practice with pre-service physical education teachers. *Journal of Physical Education, Recreation and Dance,* 82(6), 41-45. DOI: 10.1080/07303084.2011.10598644

Rotermann, M. (2012). Sexual behaviour and condom use of 15- to 24-year-olds in 2003 and 2009/2010. *Health Reports*, 23(1).

Saab, H., & King, M. (2008). Health risk behaviours. *In Healthy Settings for Young People in Canada,* 57-89. Public Health Agency of Canada.

Sallis, J.F., & Owen, N. (1997). Ecological models. In K. Glanz, F. M. Lewis, & B. K. Rimmer (Eds.), *Health behavior and health education: Theory, research, and practice.* (2nd ed., pp. 403-424). San Francisco: Jossey-Bass.

Sallis, J.F., McKenzie, T.L., Kolody, B., Lewis, M., Marshall, S., & Rosengard, P. (1999). Effects of health related physical education on academic achievement: Project SPARK. *Research Quarterly for Exercise and Sport,* 70(2), 127-134.

Saskatchewan Ministry of Education. (2009). Physical Education 6. Regina, Saskatchewan: Ministry of Education, 5.

Saskatchewan Ministry of Education. (2010). Physical Education 1. Regina, Saskatchewan: Ministry of Education, 5.

Saskatchewan Ministry of Education (2016a). Saskatchewan curriculum: Teaching physical education 4. Retrieved from: https://www.curriculum.gov.sk.ca/webapps/moe-curriculum-BBLEARNindexjsp?view=teaching&lang=en&subj=physical_education&level=4

Saskatchewan Ministry of Education (2016b). Saskatchewan curriculum: Physical education 4 outcomes Retrieved from: https://www.curriculum.gov.sk.ca/webapps/moe-curriculum-BBLEARNindexjsp?view=outcomes&lang=en&subj=physical_education&level=4

Saskatchewan Curriculum. (2016c). Health Education Aims & Goals. Retrieved from: https://curriculum.gov.sk.ca/webapps/moe-curriculum-BBLEARN/indexjsp?view=goals&lang=en&subj=health_education&level=3

Schaefer, L., Long, J., & Clandinin, D.J. (2012). Questioning the research on early career teacher attrition and retention. *Alberta Journal of Educational Research,* 58(1), 106-121.

Schaefer, L., Plotnikoff, R.C., Majumdar, S.R., Mollard, R., Woo, M., Sadman, R., Rinaldi, R.L., Boulé, N., Torrance, B., Ball, G.D.C., Veugelers, P., Wozny, P., McCargar, L., Downs, S., Lewanczuk, R., Gleddie, D.L., McGavock, J. (2014) Outdoor time is associated with physical activity, sedentary time, and cardiorespiratory fitness in youth. *Journal of Pediatrics*, ISSN 0022-3476, Retrieved from: *http://dx.doi.org/10.1016/j.jpeds.2014.05.029*

Schempp, P.G. (1983). Learning the role: The transformation from student to teacher. In T. Templin and J. Olsen (Eds.). *Teaching in physical education.* (pp. 109-117). Illinois: Human Kinetics Publishers.

Schempp, P.G. (1985). Becoming a better teacher: An analysis of student teaching experience. *Journal of Teaching in Physical Education*, 4, 158-166.

Schwartz, M., & Bouchard, C. (2005). *What the research tells us.* Runner, 41(3), 51-53.

Shephard, R.J. (1996). Habitual physical activity and academic performance. *Nutrition Reviews,* 54(4), S32-S36.

Shephard, R.J., & Trudeau, F. (2010). The legacy of physical education: Influences on adult lifestyle. *Pediatric Exercise Science*, 12(1), 34-50.

Silko, L. (1996). *Interior and exterior Landscapes: The Pueblo migration stories. Yellow woman and a beauty of the spirit* (pp. 25-47). New York: Simon & Schuster.

Silverman, S. (1991). Research on teaching in physical education. *Research Quarterly for Exercise and Sport,* 62(4), 352-364.

Sparkes, A.C. (2002). *Telling tales in sport and physical activity.* Champaign: Human Kinetics.

SPEA (Saskatchewan Physical Education Association). (2016). Retrieved from: http://www.speaonline.ca

State of Victoria, Department of Education and Early Childhood Development. (2012). *Strengths-based approach: A guide to writing transition learning and development statements.* Melbourne, Victoria: Department of Education and Early Childhood Development

Statistics Canada. (2011). *Injuries in Canada: Insights from the Canadian community health survey.* Retrieved from: http://www.statcan.gc.ca/pub/82-624-x/2011001/article/11506-eng.pdf

Statistics Canada (2012-2013). *Canadian health measures survey.* Cited in ParticipACTION, 2016

Statistics Canada. (2015). *Cyberbullying and the luring of children and youth.* Retrieved from: http://www.statcan.gc.ca/pub/85-002-x/2011001/article/11530-eng.htm#a2

Steiner, A.M. (2010). A strength-based approach to parent education for children with autism. *Journal of Positive Behavior Interventions*, 13(3) 178–190.

Story, M. (1999). School-based approaches for preventing and treating obesity. *International Journal of Obesity Related Metabolic Disorders,* 23(S2), S43–S51.

Story, M., Nanney, M.S., & Schwartz, M.B. (2009). Schools and obesity prevention: Creating school environments and policies to promote healthy eating and physical activity. *Milbank Quarterly*, 87(1), 71-100.

Strean, W.B. (2009). Remembering instructors: play, pain and pedagogy. *Qualitative Research in Sport and Exercise*, 1(3), 210-220.

Suhrcke, M. & de Paz Nieves, C. (2011). *The impact of health and health behaviours on educational outcomes in high-income countries: a review of the evidence.* Copenhagen, WHO Regional Office for Europe.

Sulz, L. & Gibbons, S.L. (in press). Whole-School approaches to health promotion in high schools: a review of four recent interventions. *International Journal of Physical Education*.

Sulz, L., Gibbons, S., Naylor, P.J., & Wharf Higgins, J. (2016). Complexity of choice: teachers' and students' experiences implementing a choice-based Comprehensive School Health model. *Health Education Journal*. Advance online publication. DOI: 10.1177/0017896916645936

Thelen, E. (1995). *Motor development: A new synthesis.* American Psychologist, 50(2), 79-95.

Tjepkema, M., & Shield, M. (2005). Measured obesity: Overweight Canadian children and adolescents. *Nutrition: Findings from the Canadian Community Health Survey*. Statistics Canada, 1.

Tischler, A. (2014). Introduction: Using case studies to analyze teaching and learning in physical education. In S. B. Flory, A. Tischler, & S. Sanders (Ed.), *Sociocultural issues in physical education* (p. ix-xiv). London, UK: Rowman & Littlefield.

Tomporowski, P.D. (2003). Effects of acute bouts of exercise on cognition. *Acta Psychologica*. 112(3), 297-324. DOI: 10.1016/S0001-6918(02)00134-8

Tompsett, C., Burkett, B., & McKean, M.R. (2014). Development of physical literacy and movement competence: A literature review. *Journal of Fitness Research*. 3(2), 53-74.

Tremblay, M.S., Carson, V., Chaput, J-P., Connor Gorber, S., Dinh, T., Duggan, M., Faulkner, G., Gray, C.E., Gruber, R., Janson, K., Janssen, I., Katzmarzyk, P.T., Kho, M.E., Latimer-Cheung, A.E., LeBlance, C., Okely, A.D., Olds, T., Pate, R.R., Phillips, A., Poitras, V.J., Rodenburg, S., Sampson, M., Saunders, T.J., Stone, J.A., Stratton, G., Weiss, S.K., & Zehr, L. (2016). Canadian 24-hour movement guidelines for children and youth: An integration of physical activity, sedentary behaviour, and sleep. *Applied Physiology, Nutrition, and Metabolism.* 41(6), S-311-S327.

Tremblay, M.S., Warburton, D., Janssen, I., Paterson, D.H., Latimer, A.E., Rhodes, R.E., Kho, M.E., Hicks, A., LeBlanc, A.G., Zehr, L., Murumets, K., & Duggan, M. (2011). New Canadian physical activity guidelines. *Applied Physiology, Nutrition, and Metabolism,* 36(1), 36-46. Retrieved from: http://www.nrcresearchpress.com/doi/abs/10.1139/H11-009#.Va0mNbe05b0

Trost, S.G. & van der Mars, H. (2010). Why we should not cut P.E. Educational Leadership. 64(4), 60-65. Retrieved from: http://eprints.qut.edu.au/72258/1/72258(pub).pdf

Trudeau, F., & Shephard, R. J. (2008). Physical education, school physical activity, school sports and academic performance. International *Journal of Behavioral Nutrition and Physical Activity,* 5(1), 1.

Trost, S.J., & van der Mars, H. 2010, Why we should not cut P.E., *Educational Leadership,* 67(4), p. 60-65.

UNESCO. (2015). *Education: Addressing exclusion.* Retrieved from: http://www.unesco.org/new/en/education/themes/strengthening-education-systems/inclusive-education/browse/6/

UNESCO (2005). G*uidelines for inclusion: Ensuring access to education for all.* Paris, France: UNESCO

UNESCO (2013). *Quality physical education (QEP): Guidelines for policy makers.* Paris, France: UNESCO

UNESCO (2015). Quality physical education policy project. Downloaded from: http://www.unesco.org/new/en/social_and_human-sciences/themes/physical-education-and-sport/policy-project/

UNESCO (2016). Addressing exclusion. Retrieved from: http://www.unesco.org/new/en/inclusive-education/

UNESCO (2016) International Charter. Accessed May 2016 from: http://www.unesco.org/new/en/social-and-human-sciences/themes/physical-education-and-sport/sport-charter

UNESCO (2017). "Literacy For All". Accessed March 23, 2017. http://www.unesco.org/new/en/education/themes/education-building-blocks/literacy/un-literacy-decade/un-resolutions-and-other-related-documents

Valois, R.F., Umstattd, M. R., Zullig, K.J., & Paxton, R. J. (2008). Physical Activity Behaviors and Emotional Self-Efficacy: Is There a Relationship for Adolescents? *Journal of school health,* 78(6), 321-327.

Veugelers, P.J., & Fitzgerald, A.L. (2005). Effectiveness of school programs in preventing childhood obesity: a multilevel comparison. *American Journal of Public Health,* 95(3), 432-435.

Veugelers, P.J., & Schwartz, M.E. (2010). Comprehensive school health in Canada. *Canadian Journal of Public Health/Revue Canadienne de Sante'e Publique,* S5-S8.

Vickerman, P., & Hayes, S. (2013). *Special educational needs and disability in physical education.* In G. Stidder & S. Hayes (Eds.), Equality and inclusion in physical education and sport (pp. 51–65). New York, NY: Routledge.

Vidourek, R.A., King, K.A., Bernard, A.L., Murnan, J., & Nabors, L. (2011). Teachers' strategies to positively connect students to school. *American Journal of Health Education.* 42(2), 116-126.

Voss, M.W., Carr, L.J., Clark, R., Weng, T. (2014). Revenge of the "sit" II: does lifestyle impact neuronal and cognitive health through distinct mechanisms associated with sedentary behavior and physical activity? *Mental Health and Physical Activity.* 7(1), 9-24.

Wall, J., & Murray, N. (1994). *Children and movement.* Dubuque, IO: WMC Brown

Wankel, L.M. (1993). The importance of enjoyment to adherence and psychological benefits from physical activity. I*nternational Journal of Sport Psychology.*

Wenger-Nabigon, A. (2010). The Cree Medicine Wheel as an organizing paradigm of theories of human development. *Native Social Work Journal,* Vol. 7, 139-161.

Whitehead (2010) *Physical literacy: Throughout the lifecourse.* London: Routledge.

Whitehead, M. (2013). International Physical Literacy Conference. Conference presentation and materials, Banff, Canada.

Williams, N. (1992). The physical education hall of shame. *Journal of Physical Education, Recreation and Dance,* 63(6), 57–60.

Williams, N. (1994). The physical education hall of shame, part II. *Journal of Physical Education, Recreation and Dance*, 65(2), 17–20.

Williams, N. (1996). The physical education hall of shame, part III. *Journal of Physical Education, Recreation and Dance*, 67(8), 45–48.

Wood, T. (2003) Assessment in physical education: The future is now! In S. J. Silverman & C. D. Ennis (Eds.), Student learning in physical education. Champaign, IL: Human Kinetics.

Woodward Loeps, G., Kao, J., & Ritchie, L. (2011). To what extent have sweetened beverages contributed to the obesity epidemic? *Public Health Nutrition,* 14 (3), 499-509.

World Health Organization. (2016) Physical activity and young people. Retrieved from: http://www.who.int/ dietphysicalactivity/factsheet_young_people/en

Wrench, A., & Garrett, R. (2012). Stories told in learning to teach physical education. *Sport, Education and Society,* 17(1), p 1-19.